Cases in Environmental Management and Business Strategy

Richard Welford

Professor of Business Economics
School of Business, University of Huddersfield

PITMAN
PUBLISHING

For Chris, Oscar and Emily

PITMAN PUBLISHING
128 Long Acre, London WC2E 9AN

A Division of Longman Group UK Limited

© Longman Group UK Limited, 1994

First published in Great Britain 1994

British Library Cataloguing in Publication Data
A CIP catalogue record for this book can be obtained from the British Library.

ISBN 0 273 60313 2

Typeset by Mathematical Composition Setters Ltd, Salisbury, Wiltshire
Printed and bound in Great Britain by Bell and Bain Ltd, Glasgow

The Publisher's policy is to use paper manufactured from sustainable forests.

CONTENTS

PREFACE

Environmental issues continue to be a matter of public concern and over the past five years we have seen quite considerable changes in both the attitudes and practices of the industrial and commercial world. However, businesses are still identified as the major source of pollution. It is difficult for industry to deny this or to refute the general need for environmental protection. There are increasing numbers of sources to which industry can turn for help and advice in terms of environmental strategies but, to date, there has been little written on what firms are actually doing, which can, in turn, be used as a resource for other organisations. Such case-based, practical guidance relating to how real progress might be made is the central focus of this book. We need now to develop practical solutions to meet the environmental challenge and, by examining what we have identified as both best practice and the impediments to improvement, we can develop workable strategies to ensure that we protect the world in which we live.

This book is a companion to the textbook *Environmental Management and Business Strategy* written by myself and Andrew Gouldson. It is intended to add some real examples to the strategies discussed in that book and present a picture of current best practice in industry. It clearly provides a snapshot of the strategies currently being developed by leading companies, begins to consider impediments to improvement (particularly amongst small businesses) and looks at some key strategies for moving towards sustainability.

The book is divided into five parts. Part 1 examines the key challenges faced by firms who, increasingly, are being forced to adopt environmental management strategies, and it looks briefly at the tools of environmental management. Thus Chapter 1 examines the key issues to be addressed in the 1990s and examines the concept of sustainable development. Chapter 2 briefly outlines the principles and tools of environmental management, and readers who want to consider these issues in more detail are referred to the companion text.

Part 2 of the book examines environmental management strategies in four leading firms. Chapter 3 stresses the need to take a systems-based approach to environmental management strategies and does so by examining the activities of IBM. Chapter 4 focuses on the activities of British Telecommunications (BT) in relation to the need for the establishment of commitment in the organisation. Chapter 5, on the Volkswagen Audi group, focuses on product innovation and life-cycle assessment. The environmental strategies of The Body Shop are examined in Chapter 6, where, it is argued, the most advanced and innovative environmental strategies are being pursued.

Part 3 of the book examines some wider environmental issues based on the activities of a number of firms, industries and sectors. Chapter 7 begins with examining the important issue of the prevention of environmental accidents and disasters by a discussion of the Exxon Valdez and Bhopal incidents. Chapter 8 examines the retail supermarket sector and, through a discussion of the strategies of Sainsbury's, Safeway and Tesco, shows that it is not just in the production sector that environmental improvement can be made. The car transport sector is discussed in Chapter 9 and it is suggested that, in a sector where there is massive environmental impact, legislation and the threat of legislation have an important role to play in encouraging companies to be more environmentally proactive. Chapter 10 focuses on impediments to environmental improvement, with a particular reference to the results of a survey of small- and medium-sized enterprises, and Chapter 11 shows what can be achieved with regional environmental strategies by examining such a project in Ireland.

Part 4 of the book brings together many of the issues raised in the case studies and, in a critical analysis, points to both the achievements which the case studies highlight and to the issues which still need fundamental attention if we are to achieve the principles of sustainable development. Finally, Part 5 of the book provides some exercises for consideration and discussion.

This book would not have been possible without the help and cooperation of many people. As well as the contributors to the text, thanks should go to Jennifer Mair of Pitman Publishing, who initially persuaded me to write the book, and to Penelope Woolf, who has been supportive throughout the whole process. For help, encouragement and tolerance at home I will always be indebted to Chris Maddison.

Richard Welford
November 1993

CONTRIBUTORS

Andrew Gouldson is a lecturer in Human Geography in the School of Geography and Earth Resources, University of Hull. He is an editor of the journals *European Environment* and *Eco-Management and Auditing*.

Peter Hopkinson is a lecturer in Environmental Economics and Management in the Department of Environmental Sciences at the University of Bradford. He is a member of the Business and Environment Research Unit at the University.

Donal O'Laoire is a director of Environmental Management and Auditing Services Ltd, based in Dublin, Ireland.

Nigel Roome is Professor of Environmental Management at York University, Canada. He was formerly a Fellow in Corporate Responsibility at Manchester Business School.

Mark Shayler is a research officer in the School of Geography, University of Leeds. He is also a researcher at Earth Resources Research.

Geoff Taylor is a freelance consultant, formerly a researcher with the Business and Environment Research Unit at the University of Bradford.

Richard Welford is Professor of Business Economics at the University of Huddersfield. He is an editor of the journals *Business Strategy and the Environment*, *Eco-Management and Auditing* and *European Business Review*. He was formerly Head of the Business and Environment Research Unit at the University of Bradford.

SUGGESTIONS ON HOW TO USE THIS BOOK

Although this book is a stand-alone text in its own right and will be useful to readers who are looking for practical examples of environmental management strategies in practice, it is also designed to accompany its sister textbook entitled *Environmental Management and Business Strategy* (Welford and Gouldson, 1993), also published by Pitman Publishing.

Increasingly courses are becoming modularised and both textbooks fit well into ten- or twelve-week courses on environmental management and business strategy. A possible outline of a twelve-week course is provided in the table shown. At MBA level, where ten-week modules are sometimes more common, it is suggested that weeks 1 and 2 and weeks 7 and 8 might be combined.

Possible course outline

Week	Topic	Relevant chapters of textbook	Relevant chapters of cases book
1	Introduction to the environmental challenge	Chapter 1	Chapter 1 Chapter 2
2	The legal framework of environmental management	Chapter 2	Chapter 9
3	Environmental impact assessment	Chapter 3	Relevant parts of Chapter 3
4	Corporate environmental policies	Chapter 4	Relevant parts of Chapters 3, 4 & 6
5	Environmental management systems	Chapter 5	Chapter 3 Chapter 4 Parts of Chapter 12
6	Environmental reviews and environmental auditing	Chapter 4 Chapter 6	Chapter 6
7	Waste management	Chapter 7	Parts of Chapter 5
8	Life-cycle assessment	Relevant parts of Chapters 7 and 8	Chapter 5 Chapter 6
9	Green marketing	Chapter 8	Chapter 8
10	Environmental management in small businesses	Chapter 9	Chapter 10
11	Regional environmental management	Chapter 10	Chapter 11
12	The management of risk and disaster prevention		Chapter 7

PART I

Environmental Challenges and Environmental Management

CHAPTER 1

Where are we now and where are we going?

Richard Welford

INTRODUCTION

Businesses are at the core of the environmental debate and are central both to the pollution problem and to the solution. To date, a small number of larger businesses have been proactive, for one reason or another, in promoting environmental improvement across their activities. However, only a small number of those have taken the thorough systematic approach which is necessary if they are to be successful in improving their environmental performance. Fewer still have adopted environmental strategies for ethical reasons. Nevertheless, a number of firms, identified in this book, are changing the way in which they do business and are putting pressure on others to change. Such change is necessary and fundamental to the continued existence of the planet which we share with other species and future generations.

Until recently, businesses have, in the main, been negligent towards their wider social, ethical and environmental responsibilities. We are beginning to see that situation change as a result of increasing legislation, greater awareness on the part of consumers, coupled with a willingness to make their views known, and more effective and more consistent management practices.

Businesses and the market mechanism in which they operate are central to the way in which we organise society. Other organisational forms have either failed or remain to be defined and, therefore, we must attempt to improve the environment in which we live, not by starting all over again, but by re-examining the ways in which we do business. By providing the goods and services demanded by all of us, businesses fulfil many vital social needs and many not-so-vital social wants. The activities of industry provide employment, and investments drive economic growth. However, in doing so, be it because of the resources that they consume, the processes they apply or the products that they manufacture, business activities are a major contributor to environmental destruction. To protect the environment, we must find ways to meet the needs of both current and future generations. In part we need to find new technologies but we cannot rely on science and technology to provide all the answers. Businesses themselves need to develop more efficient methods of sourcing raw materials, of processing them and producing final goods, and of distributing them, managing them in use, and disposing of them after use.

Individual businesses have always been faced with a range of competitive market conditions which threaten their survival. In many cases, requirements for improved environmental performance are perceived to add to this threat. It is now clear, however, that the demands placed upon industry to improve its environmental performance will continue to grow. Companies which respond to this challenge will see themselves at the forefront of industry, developing new products in new markets and gaining a competitive edge over their competitors. Not only is it ethical for a company to improve its environmental performance, but it is sound business practice. Other pressures on industry and a lack of relevant expertise mean that businesses cannot change overnight. We can nevertheless expect a gradual and continuous effort to improve environmental performance based on lessons of best practice elsewhere. This, in time, may begin to move the global economy towards a more sustainable pattern of activity.

SUSTAINABLE DEVELOPMENT

The concept of sustainable development is based on the premise that there is a trade-off between economic growth and the sustainability of the environment in which we live. Over time, growth can cause pollution and atmospheric damage leading to environmental degradation. The concept of sustainable development therefore stresses the interdependence between economic growth and environmental quality. In theory at least, it is possible to make development and environmental protection compatible by following sustainable strategies and by not developing the particular areas of economic activity that are most damaging to the environment.

The Brundtland Report, commissioned by the United Nations to examine long-term environmental strategies, argued that economic development and environmental protection could be made compatible, but that this would require quite radical changes in economic practices throughout the world. It defined sustainable development as development that meets the needs of the present without compromising the ability of future generations to meet their own needs. In other words, a continued growth in consumption is not possible indefinitely and if society today acts as if all non-renewable resources are plentiful, eventually there will be nothing left for the future. But, more importantly than that, mass consumption may cause such irreparable damage that humans may not even be able to live on the planet in the future.

The challenge that faces industry and the economic system is how to continue to fulfil a vital role within modern society in a way which is consistent with sustainable development. Complying with the principles of sustainability may take some time. However, both for entire economies and for individual businesses, there is hope that sufficient progress can be achieved within the time-scales which appear to be necessary to avoid environmental catastrophe.

Sustainable development is made up of three closely-connected issues and, to ensure a truly sustainable approach to business activities, industry must consider each of the following aspects:

- **Environment**: The environment must be valued as an integral part of the economic process and not treated as a free good. The environmental stock has to be protected and this implies minimal use of non-renewable resources and minimal emission of pollutants. The ecosystem has to be protected so that the loss of plant and animal species can be avoided.
- **Equity**: One of the biggest threats facing the world is that the developing countries want to grow rapidly to achieve the same standards of living as those in the West. That in itself would cause a major environmental disaster if it were modelled on the same sort of growth experienced in post-war Europe. There therefore needs to be a greater degree of equity and the key issue of poverty has to be addressed. There is a need to protect and respect indigenous populations and not exploit the natural resources of developing countries.
- **Futurity**: Sustainable development requires that society, businesses and individuals operate on a different time-scale from that which currently operates in the economy. While companies commonly operate under competitive pressures to achieve short-run gains, long-term environmental protection is often compromised. To ensure that longer-term, inter-generational considerations are observed, longer planning horizons need to be adopted.

The Brundtland Report concludes that these three conditions are not being met. The industrialised world has already used much of the planet's ecological capital and many of the development paths of the industrialised nations are clearly unsustainable. Non-renewable resources are being depleted, while renewable resources such as soil, water and the atmosphere are being degraded. This has been caused by economic development but, in time, will undermine the very foundations of that development.

If economic growth is to be continued, then it must be environmentally and socially sustainable rather than unplanned and undifferentiated. This means reconsidering the current measures of growth, such as gross national product (GNP), which fail to take account of environmental debits like pollution or the depletion of the natural capital stock. While concern about the depletion of materials and energy resources continues there is also concern surrounding the environment's capacity to act to deal with waste.

One major obstacle preventing sustainability from being achieved is the overall level of consumption. Western consumers are apparently reluctant to significantly reduce their own levels of consumption. While, increasingly, governments are adopting economic instruments such as taxes, subsidies and product-labelling schemes to reduce and channel consumption towards more environmentally-friendly alternatives, industry itself must be encouraged to further increase environmental efficiency. There is a role for industry in educating consumers to be more environmentally responsible. In addition, leading companies are putting increased emphasis on the concept of product stewardship. This means accepting responsibility for products even while they are being used and helping to take responsibility for the disposal of those products after use.

Sustainability therefore challenges industry to produce higher levels of output while using lower levels of inputs and generating less waste. The problem that remains is that while relative environmental impact per unit of output has fallen, increases in the absolute level of output, and hence environmental impact, have more than offset any gains in relative environmental efficiency. In this book we begin to examine the ways in which environmental efficiency can be improved. From this, we can begin to understand some of the key practical elements needed to improve environmental performance and thus move towards sustainability.

The direction in which we should move should therefore be clear. Companies are faced with the challenge of integrating environmental considerations into their procurement, production and marketing strategies. There is always an incentive, however, for profit-maximising firms seeking short-term rewards, to opt out and become a free rider (assuming that everyone else will be so environmentally conscious that their own pollution will become negligible). European Community environmental legislation is increasingly plugging the gaps which allow this to happen, and firms attempting to hide their illegal pollution are now subject to severe penalties.

Firms clearly have a role to play in the development of substitutes for non-renewable resources and innovations which reduce waste and use energy more efficiently. They also have a role in processing those materials in a way which brings about environmental improvements. For many products (e.g., cars and washing machines), the major area of environmental damage occurs in their usage. Firms often have the opportunity of reducing this damage at the design stage and when new products are being developed there is a whole new opportunity for considering both the use and disposal of the product.

STAKEHOLDER PRESSURE

Given the internal and external demands to improve the environmental performance of a company, those companies that achieve high standards of environmental performance will benefit in a number of ways. In order to realise a competitive advantage, companies must seek to develop management strategies which will improve their environmental performance and address the environmental demands placed upon them by government, the EC and stakeholders. By incorporating the increasingly important environmental dimension into the decision-making processes of the firm, managers can seek to reduce costs and exploit the opportunities offered by increased public environmental concern within a dynamic marketplace. Such a strategy must be proactive and honest and be based on the concept of sustainability. It should also involve a degree of education and campaigning such as that undertaken by The Body Shop. Ultimately, it must be ethical.

Individual businesses interact with a number of stakeholders, all of whom have an interest in the performance of that company. Traditionally the main focus of stakeholder interest has been upon the financial performance of the company. Increasingly however, stakeholder pressure is concentrating on the environmental performance of the company and other issues. The relationship between a company and its customers is obviously of paramount importance. In relation to environmental considerations, the potential importance of green consumerism cannot be overstated. The range of characteristics that underlies their own purchasing decision is also a fundamental consideration for all businesses. At present, however, the influence of green consumerism on most businesses is marginal. Of the myriad products that each consumer buys, very few are chosen on the basis of their environmental credentials alone. Nevertheless, it is certain that credible claims relating to environmental performance constitute an increasingly important element amongst the many characteristics upon which consumers base their purchasing decision. Companies which can communicate an honest and verifiable message about the environmental performance of their products will enhance their competitive position.

National governments and the EC institutions are also seeking to increase the potency of green consumerism by providing the consumer with the information necessary to make an informed choice in relation to the environmental performance of each product within the product range. For this reason, for example, we saw the introduction of the EC's eco-labelling scheme in 1993. Increasingly, we are seeing a move away from additional command and control instruments of environmental policy, towards more market-driven policies which attempt to integrate environmental considerations with economic objectives. Whether this shift in emphasis will be effective remains to be seen, however.

Many businesses do not sell into 'end-consumer' markets and may therefore perceive themselves to be remote from any consumer pressures to improve their environmental performance. But, increasingly, pressure to improve environmental performance is also emanating from trading partners. In efforts to improve overall environmental performance, many companies are exercising their own rights both as purchasers and as vendors and are demanding that all companies within their supply chain seek to minimise their own environmental impacts. Demands to improve environmental performance at all stages in the supply chain are building up a momentum which will push best practice beyond those companies that are directly exposed to the pressures of green consumerism. We shall see in the cases which follow that an increasing number of companies are preferring to buy their resources from, or sell their products to, other companies which meet certain standards of environmental performance.

Industry shares its surrounding environment with the local population both now and in the future. Increasingly this population is demanding a high level of environmental performance from its industrial neighbours, and seeks some degree of reassurance that they are not exposed to significant environmental risk due to a company's operations. In addition, local communities expect their environment to remain risk free for their children and future generations. Trends towards freedom of access to environmental information will give greater power to local communities when they question the activities of local industrial co-habitants. In order to foster a positive working relationship, companies must protect their neighbours, improve their environmental performance and communicate their efforts openly and honestly to the surrounding communities.

Businesses also have a clear responsibility towards the people they employ. The pressure to provide a healthy living environment is magnified within the workplace. Employees are entitled to healthy and secure working conditions, and can draw on an established framework of health and safety legislation in this respect. However, employees also have the right to expect good environmental performance from their employers. Increasingly people wish to work for ethical and responsible companies. In turn, companies that reflect the environmental concerns of the public will find it easier to attract, retain and motivate a quality workforce.

Lenders, investors and shareholders of a company also exert pressures to improve environmental performance. The rapid growth of ethical investment schemes reflects the desire of many investors only to lend their financial support to companies which behave in a responsible manner. There are a number of very good reasons why investors prefer to work with companies that have a good track record of environmental performance. The structure of liability for environmental damage dictates that any party that causes environmental damage may be fined and required to bear the costs of remediating any damage and to compensate the affected parties for any associated losses. It is increasingly difficult and expensive to obtain insurance to cover such costs. Consequently, companies associated with a significant environmental incident may suffer significant financial losses. These losses are then translated into reductions in share prices and dividends. For similar reasons, commercial lenders are increasingly reluctant to lend money to any company which may develop any environmental liabilities or to secure loans on the value of an asset which may be eroded through contamination. Companies which cannot demonstrate a high level of environmental performance associated with low environmental risks will find it increasingly difficult and expensive to obtain loans and retain investment and insurance for their operations.

It is pressure groups who have often been happy to expose the worst environmental practices of industry and who have pushed businesses to be more proactive. A combination of increased public awareness of environmental issues and freedom of access to information on the environmental impact of companies' activities is increasing the media and pressure group interest in the environmental performance of industry. In order to manage media and pressure group attention, companies must be able to show that they have made real efforts to improve their environmental performance. However, any claims which are made must be capable of being substantiated. Companies which seek to communicate responsible environmental performance must base any claims that they make to this effect on hard facts which they are willing to communicate. This requires an open and honest communications strategy and a move away from more traditional marketing hype.

STRATEGIC CONSIDERATIONS

Given the growing internal and external demands to improve the environmental performance of a company, which we have identified, those companies that achieve high standards of environmental performance will benefit in a number of ways. Many of these benefits are directly related to cost reduction and as such are not inconsistent with principles of profit maximisation. But cost minimisation is no panacea and the real benefits are associated with a more ethical approach to business where profits are not the sole motivation and where responsibility towards the environment and a commitment to sustainability are integral parts of doing business over longer planning horizons. Strategies need to be developed which are consistent with these aims.

In order to achieve a more widely defined competitive advantage based on sustainable principles, companies must seek to develop effective strategies which translate actions into benefits, improving their environmental performance and addressing the environmental demands placed upon them by stakeholders. By incorporating the increasingly important environmental dimension into the decision-making processes of the firm, managers can seek to reduce costs and address the opportunities offered by increased public environmental concern within a dynamic marketplace. Such a strategy must be proactive and honest. In turn, it needs to be evangelical, educating and campaigning and, above all, it must be ethical. Sustainable development is too important an issue to be treated as a marketing gimmick for short-term economic advantage.

The focus of any environmental strategy must be commitment and integration. These common elements imply that firms must examine every aspect of environmental performance. Priorities and clear targets should be set and every aspect of an organisation's environmental impact must be recognised and measured. Strategies must be defined that are holistic rather than piecemeal. It is inadequate to improve the environmental impact of one part of a firm's activities if this simply means shifting environmental damage elsewhere. Real environmental improvement involves looking at the broader picture and constantly reassessing the effectiveness of corporate strategies both now and into the future.

Environmental strategy must therefore begin with real commitment on the part of the whole organisation. This may mean a change in corporate culture, and management inevitably has an important role to play. In leading that commitment and laying out the organisation's corporate objectives with respect to the environment, management has to be the catalyst for change. Moreover, that change has to be on-going, and management must be ever mindful of the full range of objectives to which it is subject. Management has to find compromise between these objectives if they conflict, and design corporate strategies which are operational, consistent and achievable.

Environmental management has to be addressed in a systematic way, dealing with the company as a whole rather than in a compartmentalised way. Corporate structures need to be flexible and everyone must identify and respond to the role they must play in improving environmental performance. When it comes to the integration of environmental considerations, cooperative strategies provide a way forward. To date, competition has been the dominant ideology in business, but cooperative strategies between businesses, also involving the public and regulatory agencies, can bring about benefits which are sustainable. Single-minded competitive strategies which seek to exploit profitable opportunities without regard to their environmental consequences are unethical.

We therefore need to translate the philosophies associated with sustainable development into practical strategies to improve corporate environmental performance. Statements of principle and environmental policies are important in gaining the commitment needed to implement environmental improvement, and in telling stakeholders about this commitment. But in order to introduce effective environmental management, environmental information and analysis are also required. Industry is in the process of developing ever more sophisticated tools to achieve this, although much more research is needed in defining measures of environmental performance. Increasingly, there is a set of environmental management tools available to companies. Many of these are being adopted by the companies discussed in this book, but it is worth summarising their role and contribution to the overall company approach.

Environmental impact assessment (EIA) is the starting point for new developments. It provides companies and the public with information on and analysis of the development of a plant or facility. Baseline environmental reviews offer a snapshot of an existing plant's environmental performance at one point in time and environmental audits provide an on-going check on a company's environmental improvement. Techniques associated with waste reduction and waste management are central in considering aspects of product and process design. These techniques form the basic tools of analysis in a company's overall environmental management system which should, in turn, be based on a systematic and integrated approach to the improvement of environmental performance.

The company should also consider the range of tools available to it which are associated with its marketing strategy. Environmental considerations need to be firmly encapsulated within a company's traditional marketing mix. Green products, for example, must be assessed from cradle-to-grave, that is, their environmental impact must be assessed on the basis of raw material inputs, product processes, use and disposal. Accepting responsibility for a product once it has left the factory gates is fundamental to environmental performance, and techniques associated with life-cycle assessment (LCA) mean that we can identify the widest aspects of a product's environmental impact.

EUROPEAN INTEGRATION, LEGISLATION AND THE ENVIRONMENT

In Europe, environmental management has to be set within the context of the process of the European integration. Surprisingly, the original Treaty of Rome was concerned with stimulating economic growth but contained no specific reference to the environment. Since then, though, EC environmental policy has developed in line with general concerns in Europe and the deteriorating environmental position in which Europe finds itself. By 1990, 160 pieces of environmental legislation had been passed covering pollution of the air and water, noise pollution, chemicals, waste, environmental impact assessment, the prevention of industrial accidents and wildlife protection.

However, few Member States have been able to enforce fully EC legislation. Denmark is probably the only country with a consistently good record and the Southern European countries have consistently bad records. Once again this highlights the emphasis often given to economic growth rather than environmental protection, with the primary aim of countries such as Spain and Portugal being the attainment of similar living standards to the rest of the Community.

The Single European Act gave environmental policy a boost stating that there is not only a need for such legislation but that the laws should meet three key objectives:

- preservation, protection and improvement of the quality of the environment;
- protection of human health; and
- prudent and rational use of natural resources.

These objectives must be met by applying four principles:

- prevention of harm to the environment;
- control of pollution at source;
- the polluter should pay; and
- integration of environmental considerations into other Community policies.

The relationship between economic growth and the environment has therefore taken on a new importance within the EC. There now exists a major opportunity to put into place the appropriate financial and regulatory mechanisms that would make the single European market environmentally sustainable. The extent to which this happens will be seen over time, but the Single European Act provides the necessary constitutional basis for a forceful environmental response. Perhaps the strongest part of this is the requirement that policy makers should make environmental considerations a component of all the Community's other policies.

In 1992 the European Community's Fifth Environmental Action Programme was introduced. The first environmental action programme in 1973 set out a number of principles which have formed the basis of environmental action in the EC ever since. The aims are clearly set out, stating that:

1. Prevention is better than cure.
2. Environmental effects should be taken into account at the earliest possible stage in decision making.
3. Exploitation of nature and natural resources which causes significant damage to the ecological balance must be avoided. The natural environment can only absorb pollution to a limited extent. Nature is an asset which may be used but not abused.
4. Scientific knowledge should be improved to enable action to be taken.
5. 'The polluter pays' principle; the polluter should pay for preventing and eliminating environmental nuisance.
6. Activities in one Member State should not cause environmental deterioration in another.
7. Environmental policies of Member States must take account of the interests of developing countries.
8. The EC and Member States should act together in international organisations and also in promoting international environmental policy.
9. Education of citizens is necessary as the protection of the environment is a matter for everyone.
10. The principle of action at the appropriate level; for each type of pollution it is necessary to establish the level of action which is best suited for achieving the protection required, be it local, regional, national, EC-wide or international.
11. National environmental policies must be coordinated within the EC without impinging on progress at the national level. It is intended that implementation of the action programme and gathering of environmental information by the proposed European environment agency will secure this.

(Source: Haigh, N. (1992) and *Official Journal of the European Communities*: C112 20 December 1973)

The main activities of the EC in the environmental policy arena, until 1987, were centred on the application of nearly 200 command and control Directives in areas as diverse as lead in petrol and aircraft noise. More recently, in realising that environmental policy is of little use unless enforced, EC environmental policy has given increased emphasis to the improved enforcement of existing legislation. Emphasis has also shifted from the use of traditional legislative instruments in environmental policy to the application of economic market-based instruments such as the proposed carbon tax, and voluntary agreements such as the eco-labelling and eco-management and audit schemes. The aim of such measures is to encourage change in all sectors of industry and society in a more general way than can be achieved through the use of tightly defined legislative instruments. The use of economic instruments and voluntary measures is seen as a complement rather than a substitute to the more traditional application of command and control measures. This shift means that the role of businesses in being more responsive to environmental demands is of greater importance. Since they are not going to be forced along a path towards sustainable development, it is important that they act ethically and move in that direction voluntarily.

The EC view of the future of environmental policy and its interface with industrial development is clear. With some 340 million inhabitants, the Community is the largest trading block in the world, and is therefore in a critical position to take the lead in moving towards sustainability. The European Commission does accept that tighter environmental policy will impact on the costs of industry. But it views this as a cost well worth paying, and indeed environmental protection has become not only a policy objective of its own but also a precondition of industrial expansion. In this respect, a new impetus towards a better integration of policies aiming at consolidating industrial competitiveness, and at achieving a high level of protection of the environment, is necessary in order to make the two objectives fully mutually supportive.

These views are given more substance within the Fifth Environmental Action Programme. While this programme sets out the likely developments of EC environmental policy in a general sense, a number of specific measures relating to industry are included. Perhaps most importantly the commitment of the EC to strengthen environmental policy is underlined. The EC shares the view that urgent action is needed for environmental protection, and that many of the great environmental struggles will be won or lost during this decade. Further, it states that achieving sustainability will demand practical and political commitment over an extended period and that the EC as the largest trading block in the world must exercise its responsibility and commit itself to that goal. Such objectives include a commitment to considering wider aspects of sustainability, particularly where these affect the developing economies and indigenous populations.

For industries and companies that are facing a rising tide of environmental legislation, it is essential that attempts are made to find out about, and then positively address, the legislative pressures under which they find themselves. However, the Fifth Environmental Action Programme focuses on the improved enforcement of existing legislation rather than the adoption of new legislation. To some extent this should allow industry to take stock of the rapid increase in environmental legislation that has taken place in recent years and to focus on strategies for improving other aspects of environmental performance.

The Maastricht Treaty and the Fifth Environmental Action Programme require that environmental policy should be fully incorporated into all other Community policies. Therefore, while it may become easier to track the development of policies which are explicitly environmental, it will become more difficult to monitor the development of environmental policy throughout the activities of the Commission as a whole. The establishment of the European Environment Agency which will collect data and monitor compliance throughout the Community will help to disseminate information to all interested parties. More than ever, therefore, companies need to be proactive in their responses to change. To be at the forefront of environmental management strategies, they need to act before they are forced to do so, and they need to push forward the frontiers of understanding and continually to develop more effective environmental strategies.

Tackling environmental problems always requires a concerted and cooperative effort and in the EC success will depend on the extent to which Member States are politically committed to the environmental philosophy and the extent to which they are willing to cooperate. The balancing of the economic growth/environment trade-off is likely to determine the Europe-wide success of any policies. But there also need to be concerted and cooperative political motivations. There will be those who will therefore argue that the attainment of an effective and concerted environmental policy in Europe will require political and economic union. However the EC and national governments legislate over environmental protection and police offenders, significant environmental improvement will only be attained with the cooperation and commitment of producers. There is therefore a need for firms to institute the type of environmental management practices outlined in this book.

WHICH WAY FORWARD?

Companies need to do more than simply base their own environmental management strategies on benchmarking exercises where, in effect, they copy best practice elsewhere. This is nevertheless a starting point and much of the information about the real strategies outlined in this book can provide the basis for other companies' strategies.

Ultimately, though, there is a need for a change in corporate cultures where environmental issues are pushed up the hierarchy of corporate objectives. This has been achieved in some of the cases examined below but is more often an on-going process. New environmental laws have pushed some firms into thinking more widely about how they do business and integrating environmental considerations into their other activities. Industry tends to be wary of more legislation, but in order to maintain a level playing field across Europe, it may well be in the interests of industry to campaign for that legislation to be tightened up and implemented equally everywhere. The most environmentally-aware companies implement the highest standards of environmental management regardless of location and this goes some way in protecting the less developed countries who are still suffering from widespread exploitation of their natural and human resources.

Environmental management based on principles of sustainable development challenge industry to take a longer-term view of their business activities. The satisfaction of human wants now is not justifiable if that means that the needs of future generations cannot be met. Thus non-renewable resources should be used sparingly and responsibly. We cannot rely on science and technology to provide solutions to over-consumption. Too many of our past actions have assumed that technical progress will solve the problems we create today, sometime in the future.

At the core of any environmental strategy has to be a consideration of ethical issues associated with doing business. That requires industry to be more open, honest and credible than it has been in the past. We need to search for new economic paradigms which stress the importance of environmental issues and integrate ever-wider ethical aims.

We are rapidly developing a number of core techniques (environmental auditing, life-cycle assessment, etc.) for managing change and environmental improvement. These should become the centre of any company's attempt to improve its environmental performance. Companies need to push along the learning curve, developing ever more effective strategies to protect the environment and developing new measures of economic performance based on the central concept of sustainable development. Companies are unlikely ever to reach the ultimate aim of having no negative impact on the environment, so there is always more they can do. Following a committed and continuous cycle of environmental improvement is therefore a fundamental strategy which will never end.

Note: For further information on the topics raised in this chapter, please refer to Chapter 1 of *Environmental Management and Business Strategy* by Richard Welford and Andrew Gouldson (Pitman Publishing, 1993).

CHAPTER 2

The principles and tools of environmental management

Richard Welford

INTRODUCTION

Having established the need for environmental management strategies at the corporate level, it is now useful to take an overview of the key strategies available to companies. These will relate not only to internal procedures but also to external marketing strategies and a recognition of the benefits which can be derived from cooperating with other organisations. At the heart of any corporate environmental strategy has to be a systematic, open and honest approach. Moreover, any environmental action has to be taken within an ethical framework which aims to move the company towards a sustainable position, rather than aiming to maximise short-term profitability through spurious environmental claims. Long-term competitive advantage comes about through real commitment based on sound environmental principles and not short-term cynicism.

Commitment in the organisation is central to developing the systematic approach and it must be recognised that such commitment is achieved through the involvement of workers. Consultation and participative strategies need to be developed in the recognition that those people working on the processes which have an impact on the environment, are in the best position to deal with them. Management has a role in directing, organising and monitoring the system, and showing their own commitment to environmental improvement.

ENVIRONMENTAL POLICIES AND COMMITMENT TO ENVIRONMENTAL IMPROVEMENT

For any company committed to improving its environmental performance, the starting point must be to make a clear statement of that commitment through an environmental policy. The policy needs to be thorough and must reflect the company's key objectives in a document to be communicated to as wide an audience as possible. Once committed to environmental objectives, the company opens itself up to assessment and investigation, so a weak policy statement is inadequate because it will soon be exposed by competitors and pressure groups. In effect, an environmental policy is an organisation-based statement of objectives which must clearly outline the firm's commitment to environmental improvement. In so doing it should be detailed enough to define future actions and provide information so that management and workers can clearly determine their areas of responsibility and authority, and so that workers, consumers, shareholders and the general public are aware of that commitment. It must relate enterprise functions to specific laws, national and EC environmental standards, society's perceived expectations and the degree and level of enforcement to be used. The ideal environmental policy will be proactive and commit the company to going beyond minimum legislative and regulatory requirements. Examples of the policy statements of BT, IBM and The Body Shop can be found in later chapters of this book.

All aspects of a company's operations, from accounting and purchasing, to product design, manufacture, sales, marketing, distribution and the use and disposal of the product will have an impact on the environment, and the environmental policy should reflect a recognition of this. The policy needs to be comprehensive and detailed but it should not contain statements or targets which the firm cannot hope to achieve. This will do more harm than good if exposed. The content of any policy will vary from firm to firm and be influenced by the activities of that organisation. Although policies will differ between organisations, there are some general principles which can be applied to the content of the policy statement:

- Adopt and aim to apply the principles of 'sustainable development' which meet the needs of the present, without compromising the abilities of future generations to meet their own needs.
- Strive to adopt the highest available environmental standards in all site locations and all countries and meet or exceed all applicable regulations.
- Adopt a total 'cradle-to-grave' environmental assessment and accept responsibility for all products and services, the raw materials you use and the use and disposal of the product.
- Aim to minimise the use of all materials, supplies and energy and wherever possible, use renewable or recyclable materials and components.
- Minimise waste produced in all parts of the business, aim for waste-free processes and, where waste is produced, avoid the use of terminal waste treatment, dealing with it, as far as possible, at source.
- Render any unavoidable wastes harmless and dispose of them in a way which has least impact on the environment.
- Expect high environmental standards from all parties involved in the business including suppliers, contractors and vendors and put pressure on these groups to improve their environmental performance in line with your own.
- Be committed to improving relations with the local community and the public at large and where necessary introduce education and liaison programmes.

- Adopt an environmentally-sound transport strategy and consider, in particular, the need for company cars.
- Assess on a continuous basis the environmental impact of all operations and procedures via an environmental audit.
- Assist in developing solutions to environmental problems and support the development of external environmental initiatives.
- Preserve nature, protect ecological habitats and create conservation schemes.
- Accept strict liability for environmental damage, not blaming others for environmental incidents and accidents.

Environmental policies should identify key performance areas and form a sound basis for setting corporate objectives. They need to be detailed enough to demonstrate that the commitment of the company goes beyond lip-service. A clearly defined environmental policy should be implementable, practical and relate to the areas in which the company wishes to improve its environmental performance. In particular, when designing an environmental policy, the organisation needs to think hard about how it is going to quantify its objectives and measure its environmental performance. The whole issue of measurement is difficult and companies need to have clear targets which reflect a move towards sustainability.

To be successful, environmental management strategies need to be truly company-wide and therefore commitment is required from the whole workforce. Middle management has an important role to play in not only grasping the concepts themselves but also explaining them to the people for whom they are responsible. Commitment towards environmental improvement is central and needs to come from the top of the organisation. Therefore the Chief Executive has to be seen to be fully supportive of plans for environmental improvement. Upon the design and implementation of a company's environmental policy there needs to be appointed a board director either solely or, depending on the size of the organisation, partly responsible for the implementation of that policy and the improvement of processes which will improve environmental performance.

The introduction of environmental initiatives will often spur management on to consider wider aspects of their whole company performance. Arguably, the main focus of so many firms is the operation of the firm so as to minimise costs. Indeed in the early 1990s, when we observed the introduction of so many new environmental initiatives and much heightened interest in environmental management, the recession was forcing firms to focus on simple cost management. But increasingly firms are recognising the benefits of moving away from short-term, narrow objectives towards a more strategic, integrated and holistic management approach. At the centre of this strategy has to be a systems approach to environmental management.

THE SYSTEMS APPROACH TO ENVIRONMENTAL IMPROVEMENT

An effective management system pulls together all the other tools and strategies for the avoidance of environmental damage. Quite simply, a management system should be developed and implemented for the purpose of accomplishing the objectives set out in a company's or organisation's policies. Each element of the system will vary in importance from one type of activity to another and from one product or service to another. The system needs to be comprehensive, covering all the activities of the organisation. Gaps must not occur in the coverage of the system since this is where errors and mistakes will occur and where accidents and disasters may happen. Every part of an organisation must be involved in the implementation of the system and every person must recognise his or her responsibility for putting the system into practice.

The procedures within that system need therefore to be understandable to everybody involved. If roles and duties are not specified in an understandable way, they may not be carried out. This will usually involve documenting the system, training people fully in their tasks and responsibilities, and reviewing or auditing what is actually happening periodically. It requires that the system and all its elements are monitored and if the system breaks down it must be rectified quickly.

The system must be open to review and there must be a commitment to a continuous cycle of improvement in the operations of the firm and in the quality of products or services it will produce. This continuous cycle of environmental improvement should aim for an ultimate goal of zero negative impact on the environment. Everybody has a role in the system and therefore participatory styles of management are usually superior to hierarchical ones. Management pyramids often need to be flattened to allow for a freer flow of information from both top to bottom and bottom to top.

An effective organisational structure of any management system is vital and should be clearly established within the organisation. Clear lines of authority and communication channels need to be defined. All activities of an organisation should be identified and defined and appropriately documented. General and specific responsibilities and authorities should be defined to particular groups and individuals, and where these are assigned to individuals somebody else should be made responsible in their absence. A management representative, preferably independent of other functions, should be appointed to resolve disputes and problems and the interface and coordination between different activities need to be clearly defined.

Although the case studies of organisations and industries discussed in this book can provide useful information, it is dangerous to imagine that success stories or accounts of disasters are universally applicable, because organisational culture, operating conditions, people, history, processes, products and services are rarely exactly comparable. Management needs fully to appreciate the critical nature of the factors involved in operating systems and decide what reliance can be placed upon assumptions made. There is no real alternative to taking a good hard look at every aspect of one's own organisation and systems. Moreover, this is not a once-and-for-all process but an ongoing requirement if risks of failure are to be minimised.

A central aspect of any management system will revolve around decision-making. Senior management is ultimately responsible for making balanced judgements. But modern management methods highlight the need for flexibility and participation and this usually involves decisions being taken further down the hierarchy. In arriving at decisions the calibre and personal integrity of staff are of fundamental importance and management needs to ensure that each person in the organisation understands their role in decision-making and the consequences of their actions. Decisions are often of a higher quality when they are participative and systems need to avoid giving single individuals too much power. The quality of decisions is also closely linked to the availability of adequate education and training programmes for all employees, and such programmes need to be built into organisation-wide systems.

There is therefore a need to develop comprehensive environmental management systems. For most organisations the ultimate aim of zero negative impact on the environment, widely defined, simply cannot be met. But never-ending or continuous improvement is an achievable goal. The environmental management system has to be firmly tied to other corporate objectives and the central importance of commitment must not be lost. A never-ending improvement cycle will mean that the organisation learns from its successes and failures and improves operations and outputs. This has to be done in a planned, systematic and documented way in order to create an organisational culture which protects the environment and the reputation of the company, and which permeates the whole organisation.

ENVIRONMENTAL REVIEWS AND ENVIRONMENTAL AUDITING

After an initial policy has been formulated, an environmental review of the company is undertaken in order to provide a detailed snapshot of the company's present position and, given this information, the company will need to revise and fine-tune its environmental policy to the particular needs and objectives identified in the review.

One of the major outcomes of the environmental review will be the development of an action plan on how to manage and ensure environmental improvement. This action plan must be implemented by the organisation, and the extent of environmental improvement will be assessed regularly by means of an environmental audit. After each audit-finding has been considered there will be a need to further consider the organisation's environmental policy and action plan.

Environmental reviews and audits are usually carried out by teams which include lawyers, management consultants, engineers, scientists and environmental generalists drawn from industry, government and consultancy companies. The US Environmental Protection Agency has been instrumental in promoting environmental audits in the USA and has published policy guidelines which recommend going beyond the minimum legal requirements to identify actual and potential environmental problems. The International Chamber of Commerce has also drawn up audit guidelines which promote the need for self-regulation by the business community in the spirit of responsible care.

The definition of an environmental audit provided by the International Chamber of Commerce (ICC) (1989) is:

> A management tool comprising a systematic, documented, periodic and objective evaluation of how well environmental organisation, management and equipment are performing with the aim of helping to safeguard the environment by: (i) facilitating management and control of environmental practices; and (ii) assessing compliance with company policies, which includes meeting regulatory requirements.

An environmental audit is central to a company committed to the implementation of an environmental management system. The environmental audit should not be seen in isolation, but rather as one component of a comprehensive approach to environmental management. The role for senior management is therefore crucial. Without top management support an internal environmental audit programme will not succeed. Moreover, management needs to be fully committed to environmental compliance and to correcting any deficiencies uncovered by the audit programme. It is important that management from the highest levels overtly supports a purposeful and systematic environmental auditing programme.

An environmental review or environmental audit is more than a simple inspection or assessment which offers an opinion based primarily on professional judgement. It has to be a methodological examination of a facility's procedures which will include analyses and testing in order to verify that legal requirements and internal policies are being met. In this context, auditors will base their judgements of compliance on evidence gathered during the audit. An audit can look at particular issues facing the company or it can be a wide-ranging audit which includes a full assessment of the effectiveness of an environmental management system as well as compliance, safety and quality control.

The audit is not a one-off activity. It needs to be seen as an on-going programme where the audit is not only repeated periodically but also developed in terms of scope and sophistication over time. Seeing a single audit as a panacea would not only be wrong but is likely to lead to more problems than it solves. Central to the audit programme therefore is a commitment towards continuous improvement. In effect, an auditing system helps the firm anticipate environmental damage and therefore prevent it from happening.

The overall aim of environmental auditing is to provide an on-going status check which will enable environmental improvement within the organisation to continue and in so doing, will help to safeguard the environment and minimise the risks to human health. Although auditing alone cannot achieve environmental improvement, it is a powerful managerial tool. The key objectives of the environmental audit are:

- to determine the extent to which environmental management systems in a company are performing adequately;
- to verify compliance with local, national and European environmental and health and safety legislation;
- to verify compliance with a company's own stated corporate policy;
- to develop and promulgate internal procedures needed to achieve the organisation's environmental objectives;
- to minimise human exposure to risks from the environment and ensure adequate health and safety provision;
- to identify and assess company risk resulting from environmental failure;
- to assess the impact on the local environment of a particular plant or process by means of air, water and soil sampling; and
- to advise a company on environmental improvements it can make.

There are a number of benefits to firms in having an environmental audit undertaken. These include: assurances that legislation is being adhered to and the consequent prevention of fines and litigation; an improved public image which can be built into a public relations campaign; a reduction in costs (particularly in the area of energy usage and waste minimisation); an improvement in environmental awareness at all levels of the firm, and an improvement in overall quality. Many environmental audit programmes are established on the direct orders of top management for the purpose of identifying the compliance status of individual facilities, thereby providing management with a sense of security that environmental requirements are being met. Increasingly, ignorance will not be tolerated as an excuse when environmental litigation is being pursued.

On the other hand, there are some potential disbenefits of the audit. These include the initial costs of the audit and the cost of compliance with it and the temporary disruption of plant operations. It is also vital that management sees that the recommendations of the environmental auditor are adhered to otherwise an audit report could be incriminating in a court case or insurance claim. An audit report is a 'discoverable' document and may therefore be used in any legal proceedings which may follow. Before an audit is undertaken therefore, management must recognise that the audit may recommend changes which require immediate action because faults are either illegal or hazardous to human health. There is a need therefore to establish a contingency budget to cover expenditure which may be required in response to such recommendations.

There is also often a natural reluctance on the part of management and workers to see outsiders entering the organisation and assessing their own performance. In particular, management can become unhappy about its line of responsibility being invaded. The legitimacy of any auditing team, which may not have the same level of knowledge of an industry as do personnel, will often be challenged. In these respects therefore it is vital that senior management are seen to be supportive of both the audit team and the process.

EVALUATING THE IMPACT OF PRODUCTS VIA LIFE-CYCLE ASSESSMENT

Taking a systems approach to environmental improvement and carrying out environmental audits of sites and organisations are, however, just one half of the picture. There is also a need to consider the environmental impact of products being produced. Life-cycle assessment (LCA) seeks to highlight those areas in the environmental profile of a product where producers should focus their attention in order to minimise their environmental impact through redesign. Should the major area of environmental impact be that of production, then efforts to reduce the impact of the good should centre on the production facility. Alternatively, if the major area of environmental impact occurs as a result of the source of the raw materials used, then alternative sources should be sought. In all cases, those aspects of the product and its production which generate significant environmental impact should be revised.

Life-cycle assessment, also known as cradle-to-grave assessment, attempts to provide information on all facets of a product's environmental performance. The results of LCA must be incorporated into the overall environmental management strategy of the firm to provide an integrated and comprehensive profile for a particular product. As process and product design are inextricably linked, the importance of an integrated approach which aims to minimise the overall environmental impact of a company cannot be over-emphasised.

Undertaking LCA necessitates a number of stages. Briefly, the stages are:

- to identify the areas of environmental impact in order to enable further study;
- to quantify energy and material inputs and emissions within these areas;
- to assess the environmental impact of inputs and emissions at all stages; and
- to establish the options for improving any stage of the life-cycle of the product.

The chosen options should then be incorporated into the wider objectives that are being worked towards through the environmental management system.

While many of the outputs of the LCA may appear to be obvious, the systematic and objective collation of quantitative data will firmly establish the extent of the impact and the scope for improvement. Merely undertaking the LCA will put focus on issues which are normally taken for granted, will confirm or challenge preconceptions and will facilitate a greater understanding of the issues involved. Measuring and documenting the findings of the LCA will enable many of the lessons learned to be transferred throughout the company to change the attitudes and behaviour of those concerned with producing the good. As an internal management tool aiming to achieve results such as these, the benefits of LCA are clear and unequivocal.

If we consider the potential scope of an LCA, then it becomes clear that before beginning the process of LCA, it is important to decide upon the scope and objectives of the exercise. Should a company wish to select the best environmental option in each link in its supply chain, then in theory at least, all of the options available in the supply chain should be assessed. Clearly it is necessary to set the boundaries of the LCA within manageable limits. Current applications of LCA select those facets of the process which are likely to provide the most relevant information, for instance in highlighting any inputs which are especially damaging, or any stages of packaging, distribution, use or disposal which can readily be improved. In practical terms, LCA provides a systematic framework through which the constituents of the product and their environmental impacts, which are selected for study, can be analysed and the potential for impact reduction assessed. For internal use, the scope of LCA may be very selective: however, for external use where comparative measures of total environmental impact are needed, the LCA must be much more comprehensive.

Focusing on the use of LCA as an internal management tool, there are a number of generally accepted stages in its methodology as set out below.

1. Inventory analysis

Inventory analysis gathers information relating to the material and energy inputs into a product and its production and any emissions associated with this. The analysis should relate to all stages of the life-cycle from extraction and cultivation, to processing, transportation, manufacture, packaging, distribution, use and disposal. Resources used and emissions generated should be measured per unit of output produced. Although this stage may demand extensive research, particularly for companies which use a large number of inputs or operate within long supply chains, it is relatively straightforward.

2. Impact analysis

Impact analysis is much less straightforward than inventory analysis. It involves establishing the environmental impact of each of the areas documented under the inventory analysis. This may be extremely complicated because, in many cases, the impact of an emission depends upon the nature of the emission, the environment into which it is emitted and the interaction of a significant number of ecological characteristics. The boundaries of this stage of LCA will therefore be defined by the depth of analysis which is deemed both necessary and possible.

3. Impact assessment

Once the scope and level of environmental impact has been established, some assessment or measurement of this impact is necessary. Impacts can be established both quantitatively and qualitatively. Quantitative impact assessment develops a list of the amounts of emissions and some measurement of their impact. In many cases, factual assessment is difficult and qualitative judgements will have to be made. Comparisons of firms across an industry through benchmarking is useful here.

4. Improvement analysis

The final stage of LCA is that of improvement analysis where the environmental profile of the product is altered through redesign of the product and the methods of its manufacture. A formal and systematic appraisal of the product's environmental impact will often reveal areas where relatively simple fine-tuning will reduce environmental impact. Improvement analysis will therefore assess the technically and economically feasible options available at all stages of the product's life which can be utilised to improve the environmental impact of the good. Obviously, the attention should focus on those areas of their operations where the environmental impact and the potential for its reduction are highest.

The LCA process may not always necessitate such a comprehensive analysis. LCA can be simplified in a number of ways. Different components of the study can be collated in relation to separate impacts, for instance in all those areas where solid waste is generated, energy is consumed and so on. This will reduce the number of variants and simplify the process considerably. Also, for some commonly-used inputs, such as energy, databases of environmental impact are being established in order to provide common LCA solutions. These databases will offer standardised impact assessments for a range of energy and material inputs. Further, developing a selective list of criteria to be assessed may also simplify the process while still enabling internal baseline comparison and external ranking, should the same criteria be consistently applied. The selection of these criteria will in itself be a subjective decision, and once these criteria have been published, products may be designed to minimise environmental impact according to these criteria while ignoring all other areas.

However, as the experience of LCA progresses, the present levels of subjectivity in impact assessment will be reduced. The application of LCA under the EC eco-labelling scheme will scrutinise the data and methodology used and will offer external verification and peer-review of the claims made relating to aggregate environmental impact. Further, as LCA becomes more widely applied, the availability of widely accepted data will increase and hence the process will be simplified.

GREEN MARKETING STRATEGIES

Strategies for green marketing must be at the heart of any company's forward planning. This is where environmental differences will be communicated and where a company's commitment will often be judged. It is also where companies' performance is assessed by consumers and the wider public, and it is important that the integrated approach developed in the environmental management system continues. Legislation requires companies to address their own environmental impact and what is voluntary now may be regulatory in the future. From a marketing perspective there is a need to recognise the potential gains which can be achieved by being proactive and therefore in control of your own destiny. This has been the experience of companies like The Body Shop, Sainsbury's, Safeway and Tesco (discussed in this book) who have successfully integrated environmental considerations into their activities.

One of the key marketing challenges of the 1990s is to re-examine product portfolios as consumers switch to buying more environmentally-friendly goods. This will involve the company in new areas of market research and new marketing strategies to inform consumers about the environmental attributes of their products, and to persuade consumers to buy these products rather than others. This whole process will bring with it a range of new opportunities and threats. However, green marketing, which has too often been treated as a gimmick in the past and ridiculed for its cynicism, is more than about changing the characteristics and advertising of a product. It must be part of an overall philosophy for business which is consistent with the systems-based approach.

Marketing has to be seen as a key part of a corporate philosophy concerned with the identification, development and promotion of products and markets. Marketing strategies aim to satisfy the consumer and should therefore be seen from the customer's point of view. It is, in effect, the management process for identifying, anticipating and satisfying customer's requirements at a profit. The key task of the organisation must therefore be to determine the needs and wants of the target markets and to adapt the organisation to delivering desired satisfactions more effectively and efficiently than its competitors. Green marketing requires that this is done in a way which improves the environmental performance of products and of the business, and therefore enhances consumers' and society's well-being.

A key problem or contradiction often exists in this strategy, however, because consumers' wants do not always coincide with the long-term interests of the environment, and a key element in any green marketing strategy needs therefore to be education and the provision of accurate information. Simply claiming that a product is green without any real basis is unlikely to make a real difference to sales in the long run. But explaining to consumers the real environmental benefits of one product over another is likely to have more far-reaching effects.

A good starting point for analysing any corporate strategy is to examine the demands being made of that strategy. There will be a need to satisfy a whole range of often disparate demands. This will include demands from customers for environmentally-friendly products at reasonable prices with high-quality attributes, demands from shareholders for profitability and growth, and demands from employees for reasonable wages and job security. Although difficult, firms must try to satisfy these demands and reduce the tensions which exist between competing objectives. This approach which has been alien to so many organisations in the past must be part of an organisation's corporate culture if the company is to honestly claim that it is seeking to improve the whole of its environmental performance. Local communities need to be informed about the activities and potential dangers of a site, for example. This is not only paramount in the case of an accident, but it is also necessary for maintaining good relations with those living near to a site. Some sort of report following the implementation of environmental audits needs to be disseminated to the local community as a minimum.

Although environmental considerations are increasingly important to the consumer, environmental attributes alone will be insufficient to sell a product. The product must still be fit for the purpose for which it was intended, have the desired quality and delivery attributes and be price-competitive. Failure to meet these basic requirements will result in failure of the product. Therefore green marketing has to be integrated marketing. Indeed green marketing is no different from traditional marketing insofar as its aim must be to satisfy the end consumer and provide an acceptable profit margin.

Green marketing cannot therefore be looked at in isolation. The effects of launching a new product or reorienting an existing one to have superior environmental attributes will have ramifications for procurement, finance, human resources, production processes and delivery. The fundamental key to a green marketing strategy is to approach the problem systematically and to undertake appropriate research and planning. The general approach may be little different from a conventional marketing strategy but if 'greening' is to be a consideration at the outset, a number of questions will have to be addressed:

- Has the marketing plan identified the key environmental considerations involved in the market for the product?
- Has sufficient scientific and technological research been undertaken to ensure that the product will have superior environmental performance to that produced in the past?
- What effect will new environmental attributes have on costs, revenue and profitability?
- Has the company planned on changes in the overall size of the market which may result in changing consumer attitudes?
- How much new investment will be required in the modification or development of the product in question?
- Has the whole environmental impact of the product from cradle to grave been assessed?

- Has the product undergone sufficient testing to establish its environmental credentials?
- Have environmental pressure groups been consulted and is the company prepared for any adverse criticism of its product?
- Do the communication strategies relating to the product emphasise environmental aspects and benefits?

Consideration of different time-scales for different activities is also important. While we have recognised the importance of longer-term strategic planning, the day-to-day operation and success of the company cannot be neglected either.

ENVIRONMENTAL MANAGEMENT STRATEGIES IN THE SME SECTOR

Small- and medium-sized enterprises (SMEs) have an important role to play in environmental management and although it might be argued that their individual contribution towards environmental degradation is small, taken together they have a very large impact. An obvious problem is that small-business managers do not have access to information concerning environmental management and, in addition, many small firms lack the capital to invest in environmentally-friendly technology. Nevertheless, there are things that they can do at very little cost, and if they can integrate environmental considerations into their everyday activities they are likely to save money, rather than spend it, in the longer term.

One key aim of the environmental challenge must be to help small- and medium-sized enterprises develop and become resource efficient, competitive, technically advanced and environmentally friendly. We have already noted that it is very difficult for the small enterprise alone to achieve all these requirements. The sort of technical expertise which large firms will have in-house to help with their environmental management, will probably be lacking, and few small businesses will have the money to buy in consultants to do these important tasks. A clear way forward for the SME sector revolves around cooperation and networking. This entails creating links between small firms and between firms and institutions. For example, a useful and often unexploited link might be between businesses and local universities, or between firms and economic development units of councils. Natural, geographical links often exist which can also be exploited. By networking and cooperating beyond even the boundaries of the firm, managers can learn from other people's experiences and errors. What small businesses need therefore is a framework within which to achieve such advantages. These can be created by the establishment of industry-specific or multi-sectoral forums, or simply forums within localities, but the common element which will determine the success of any of them is cooperation.

The development of environmental networks among small businesses, voluntary organisations and the public sector, will enable controlled and sustainable growth to occur. Ultimately what we do with our environment affects us all, also future generations. If the environment is important then we should recognise that the systems and processes used in businesses are also important. There is a need for small businesses to be given incentives to undertake environmental change. Some of these incentives are provided by the legislative framework and a need to survive in a more competitive and environmentally aware marketplace. In addition, larger firms will push environmental improvement along the supply chain. But there is still a need to convince small businesses that environmental improvements will reduce costs in the long run, and this can only be achieved by demonstration of best practice. There is a clear role here for government and local authorities in supporting innovative developments and providing a forum where information can be exchanged.

REGIONAL ENVIRONMENTAL MANAGEMENT AND ECONOMIC DEVELOPMENT

The original Treaty of Rome did not give the EC explicit powers to legislate on environmental matters but this was amended by the adoption of the Single European Act 1987, which now provides a firm legal basis for Community legislation on the environment. One of its provisions states that environmental protection requirements should be a component of all other policies based on the indisputable fact that measures in the sphere of other policies may have a significant positive or negative impact on the environment. This must be viewed as an important provision as it establishes a requirement that environmental protection must form an essential component of all Community policies, including economic development policies.

The EC's Fifth Environment Programme, which was introduced in 1993 and will run to the end of the century, has as a major theme the promotion of information and education of the Community's citizens towards the protection of the environment, and the direct involvement of the Community in achieving environmental protection through the use of voluntary agreements, codes of conduct, and economic and fiscal measures.

There will be a move away from dealing with environmental issues on an individual media basis, i.e., air, water, noise, waste, etc., to handling issues on a sectorial and regional basis involving local communities and local and national governments. This approach further emphasises the need for regional conversion plans, which means the integrated development of the economy and the environment involving all sectors of industry, the local community, and local authorities.

Integrated preventive action encourages actions to be taken to protect the environment at an early stage, requiring environmental management to go beyond the question of repairing damages, to stopping pollution from occurring in the first place. 'The polluter pays' principle is an important instrument enabling the market to be adjusted to reflect the true costs of the production of goods and services, and is being adopted by both the EC and Member States' governments. Pressures for regulatory compliance will be met, in the main, through the initiation of continuous and sophisticated monitoring systems, waste minimisation, more effective investments in process technology, and research and development. As these costs begin to impinge more heavily on an organisation's operating and capital costs, evidence of good practice will become a precondition for access to the wider investment community.

These trends confirm that industry will need to adopt a more strategic view of environmental problems. It needs to move away from predominantly short-term solutions to actual problem-solving and towards the development of pre-emptive control strategies striking a balance between regulation and the need to turn those regulations into competitive advantage abroad. The development of a regional environmental management system (REMS) can help significantly here. Not only does it allow for a cooperative environmental effort on the part of firms in the region, which can lead to synergy in research and development, waste management and energy efficiency, but also a significant advantage can be derived from a common marketing approach. A regional conversion plan aims at focusing the marketing instrument not only on the company but also on the region in which the company is based. The region can develop a competitive advantage by way of an integrated proactive environmental policy and by way of an integrated proactive regional environmental management system. In other words, the product will be produced to the highest environmental standards in a geographical region where the quality of the environment is maintained through an efficient REMS.

Where a region is already polluted or environmentally damaged, the common approach to tackling problems is to deal with specific point sources of pollution using regulatory controls. In addition, over time, individual impact assessments can mitigate environmental damage, but they do not necessarily alter the larger picture. The effect of this ad hoc approach on the regional environment can often be seen as 'two steps forward, one step back'. Because of the non-integrated and non-coordinated approach, what is beneficial or, more often, 'not harmful' for one industry, may well be harmful to another.

It must be recognised that the environment responds as a whole when stressed at a particular point, but the traditional piecemeal approach to environmental management does not provide any information about how the whole system reacts. There is therefore a need to develop a more integrated REMS which is capable of exploring the synergistic effect of applying environmental management policies to all sectors of activity. This change from a piecemeal to a holistic approach can be seen as an important part of a 'sustainable development' approach. The concept of sustainable development recognises that there is an interdependence between the economy and the environment, not only because the way we manage the economy has an impact on the environment, but also because environmental quality has an impact on the performance of the economy.

Central to the development of a REMS is the cooperation and commitment of regional and local resources facilitated through partnerships between individuals, businesses, public sector institutions and other agencies. A regional strategy of regional environmental management is required which promotes and stimulates community-implemented development. It is particularly important, therefore, to involve the business sector and to make it clear that there are significant benefits to that sector in becoming involved. This process must begin through the provision of information, continue through education and training, and lead, subsequently, to the the provision of support, advice, and capital for local initiatives. Any environmental management system starts with, and depends strongly upon, the development of understanding and commitment from all people involved, and the REMS is no exception.

There is also a need to have a clear policy for the region which integrates both regional objectives and industrial aspirations. Such policies are already in place where local authorities have followed Friends of the Earth advice in introducing a declaration of commitment to environmental protection and policy development in the areas of recycling, energy, transport and planning, environmental protection and enhancement, health, and the monitoring and minimisation of pollution. Some authorities have also introduced regular environmental audits and invited public and industrial participation. However, the regional environmental management system policy needs to go beyond this and fully integrate the needs of the region, industry and the public into a plan which binds them together with the objective of significantly improving all aspects of the region's environmental performance.

Industry itself can benefit greatly by the additional help which will be provided by firms working together cooperatively with the support of a regional team. The REMS will complement the firm's own internal environmental management system and further add to the firm's competitive advantage if the region can attract a 'green label'. To a large extent the future of the environment and of the planet requires more cooperation, and the concept of the regional environmental management system extends much of the best practice discussed in this book. A key concept of environmentalists has long been associated with local action, global impact. At the centre of this concept is the need for increased cooperation and the REMS extends what firms alone can do towards achieving this important objective.

CONCLUSIONS

The case studies in this book highlight how many of the principles outlined above have been put into practice. Different firms have different ways of translating rhetoric into reality but it will be seen that these basic principles are being adopted in order to bring about environmental improvement. In most of the cases examined it is clear that there either is, or there needs to be, a systematic approach taken to environmental improvement. Central to the process is measurement and, although measures are lacking in definition, it is the role of the environmental audit to assess the improvements which have been made over time.

At industry level or regional level, we must accept that there are inherent risks in treating economic forces and the environment as if they were separate and non-interacting elements. Economic policy which neglects to take into consideration environmental risks and damage is not sustainable. This is exemplified in so many semi-rural areas where economic development has resulted in the exploitation of the natural environment, leaving rivers biologically dead, and parts of the landscape aesthetically degraded and sometimes contaminated. We shall see that cooperative strategies have much to offer in a world where we treat the environment as the important resource which it is.

Note: For further information on the topics raised in this chapter, please refer to Chapter 1 of *Environmental Management and Business Strategy* by Richard Welford and Andrew Gouldson (Pitman Publishing, 1993).

PART 2

Company Case Studies

CHAPTER 3

Taking a systems approach to environmental improvement: the case of IBM UK

Geoff Taylor and Richard Welford

INTRODUCTION

Founded in the USA in 1914, IBM is now the world's largest computer company. Although its activities are not considered to be of the highest environmental impact, the company does use significant quantities of both chemicals and energy. Formal awareness of corporate environmental responsibility has existed within the corporation for some time, with the first corporate environmental policy statement dating back to 1971.

IBM UK's operations have been particularly proactive in responding to environmental issues. In addition to the regular audits required under corporate guidelines, IBM UK has undertaken a comprehensive internal review of its activities, the results of which, together with a list of future objectives and targets, were published in the 'Environmental Programmes for the 90s' document. A key recommendation of this report was that the company should commission an external review of its management policies and systems. This activity was completed by the environmental consultancy Sustainability in 1992 and the resulting report made public.

The impact of continuing poor financial performance, a changing marketplace and new senior management at corporate, and UK level is as yet unclear. There is little doubt, however, that the company will see further radical restructuring in the near future. In spite of this, UK senior management have indicated a commitment to environmental performance as a core issue in the development of future business strategies.

CORPORATE ENVIRONMENTAL POLICY AT IBM

IBM produced its first environmental policy document in 1971 in the form of Corporate Policy Letter 129. Since its initial issue, that statement has been modified on several occasions in response to: changes in legislation; greater

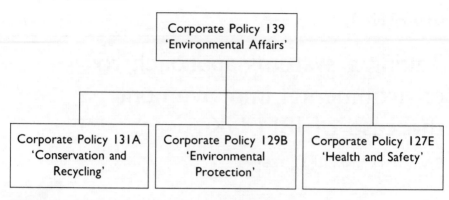

Figure 3.1 IBM environmental policy statements

scientific understanding; experience gained through the development and implementation of environmental programmes; and social concerns.

The latest update to IBM's environmental policy statement occurred in November 1990, with the publication of Corporate Policy 139 – 'Environmental Affairs' (see Appendix, page 56). This document integrates policy letters on environmental protection, conservation and recycling and health and safety (see Figure 3.1), into a comprehensive policy framework, which commits IBM to a proactive stance with regard to environmental concerns. This position has been acknowledged in public by senior management, with IBM's Vice President of Environmental Affairs stating that the corporation's proactive environmental strategy is to conduct itself in such a way that it is never forced (through new legislation) to do anything. As with earlier environmental policy letters, Corporate Policy 139 is binding on all IBM operations world wide, ensuring that environmental standards operate equally in all locations. This approach ensures that coordination of policy, procedures and programmes is optimised within the corporation as a whole, while reducing the opportunity for the development of conflicting priorities and strategies.

ORGANISATIONAL STRUCTURE: ENVIRONMENTAL AFFAIRS

Relationships and responsibilities, with regard to environmental management and policy development at IBM, are illustrated in Figure 3.2. Overall responsibility for environmental affairs within the IBM Corporation, lies with the Corporate Environmental Advisory Council. This body is chaired by the IBM Corporate Vice President of Environmental Affairs. Within Europe, policy objectives and standards are set by the European Environmental Advisory Council, subject to consultation with corporate headquarters.

Within IBM UK, executive responsibility for environmental affairs at Main Board level, has been assigned to the Director of Personnel and Corporate

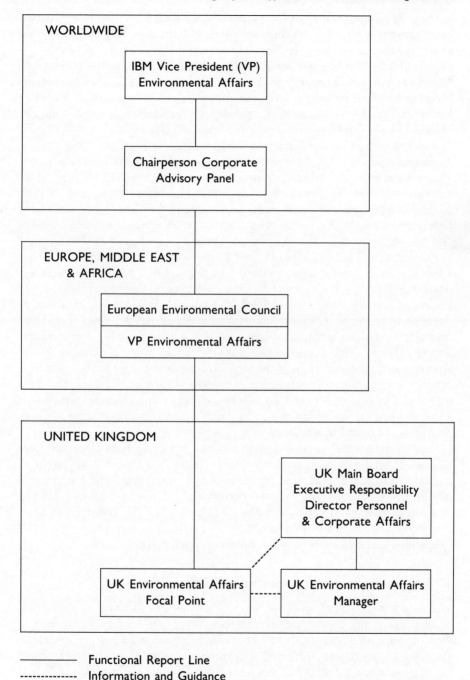

WORLDWIDE

IBM Vice President (VP)
Environmental Affairs

Chairperson Corporate
Advisory Panel

**EUROPE, MIDDLE EAST
& AFRICA**

European Environmental Council

VP Environmental Affairs

UNITED KINGDOM

UK Main Board
Executive Responsibility
Director Personnel
& Corporate Affairs

UK Environmental Affairs
Focal Point

UK Environmental Affairs
Manager

———————— Functional Report Line
-------------- Information and Guidance

**Figure 3.2 IBM global organisational structure for environmental
affairs**

Affairs. Environmental issues are currently scheduled for discussion at two meetings per year. To develop appropriate strategies to meet corporate environmental objectives, the 'IBM UK Environment Council' has been established. This body meets quarterly and is chaired by the Regional Procurement Manager, Northern Europe, and consists of representatives from all the major business functions including development, procurement, manufacturing, marketing and property management. Senior management is therefore centrally involved in the implementation of environmental strategy.

Implementation of the Environmental Strategy Council's decisions is the responsibility of the 'UK Environmental Operations Council'. This body consists of representatives from operational functions within IBM UK and meets six times per year. To ensure clear lines of responsibility, 'ownership' of each of the 36 environmental 'focus areas' – identified in the 'IBM UK Environment Programmes for the 90s' – has been assigned to an Executive Board Member and a representative of the Operations Council.

Environmental activities within the UK operations are coordinated through Environmental Affairs Coordinating Meetings (EACMs). These meetings draw together the Environmental Affairs Country Coordinators and are chaired by the UK Environmental Affairs Manager. EACMs are scheduled to occur six times per year. Responsibility for the day-to-day activities of environmental management within IBM UK is in the hands of the UK Environmental Strategy Team. This group consists of the Environmental Affairs, Public Affairs and Communications Managers. Thus environmental issues are spread across the organisation, with teams of managers meeting regularly to assess progress. The emphasis of the teams is to coordinate and monitor, rather than become involved in problem solving, this activity being practised where problems are found to occur.

Implementation of corporate environmental policy by IBM UK is through a series of well-defined procedures and practices (see Figure 3.3). Environmental assessment of plant and processes is carried out regularly, both internally by UK staff and using external personnel, under programmes organised at a corporate level. A key point to be made here is that the approach adopted is systematic and well planned.

Essentially the strategy is based on the following six activities.

1. Site environmental assessment (SEA)

SEAs are undertaken prior to the purchase of any new site, with the intention of identifying any environmental factors which potentially may: hinder site development, in terms of either limitations on intended use or increased remedial costs; present IBM with a continuing pollution problem; or, have an adverse affect upon IBM's public image. This not only enables IBM to satisfy itself, at the earliest opportunity, that no unacceptable environmental impact occurs as a result of a new acquisition, but it also demonstrates to local

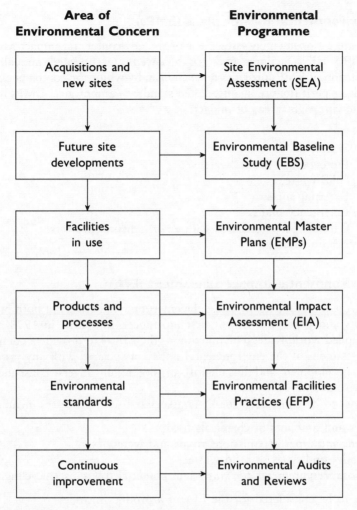

Area of Environmental Concern	Environmental Programme
Acquisitions and new sites	Site Environmental Assessment (SEA)
Future site developments	Environmental Baseline Study (EBS)
Facilities in use	Environmental Master Plans (EMPs)
Products and processes	Environmental Impact Assessment (EIA)
Environmental standards	Environmental Facilities Practices (EFP)
Continuous improvement	Environmental Audits and Reviews

Figure 3.3 Environmental practices and programmes

stakeholders that the company takes environmental issues seriously from the outset.

2. Environmental baseline studies (EBSs)

EBSs have been introduced to provide baseline statements on environmental status. They represent an integral part of any planning applications associated with future developments and are used in the development of strategies for site remediation and reclamation.

3. Environmental master plans (EMPs)

EMPs are a documented assessment of the environmental impact associated with IBM UK's facilities and are reviewed and updated annually. The introduction of EMPs provides a mechanism by which the company can begin to audit its performance against stated standards and targets. EMPs focus on the following eight areas of impact:

1. Air.
2. Water.
3. Protection of groundwater.
4. Solid waste.
5. External noise.
6. Emergency plans.
7. Capital costs associated with environmental projects.
8. Administration.

4. Environmental impact assessment (EIA)

The EIA is the tool used to assess the environmental effects of both proposed products and processes. It was first introduced into IBM in 1978 and are now applied world wide. The function of the EIA is to provide a comprehensive assessment of the environmental impact associated with any product or process development and thus identify any potentially adverse consequences to the environment.

Factors to be considered for EIAs associated with processes include:

- types and amounts of chemicals used;
- extent and types of emissions to air and water;
- quantity and types of solid waste;
- disposal requirements for waste and potential for re-use/recycling.

Factors to be considered for the EIA of a product include:

- types and quantities of raw materials used in manufacturing the product;
- transport and storage requirements for raw materials;
- disposal requirements for waste materials used in manufacturing the product;
- disposal requirements for packaging and other materials associated with the product;
- the potential for re-use/recycling;
- energy consumption of the product while operating.

5. Environmental facilities practices (EFPs)

Environmental standards as defined at corporate level, appear in the form of EFPs and Instruction Letters. The latter are mandatory, while the former provide guidance on best practice and procedures to be followed. Permission to deviate from EFPs must however be applied for. These standards apply to all manufacturing plants, laboratories and offices, and reference to these is required in the development of Environmental Master Plans.

To facilitate the transfer of products and processes across IBM's global operations, EFPs are standardised across all facilities world wide and based on the most stringent regulations in existence. This requirement, together with the presence of IBM in all the world's major markets, has resulted in IBM adopting environmental standards which are consistent with the strictest of legislative demands. In addition, the proactive approach adopted by IBM means that the organisation is in a position to pre-empt any unilateral changes in environmental regulations which may occur in any of the countries in which it operates.

6. Environmental audits and reviews

Environmental audits of IBM activities are undertaken from several perspectives. Each site undertakes an internal audit in the process of reviewing its EMPs, while a rolling programme of site audits at UK level occurs on a 3-to-5-year cycle. All UK sites are also subject to an environmental review and assessment at corporate or IBM Europe level. These audits occur approximately on a 2-year cycle and ensure that improvements in environmental performance become an on-going objective.

In addition to the series of regular audits and reviews, IBM has undertaken a comprehensive internal review of its UK operations. The results of this review were published in the 'IBM UK Environmental Programmes for the 90s' report. The principal objectives for undertaking this review were to: identify areas of major environmental impact; determine whether current policies and practices were adequate to meet the environmental problems identified; and identify new objectives.

EMERGENCY PROCEDURES

IBM has installed an extensive range of emergency procedures to meet those risks perceived to be associated with its activities. All emergency procedures are incorporated within site EMPs and are reviewed regularly both by IBM staff and by external consultants. Emergency response teams exist at all facilities and IBM UK policy stipulates that such teams must be on-call at any time when production equipment is operating.

Strict reporting standards have been established in the case of environmental incidents, with the requirement that the Vice-President, Environmental Affairs, IBM Euro-coordination, be informed within 24 hours of any event which:

- requires reporting to a government agency;
- involves death, or a reportable injury or illness;
- may result in significant impact on human health or the environment;
- results in the emission of any IBM UK chemical substances during transit, or of any such material or waste for which IBM UK is the owner or responsible;
- results in the emission of 1 kg of material classified as toxic or very toxic, 5 kg of material classified as harmful or an irritant, or 50 kg of corrosives, petroleum products or concentrate chemical solutions;
- results in a sheen or discolouration appearing on a body of water;
- may result in adverse publicity for the company.

QUALITY IMPROVEMENT PROGRAMMES AND ENVIRONMENTAL PERFORMANCE

The link between the commitment to total quality within an organisation and the environment has been widely accepted. The objective of total quality programmes is to develop and operate processes such that defects are minimised and, ultimately, prevented totally. Traditionally, management has focused on inspecting the output of processes. This approach allows errors to accumulate and thus results in waste of time and human resources, with materials to rectify. Focusing on the inputs to a process, however, enables the organisation to optimise its performance. Implementation of a total quality system enables companies to improve performance in three ways: a reduction in costs as waste is minimised and stock is controlled more effectively; the development and application of systems and tools which enable the organisation to meet more stringent specifications; and the development of systems and procedures which enable the organisation to respond more effectively to customer requirements.

The link between total quality programmes and environmental programmes is clear. By modifying processes, and introducing programmes and procedures which minimise waste, pollution and the consumption of non-renewable resources, the total environmental impact of the organisation can be reduced. The link between quality issues and environmental performance has been formally acknowledged with the publication of the British Standard for environmental management systems (BS7750). With its many similarities, this system enables organisations to build on the work they have undertaken in achieving the award of the quality system BS5750.

IBM considers quality issues to be a critical success factor in the 1990s and under its MDQ (market-driven quality) programme is dedicated to continuous improvement in all its activities. There is general recognition within the company of the link between quality improvement and reduced environmental impact with the company's quality measurement methodology proving particularly compatible with the drive for waste minimisation.

MANAGEMENT OF HAZARDOUS MATERIALS AND CHEMICALS

IBM UK uses a variety of materials with the potential for significant environmental impact. Well-defined procedures have been established for the handling and disposal of those materials harmful to health, or which have the potential of polluting the environment. Targets have also been set, both at corporate level and by IBM UK, to reduce consumption of materials which, through their use or disposal, will have an adverse affect upon the environment.

Chemicals management at IBM UK is defined within a series of detailed procedures bounded by UK and EC legislation, and by an IBM instruction letter. The importance of the correct management of chemicals with regard to environmental performance, has been recognised, with the identification of this issue as an 'Environmental Focus Area' in the 'Programmes for the 90s' programme.

IBM UK has found meeting corporate environmental guidelines sometimes involves considerable expense. This was evident with the introduction of large-scale chemical processing at IBM UK's Havant site. The company was required to provide extensive safety measures to protect groundwater and, to date, no underground chemical storage facilities have been introduced either at Havant or any other IBM UK site. Storage and disposal procedures for hazardous materials are monitored through site EMPs. To ensure that both IBM UK's practices in this area, and those of its waste disposal contractors, are seen to be operating correctly, external audits are undertaken by the Waste Site Inspection Group. This group is an international organisation funded by multinational companies, which funds environmental audits of hazardous waste contractors world wide.

Chemicals widely criticised for their environmental impact are PCBs (polychlorinated biphenyls). These materials are bioaccumulative and their use was banned by law in 1979, although they are still to be found in some older electrical components. IBM has produced detailed guidelines for their handling and disposal.

Inclusion of these chemicals in IBM products is no longer allowed, and the risks posed by asbestos to the health and safety of its workforce, and to the wider environment, have been acknowledged by IBM UK. In 1974 the company stated that it would no longer be introducing asbestos into newly-acquired property. During the period 1984–89 the company completed an extensive survey of all of its facilities to identify the location of all asbestos material. The company addressed the risk associated with this material by undertaking an extensive removal programme over the period 1986–90. However, as asbestos removal involves stringent procedures and is time consuming, in the case of sites judged to present only negligible risk, the company has chosen to record the presence of asbestos, while deferring removal to such time as a general refurbishment is undertaken.

Damage to the ozone layer is one of the major environmental issues facing the world. Although not a major user of chemicals generally, IBM processes do use ozone-depleting chemicals such as CFCs (chlorofluorocarbons), methyl chloroform and halons. The adverse impact of these chemicals on the environment has been recognised by IBM and the following corporate targets have been set: .

- cease using CFCs in products and processes, at all operations world wide by the end of 1993;
- cease using methyl chloroform in products and processes, at all operations world wide by the end of 1993;
- cease use of halons as viable alternatives become available.

CFC use in processes was phased out at IBM UK's Greenock and Hursley sites in 1990 and 1991 respectively. At the time of writing the Havant site was currently on schedule to eliminate use of these chemicals, as required under the corporate target. Although it is intended that CFCs will be eliminated from all products and processes, it is likely that due to the lack of viable alternatives, IBM UK will still be using these chemicals in air conditioning and refrigeration systems after 1993. IBM has, however, stated that when suitable alternatives become available the company will adopt them where possible. A further reduction in IBM's use of CFCs has been achieved through the incorporation of a clause into all new construction contracts requiring all new projects to use CFC-free insulating materials. The use of ozone-depleting chemicals, together with progress made in reducing such use, is tracked through site EMPs.

ENERGY AND WASTE MINIMISATION

IBM's Corporate Policy statement reflects recognition within the organisation of the importance of waste minimisation and recycling, as a means of conserving natural resources, thus reducing the company's environmental impact.

I. Energy consumption

IBM's operations and products consume considerable electricity. The company has been improving energy performance for some time. Under the 1984–89 Energy Plan, IBM UK set itself a target of achieving a 20 per cent reduction in energy consumption. Over this period an actual reduction of 25.6 per cent was observed, resulting in a saving of £2.6 million. The drive to improve energy efficiency continued with the introduction of the 1990–94 Energy Plan. Under this programme the company committed itself to achieving 4 per cent per annum reduction in total energy consumption over the period. IBM UK achieved a 3.4 per cent reduction in 1990 and a 4.2 per cent reduction in 1991. Continuing to match the stated objectives is, however, likely to prove increasingly difficult, as many of the easiest schemes have already been implemented. Nevertheless, this experience demonstrates very clearly that improved environmental performance can result in considerable cost savings.

The relative importance of energy consumption as a contributing factor to the environmental impact of IBM's activities, is indicated by the fact that of the 36 key areas identified in 'Programmes for the 90s' as presenting the greatest environmental impact from all the company's activities, five concerned energy. The distinct focus areas of these five are:

- Energy supply.
- Energy use in UK Internal Information Systems.
- Energy use in buildings and space.
- Energy use in manufacturing processes.
- Energy use in IBM products.

To date IBM UK's energy reduction programmes have focused on conservation and improving efficiency rather than developing alternative sources of supply. A study to assess the feasibility of using natural or landfill gas to run a CHP (Combined Heat and Power) plant at the North Harbour facility in Portsmouth has been undertaken, however the excessive pay-back period made the project unfeasible.

IBM UK's single largest use of energy is within the area of information technology services. These activities account for approximately 50 per cent of total consumption and historically have grown year-on-year. A task force is currently reviewing and implementing plans which will enable information technology service functions to contribute to the energy reduction targets stated in the 1990–94 Plan. Areas to focus on include:

- the introduction of more energy-efficient hardware;
- reviews of the service level requirements;
- introduction/updating of energy-conservation programmes within computer centres.

At approximately 30 per cent of total consumption, energy use within buildings represents a significant component of IBM UK's current energy needs. Although energy-conservation plans were introduced at all sites by the end of 1991, energy demand is projected to grow. As a result of planned improvements in working conditions, a major source of this growth will be attributable to the introduction of air conditioning to buildings previously lacking this facility. Growth in energy demands in this area are expected to exceed gains made as obsolete plant/equipment is replaced by new energy-efficient systems. However it should be noted that the considerable restructuring and down-sizing of IBM, occurring on a global scale, may significantly affect these growth estimates.

Improvements in technology, with the increasing miniaturisation of computer components, have led to a reduction in the energy consumption of IT equipment. Assessing the overall energy requirement of such equipment and comparing alternative technologies may however not prove straightforward. Although computers and associated peripherals are usually labelled, this information takes no account of any supporting energy requirements, such as cooling. Reviews of equipment assessed by IBM, indicate that overall consumption levels associated with their operation generally vary by 10–15 per cent and may vary by up to 50 per cent. Although IBM products do not, as yet, perform significantly better in this area than those of their competitors, in 1990, development and manufacturing facilities were directed to place a higher priority on reducing product energy consumption as an integral part of reducing life-cycle impact.

Although many of the easiest energy-improvement activities have been undertaken at IBM facilities, increasing energy costs and the possible future introduction of an EC carbon/energy tax, mean that further reductions in energy use are needed in order to further reduce costs in this area.

2. Non-hazardous waste

Waste disposal is becoming increasingly difficult for industry generally. Potential new landfill sites are becoming increasingly difficult to identify due to the lack of suitable locations, pressure from local communities and increasingly stringent legislation. In addition to these constraints, costs at current sites are also rising, as waste management companies adjust to meet the requirements of the Environmental Protection Act 1990. As a result of these factors, industry is under increasing pressure to identify effective solutions for the recycling/re-use of waste material. IBM set itself the goal of achieving a 50 per cent recycling rate of non-hazardous waste at its facilities by 1992. IBM UK achieved this target at the Havant and Hursley sites by the end of 1989 and 1990 respectively. Waste minimisation techniques currently employed or pioneered at Havant include the re-use of wooden pallets, and the introduction of paper and board collection points, bottle banks and aluminium can banks.

In January 1991 the company implemented EMPs at all UK facilities, to identify the types and quantities of all non-hazardous waste. In 1991 the company also developed guidelines for the provision, where feasible, of employee waste-disposal schemes for aluminium cans, paper and cardboard.

3. Packaging

The year 1990 saw the introduction of new corporate guidelines for the design of packaging which emphasise materials minimisation and recovery/recyclability. Facilities are also required to include packaging when undertaking a life-cycle assessment (LCA) of the environmental impact of products.

The issue of packaging has achieved greater importance as a result of the German Packaging Ordinance and its statutory requirement for suppliers to take back packaging. Increasingly stringent packaging legislation is also appearing in other European nations, with the Dutch Packaging Covenant and the French Packaging Decree. Furthermore, the introduction of the proposed EC Packaging Directive is likely to increase the company's need to focus on this area. Within two years of the implementation of this Directive all re-usable and recoverable packaging must carry an appropriate mark to inform the consumer about the nature of its recoverability and that it is part of an established recovery system. Furthermore, Member States will be required to achieve a 90 per cent (by weight) recovery rate for packaging waste within ten years, of which 60 per cent must be recycled. Additionally by the year 2000 all EC States must have deleted from their markets any packaging material for which there is no established re-use or recovery channel. The impact of this Directive on organisations operating within the EC will be to exert pressure on them to:

- minimise their use of packaging materials;
- identify and use packaging materials which are more readily re-usable or recyclable;
- identify or establish channels for the re-use or recycling of packaging materials.

4. Office supplies

In 1991 IBM undertook a preliminary review of the environmental impact of a wide range of office supplies. Although materials such as correction fluids do have implications with respect to both health and safety, and general environmental impact, the large volumes of paper used (200 million sheets of writing, copier and printing paper each year) by IBM UK resulted in the decision being taken to focus effort on this area of office materials.

The company is taking two approaches to reducing the impact of its paper use. Firstly the use of recycled paper, particularly for printing, has been actively supported. The main benefit to the environment is, however, likely to come through increased use of the RMDS (Report Management and Distribution System). This system enables employees to transfer reports electronically between sites, with the capability to print selected pages if wished. Full utilisation of this system, to achieve maximum environmental benefit, will require educating staff to break from the ingrained habit of printing all material they wish to review, rather than reading it from a monitor. This approach does, however, offer potentially much greater savings than simply moving to recycled paper, as it tackles the issue of the extent to which employees actually use and waste paper.

PRODUCT DESIGN AND DEVELOPMENT

Like many other companies, IBM has recognised that the environmental performance of its products is becoming an increasingly important success factor for the company. The introduction of BS7750 and the EC eco-management and audit scheme, together with the EC eco-label scheme, increases pressure, both from within the organisation and from customers, on improving the performance of products.

IBM is an active member of the pilot programme for BS7750 and award of both this standard and the eco-management and audit scheme will require the company to display improved environmental performance in all areas including product impact. As with IBM, those of its industrial customers intending to achieve award of these standards will also have to display a commitment to environmental improvement. A key factor in such a process is the identification and use of suppliers with similarly high environmental standards.

Along with adherence to the new environmental system standards, IBM is committed to achieving the award of the eco-label for its products. This scheme is of particular importance to IBM as it will enable the company to differentiate its products from those of its competitors in an increasingly competitive market where PCs are increasingly being seen as commodities. A key feature of the EC eco-label scheme is the need for an assessment of the environmental impact of products over their life cycle. Such an analysis will require reviewing the environmental impact of all components and will therefore force environmental issues onto the agenda of companies along the supply chain. As a result IBM expects its industrial customers to consider the environmental impacts and to report on both the general environmental performance of the company and that of specific products.

The development of products with a reduced environmental impact has been in the hands of the ECP (Environmentally Conscious Product) task force, established in 1990. This group has been attempting to apply LCA techniques to quantify the environmental impact of products. However, as a result of the complex nature of PCs, their many applications and the long supply chains used by IBM, the organisation has as yet been unable to develop a usable methodology. In fact, IBM has found it difficult even to identify the dominant areas of environmental impact related to its products. For this reason IBM has been able to release only provisional, qualitative guidelines to its design teams.

A particular area being focused upon is the type and combination of plastics used in IBM's products. To increase recycling capability, the company is moving towards using single polymer materials, while avoiding the use of coatings. The increasing application of clip-together technology is also seen to be of considerable importance in facilitating the recycling process. The replacement of traditional screw fastenings with such technology will improve disassembly rates, thus making materials recycling more cost-effective.

IBM UK has been operating a materials recovery, recycling and disposal scheme internally since the mid-1980s and this was expanded to its customers, in the form of its ECO (Equipment Collection Offering) scheme, in January 1991. The scheme is intended to operate on a non-profit basis, with customers being required to pay only a small fee.

IBM is currently able to recycle approximately 80 per cent (by weight) of its systems and aims to improve this to over 90 per cent by the mid-1990s. The vast majority of this recovered material is base metal, although a small amount of precious metal is also recovered. Although the quantities of these metals have made recycling of older systems very cost-effective, a problem now facing both IBM and its competitors is that improving technology has resulted in a reduction in the amount of valuable material within each system, thus also reducing the viability of the whole recycling scheme. One answer to this has been to join with other companies involved in the electronics equipment supply chain, to establish a common recycling scheme. The Industry Council for Electronic Equipment Recycling (ICER) was launched with this aim in mind and includes ICL, DEC, Hewlett-Packard, Northern Telecom and Thorn-EMI. By pooling expertise and programmes, it is hoped to increase recycling volumes and thus achieve improved cost-benefit ratios through economies of scale.

SUPPLIERS' AGENTS AND DEALERS

With an extensive supplier base, a significant element of IBM UK's environmental impact is governed by suppliers' activities. As mentioned above, with IBM UK's stated intention of obtaining the award of the EC eco-label for some of its products, together with BS7750, the company is finding it increasingly necessary to assess its suppliers' activities. IBM has recently seen a considerable reduction in suppliers from over 4,000 to approximately 2,700. This is partly a result of the development of new products which use fewer components and have a more standardised specification, and also the development of closer relationships with core suppliers.

In 1990, IBM UK established a Supplier Environmental Task Force to review and promote environmental awareness amongst the company's suppliers. In its report in May 1991 the task force concluded that on-site suppliers operate to acceptable environmental standards; however off-site suppliers either do not know what to do to improve performance, or do, but as yet have failed to fully implement environmental programmes.

To obtain a fuller picture of the performance of its suppliers, the task force began a review programme of suppliers in June 1991. This involved providing a self-assessment questionnaire to suppliers, with a more detailed questionnaire for those considered to be of high risk. Based on the responses received, IBM judges that:

- 50 per cent have a very good environmental performance;
- 25 per cent have a good environmental performance;

- 15 per cent know what to do to meet IBM's standards but have, as yet, not achieved them;
- 10 per cent do not know what to do.

Of those that have little idea of how to respond to IBM's environmental demands, all are in the Far East. These companies often respond by saying IBM should foot the bill for any environmental improvements they require. IBM's response to this has been to work with other customers to place pressure on the supplier to improve. One key problem is that under circumstances where a supplier's other customers are not prepared to pay a premium for products with a lower environmental impact, the supplier would lose these customers if forced to meet IBM's requirements. This situation has led to resistance, by suppliers, to pressure for change, and under these circumstances IBM has often changed to a new source of supply. Recently however, IBM is considering whether this approach is in fact the most effective. De-listing a supplier can have considerable adverse affects for local economies while doing almost nothing to reduce environmental damage overall. The company is now focusing on working closer with its suppliers' other customers to coordinate environmental requirements and thus encourage the adoption of environmental strategies by the suppliers. This approach is therefore proactive and goes beyond the traditional supply chain model of development.

In the UK, IBM has faced growing resentment among its suppliers who are being inundated with requests from customers to reply to questionnaires about environmental performance, or to undertake environmental audits. For this reason (and others) the company is now actively involved with the Business in the Environment organisation, developing a suppliers' code of conduct with regard to environmental performance. The introduction of this code should assist suppliers in developing an integrated and comprehensive environmental profile which can be given to customers.

One key strategy behind IBM's environmental programme is therefore to use environmental characteristics in its product range as a source of competitive advantage. The company's intentions to use environmental performance as a marketing tool, in turn, requires a consistent approach along all distribution channels. For example, attempts have been made to develop a code of conduct for agents. Failure to address this issue risks the perception by customers of inconsistency within the organisation, and a lack of clear strategic direction or commitment to environmental improvement. Moving both forwards and backwards along the supply chain is therefore an important area for development in the future. To date, failure to achieve this requirement is symptomatic of IBM's greatest potential weakness in the area of environmental management. Although the company has achieved much in terms of its own environmental performance, Sustainability noted a tendency for IBM management to be inward-looking, with little awareness of what the company's competitors may be doing in the environmental area. Although the company has been benchmarking competitors for years, this process has contained no formal assessment of environmental performance. Since the completion of Sustainability's review, the company does appear to be responding in this area. Benchmarking procedures have now changed, and a team has been established to review earlier information regarding the products and processes of key competitors, therefore the appropriate analysis of these data should provide a comparative environmental performance assessment of IBM in its marketplace. In turn, it will provide information for IBM to measure the real extent to which it holds a competitive advantage in environmental terms.

TRANSPORT AND DISTRIBUTION

Guidelines for environmental performance have operated within IBM's distribution function for many years. However, these requirements were not fully formalised until recently. The key environmental issues associated with distribution are outlined in the document 'Gearing Up For The Environment', produced in association the National Materials Handling Centre, and distributed to all UK distribution managers.

In an effort to reduce waste and storage requirements, IBM has moved increasingly to implementing 'Just-in-Time' (JIT) and 'Materials Requirements Planning' (MRP) methodologies. A common feature of both these approaches is that they are demand-led, thus ensuring that stocks are kept to a minimum. Implementation of such systems enables the organisation to reduce the capital it invests in inventories and the extent of storage facilities. By introducing such practices, the levels of hazardous materials stored can also be reduced, thus reducing risk. Drawbacks do, however, exist with regard to these approaches. IBM readily admits that as a result of the implementation of these approaches the frequency of vehicle movements has increased. Furthermore, increased warehouse centralisation has resulted in an increase in the distance of journeys. This illustrates the key environmental trade-offs to be considered between JIT and MRP principles, which reduce stock holdings and their associated transport implications.

IBM operates a significant employee car fleet. As a result of the company policy document on unleaded fuel, approximately 95 per cent of IBM's car fleet now runs on unleaded fuel, and methods of achieving greater fuel efficiency are provided through newsletters. An initiative that may significantly reduce the environmental impact of road use by company employees is the introduction of 'car pooling'. So far, a limited initiative is running at the Hursley site, supported by the company's IT facilities. Nevertheless any company which operates a significant car fleet must recognise that it is encouraging employees to use this mode of transport at the expense of alternatives such as rail. The environmental implications of maintaining the fleet and the criteria employed in allocating cars to staff need to be fully addressed.

COMMUNICATION AND EDUCATION

1. Internal communication programmes

No environmental improvement strategy will work without the full cooperation of the workforce which it affects. Employee access to information on
environmental issues is therefore of considerable importance. The application
of electronic communication tools enables IBM to provide greater access to
information, with employees being able to view UK environmental
programmes and policies through on-line office systems. The company also
employs a system of 'Speak-ups', which provide a mechanism through which
staff can communicate anonymously with management about issues which
concern them. The company has found that environmental concerns are often
voiced through this medium, with issues such as recycling and emissions from
photocopiers and laser printers being raised. General information regarding
environmental issues is also often to be found in site newsletters.

The single greatest criticism by employees, and identified by Sustainability,
relating to IBM's internal communication systems is the tendency towards
excessive bureaucracy. The company is aware of this problem and, in order
to address this issue, the 'Speak-up' system was introduced. Staff comments
indicate, however, that further work needs to be done in this area.

2. Employee training

IBM has a reputation for investing heavily in the training of its employees. The
courses 'Management in a Changing Environment' and a three-day strategy
programme, both run by IBM UK, identify environmental issues as an area to
be addressed in the development of future strategies within the company. To
provide further support for key managers involved in the development and
promotion of environmental programmes within IBM UK, the company is
developing both an internal training scheme concerning environmental, energy
and chemical management, and an MSc course at Portsmouth University.

Training is regarded as a key issue for the company but, during Sustainability's environmental review, staff indicated that training in this area was still
insufficient, particularly with regard to middle management who are responsible for implementing environmental strategies. The numbers and grades of
staff which the company enrols on its new environmental training programmes
will, therefore, be both an indicator of the further commitment of the company to environmental improvement, and crucial to the long-term success of
translating corporate environmental strategies into realisable benefits.

3. External communications

IBM is widely regarded as developing an early commitment to environmental
issues, although this image is adversely affected by the failure at corporate level

to sign up to the ICC's Business Charter for Sustainable Development. Nevertheless, within the UK company representatives are actively working with the many organisations and committees involved in policy developments in industry and the environment, including:

- ACBE (Advisory Council on Business and the Environment)
- BSI (British Standards Institute)
- BiE (Business in the Environment)
- UKCEED (UK Centre for Economic and Environmental Development)
- IIED (International Institute for Environment and Development)

The company is also represented on a variety of CBI committees and panels, formed to address a range of environmental issues.

Programmes to aid community activities and charities operating in the environmental field have included the provision of free consultancy to small charities on how best to employ IT, and the funding of three-day strategic planning courses, also for charities. Community participation by the company has been promoted through the introduction of the company's innovative LEAT (Local Environmental Action Teams) programme, which has enabled employees to take time off to become involved in voluntary environmental activities.

The company has made considerable donations in the past to the support of environmental programmes, including initiating a £3.6 million donation by several IBM companies to the United Nations Environment Programme (UNEP). The recent poor financial performance of IBM led, however, to a considerable reduction in IBM's donations budget in 1992. Furthermore it is as yet unclear to what extent the company's capacity to monitor and respond to external events is likely to be affected by the recent substantial reduction in the resources available to the Public Affairs function.

THREATS TO IBM'S ENVIRONMENTAL PROGRAMMES

Sustainability highlighted a major dilemma facing IBM in the development of its environmental strategies. If the company develops its programmes too rapidly it may find itself too far ahead of its customers and thus lose business. This issue has gained more relevance recently with the decline of IBM's dominance in the computer market. Previously the company was able to dictate developments in the market. However, with changing patterns in technology and greater competition, this control has declined and IBM is now faced with the need to respond more readily to customer needs, which do not necessarily place great emphasis on environmental concerns.

Rapid developments in IBM's environmental programmes may create further problems for the company. If suppliers are unable to match the environmental targets defined in IBM's specifications, this in turn may lead to the company being unable to meet its own targets. Such a situation is likely to have a considerable adverse impact on the ability of the company to differentiate its products through the marketing of its environmental performance.

The risks associated with pushing ahead with its environmental initiatives may therefore force the company to reduce its investment in environmental performance just as this investment could begin to pay back. Although further investment, at a later date, will enable the company again to begin a process of improvement, valuable time will have been lost, with competitors being given the opportunity to catch up with or overtake IBM.

The commitment of IBM UK's senior management does seem to have been reinforced subsequent to Sustainability's review, with the Chief Executive of IBM UK, Nick Temple, suggesting that if IBM's green record can provide any marketing advantage whatsoever, then it should be exploited to the full in pursuing the market vigorously. This, together with the introduction of competitive benchmarking of products, with regard to environmental performance, suggests that UK senior management is committed to environmental issues and reflects the need to make performance in this area more market-orientated. Having said this, however, uncertainty over IBM's environmental strategy is likely to increase in the near future. The financial difficulties currently being faced by the company, together with the changing nature of the computer market and a new corporate Chief Executive, are likely to result in a further significant restructuring of the corporation's global operations. The impact of these changes on IBM's environmental programmes is uncertain. However, cutbacks in IBM UK's donations in 1992, and a down-sizing of the Public Affairs function, represent threats to the maintenance of momentum in the drive for environmental improvement. It is likely that in future the corporation will become increasingly decentralised as corporate management attempts to introduce the necessary flexibility into the organisation, enabling it to respond more rapidly to changes in its markets. As the decision-making process is further delegated and management respond increasingly on purely regional or product levels, it may become increasingly difficult for the corporation to present a coherent strategy at a global level. If conflicting strategies are allowed to develop this will significantly weaken the company's ability to market itself as a leader in environmental performance and will reduce its capacity to influence the performance of its suppliers. This in turn may result in a competitive advantage being turned into a fragmented and piecemeal approach so often identified with other less environmentally aware organisations.

CONCLUSION

IBM UK's environmental performance, to date, has been impressive and much has been achieved. The strategy has been on a well-defined policy, a system for the management of environmental issues and the establishment of groups and teams with responsibility for implementing that policy. The company has used this mechanism in its drive to achieve commitment to environmental improvement at all levels in the organisation. The company has not only emphasised its own internal organisational strategies but is increasingly interested in the environmental performance of its products from cradle to grave. Its strategy of materials and waste management and a renewed consideration of design aspects with regard to its products, has enabled IBM to use environmental characteristics as a marketing tool. IBM's integrated and comprehensive environmental strategy has increasingly encompassed suppliers and distributors in an attempt to achieve its objectives, as well as promoting environmental issues more widely. There is still considerable scope for improvement, particularly in the area of transport and the implications of the company's current financial difficulties on the extent of investment in environmental improvement is as yet unknown. However, the process of environmental improvement is clearly under way within IBM.

APPENDIX
CORPORATE ENVIRONMENTAL POLICIES AT IBM

I. Corporate Policy 139 – 'Environmental Affairs'

IBM is committed to environmental affairs leadership in all of its business activities. IBM has long-standing corporate policies of providing a safe and healthful workplace and safe products (Policy Letter Number 127), of protecting the environment (Number 129), and conserving energy and natural resources (Number 131), which were initiated in 1967, 1971 and 1974, respectively. These policies continue to guide IBM operations and they are the foundation for the following corporate policy objectives.

- Provide a safe and healthful workplace, including avoiding or correcting hazards; ensuring that personnel are properly trained and have appropriate safety and emergency equipment.
- Be an environmentally responsible neighbour in the communities where IBM operates; act promptly and responsibly to correct incidents or conditions that endanger health, safety, or the environment, report them to authorities promptly, and inform everyone who may be affected by them.
- Maintain respect for natural resources by practising conservation and striving to recycle materials, purchase recycled materials and use recyclable packaging and other materials.
- Develop, manufacture and market products that are safe for their intended use, efficient in their use of energy, protective of the environment, and can be recycled or disposed of safely.
- Use development and manufacturing processes that do not adversely affect the environment; develop and improve operations and technologies to minimise waste, prevent air, water and other pollution, minimise health and safety risks, and dispose of waste safely and responsibly.
- Ensure the responsible use of energy throughout IBM business, including conserving energy, improving energy efficiency, looking for safer energy sources and giving preference to renewable over non-renewable energy sources when feasible.
- Assist in the development of technological solutions to global environmental problems, share appropriate pollution-prevention technology and methods, and participate in efforts to improve environmental protection and understanding throughout industry.
- Meet or exceed all applicable government requirements. Where none exists, set and adhere to stringent IBM standards and continually improve these standards in light of technological advances and new environmental data.
- Conduct rigorous audits and self-assessments of IBM's compliance with this policy; measure progress of IBM's environmental affairs performance and report periodically to the Board of Directors.

- Every employee and every contractor on IBM premises is expected to follow the company's policies and to report any environmental, health, or safety concern to IBM management. Managers are expected to take prompt action.

2. Corporate Policy 129B – 'Environmental Protection'

IBM will reduce to a minimum the ecological impact of all of its activities. Management in IBM is expected to be continuously on guard against adversely affecting the environment and to seek ways to conserve natural resources.

Although IBM is not in a business which creates severe pollution problems, IBM is committed to:

- Meet or exceed all applicable government regulations in any location.
- Establish stringent standards of its own where government regulations do not exist.
- Attempt to utilise non-polluting technologies and to minimise energy and materials consumption in the design of products and processes.
- Minimise dependence on terminal waste treatment through development of techniques to recover and re-use air, water and materials.
- Assist government and other industries in developing solutions to environmental problems when appropriate opportunities present themselves and IBM's experience and knowledge may be helpful.

3. Corporate Policy 131A – 'Conservation and Recycling'

It is IBM's policy to conserve energy and raw materials, to recycle commodities and to help protect the environment.

The oil crisis of the early 1970s forcefully demonstrated that with planning and imagination IBM was able to reduce its fuel and power consumption significantly. The solid waste disposal crisis now confronting the United States and other countries gives IBM an additional challenge to reduce waste by making more efficient use of raw materials and recycled commodities. Recognising the need for prudent energy use and global environmental protection, while maintaining a safe and healthful workplace, management must strive to keep its focus on both energy conservation and materials recycling.

Therefore, IBM expects each operating unit to cooperate fully in conservation programmes, giving high priority to the energy-efficient operation of its facilities and processes, and to the conservation of energy and raw materials in the design and manufacture of products. Emphasis should also be given to the use of recyclable packaging and components, the recycling of used commodities, and the purchase of recycled materials. Similarly, IBM expects managers at all levels to implement these policies by personal example – whether it be simply in turning off equipment or lights, or in the prudent purchase, consumption and recycling of supplies and materials.

This approach is good business practice and serves the broader purpose of helping to conserve the world's limited resources.

4. Corporate Policy 127E – 'Responsibility for Health and Safety'

IBM is committed to provide a safe and healthful work environment and safe products. There can be no compromise in protecting the health and safety of employees and customers.

All IBM managers have personal responsibility for protecting the health and safety of all persons in the work environment. They must take positive actions to avoid or correct potential health and safety hazards. To accomplish this, management must ensure that IBM employees, and others for whom they are responsible, are properly placed and trained, perform safely and, where appropriate, are provided with proper safety and personal protective and emergency equipment.

Every manager involved in the development, manufacture, installation, service or disposal of IBM products is responsible for ensuring that the product or process meets requirements for health and safety, including necessary precautions for those who come into contact with them.

Corporate staff heads, as a part of their responsibility for a functional area, will determine that the organisation's health and safety practices are reasonable, adequate, current, and thoroughly understood.

The personnel staff head is responsible for developing uniform medical and health programme policies for all IBM employees, for reviewing policy implementation, for overseeing all human health research programmes, and for effecting coordination between the different areas and staffs of the business.

The environmental affairs staff head, with the counsel of appropriate corporate staffs, will prescribe the practices that must be followed to discharge IBM's responsibility for environmental programmes. Further, the environmental affairs staff head is responsible for developing safety policy and shall have oversight responsibility for chemical management and product/process safety.

The manufacturing and development staff head, with the counsel of appropriate corporate staffs, is responsible for establishing world-wide uniform chemical management and product/process safety programmes. Appropriate reviews will be implemented to ensure control and accountability for programme activities at IBM locations.

Questions for discussion

1 Do you consider IBM's environmental strategy to have been a success? What do you consider to have been the critical success factors?

2 What methods can the company employ to encourage improved environmental performance from its suppliers/agents?

3 How can IBM more effectively market its environmental performance?

4 What methods can the company employ to raise environmental awareness among its customers?

5 IBM has introduced its 'Speak-up' programme in an attempt to circumvent excessive bureaucracy and more effectively to tap the potential of its employees. What other approaches could be employed to support this process?

6 What are the implications for the future environmental performance of IBM of both its poor financial performance and the likely radical restructuring of the company?

Note: For further information on the topics raised in this chapter, please refer to Chapters 3, 4 and 5 of *Environmental Management and Business Strategy* by Richard Welford and Andrew Gouldson (Pitman Publishing, 1993).

CHAPTER 4

A commitment to environmental improvement: the case of British Telecommunications

Geoff Taylor and Richard Welford

INTRODUCTION

British Telecommunications (BT) is both the UK's largest company and its principal supplier of telecommunications services. Currently the company is perceived by the general public as having little impact upon the environment, however senior management have recognised that in addition to the threats posed by consumer attitudes and changing legislation, new opportunities are also appearing for those organisations willing to take a proactive stance with regard to environmental issues. BT is also a major purchaser of goods and services and feels that it can have a significant influence on environmental performance, widely defined, by pushing environmental issues along the supply chain.

BT is therefore actively involved in the implementation of a comprehensive business-wide environmental management programme, which addresses all areas where the organisation impacts upon the environment. The programme focuses heavily upon integrating environmental performance into all planning activities within the company.

The increasingly dominant paradigm associated with the view that environmental performance is a quality issue with waste and poor performance being linked to quality failure, has been accepted by the organisation. Along with other large organisations investing heavily in environmental improvement, such as IBM, ICL and ICI, BT is building on experience gained through its existing Total Quality Management (TQM) programme. Central to this approach is the commitment of BT to improving its performance in line with quality standards.

Particularly important features of BT's environmental programme to date are its commitment to the annual publication of a comprehensive company environmental performance report and the development of a generic procurement standard. The latter is of particular importance in the context of the scale of BT's purchasing activities, thus the potential influence it can exert upon its suppliers to improve their performance is significant. This is likely to become a major thrust in getting smaller companies to think about their own environmental performance.

ENVIRONMENTAL POLICY AND MANAGEMENT SYSTEMS

The initial environmental review

With BT's decision to commission the environmental consultancy, Sustainability, to undertake a high-level review of its activities and practices, 1989 represented a milestone for BT in terms of its environmental programme. As a result of this review the following strategic recommendations were made:

- responsibility for environmental affairs was to be assigned to a specific Board member, thus ensuring Board level ownership of this issue and indicating the commitment of senior management;
- publication of an environmental policy statement;
- formal recognition of environmental performance as a quality issue and thus its links to its TQM programme;
- the introduction of a formal environmental management structure, with the establishment of a corporate environmental management unit to oversee environmental programmes and monitor progress.

BT's environmental policy

Subsequent to Sustainability's review, BT began work developing an appropriate environmental policy statement. A number of key requirements were identified as being important in this document. Although it was recognised that the policy statement should address BT's many varied activities, it was felt that an overly wordy document would be inappropriate. Any policy statement would have to indicate a genuine commitment to the environment and act as a catalyst for change, while at the same time recognising BT's need to act pragmatically in order to operate in a competitive business environment. The policy statement would also have to be consistent with BT's primary business objectives. Lastly, the policy statement should be written in such a manner that it would not require frequent revisions.

The final version of BT's environmental policy was published in March 1991. The purpose of the statement is to place environmental issues within the context of the company's activities. It addresses:

- the pros and cons of BT's activities in terms of its contribution to the total environmental impact of society's activities;
- the relationships between environmental issues, health and safety, total quality management and training standards within the organisation; and
- the assignment of ownership of environmental issues to a specified member of BT's Board, thus ensuring commitment of the organisation to future

environmental improvement and to communicating this to staff and stakeholders.

The policy is as follows:

In the pursuit of its mission to provide world class telecommunications and information products and services, BT exploits technologies which are basically friendly to the environment. In the sense that use of the telecommunications network is often a substitute for travel or paper-based messages, BT is contributing positively to environmental well-being and conservation of resources.

We recognise however that in our day-to-day operations we inevitably impact on the environment in a number of ways and we wish to minimise the potentially harmful effects of such activity wherever and whenever possible.

As part of our continuing drive for quality in all the things we do we have therefore developed a comprehensive policy statement which will enable us to set the targets by which our efforts towards sustainable environmental improvement can be measured and monitored on a regular basis. In this way we aim to protect the health of our own people and our customers while contributing to the future well-being of the environment.

We have undertaken to help every BT person to understand and to implement the relevant aspects of this policy in their day-to-day work through the regular communication of objectives, action plans and achievements. At Board level, the Deputy Chairman has specific responsibility for policy development, coordination and evaluation of performance. BT is committed to minimising the impact of its operations on the environment by means of a programme of continuous improvement. In particular BT will:

- meet, and where appropriate, exceed the requirements of all relevant legislation – where no regulations exist BT shall set its own exacting standards;
- promote recycling and the use of recycled materials, while reducing consumption of materials wherever possible;
- design energy efficiency into new services, buildings and products, and manage energy wisely in all operations;
- wherever practicable reduce the level of harmful emissions;
- minimise waste in all operations and product development;
- work with BT suppliers to minimise the impact of their operations on the environment through a quality purchasing policy;
- protect visual amenity by careful siting of buildings, structures and the deployment of operational plant in the local environment and respect wild life habitats;
- support through its community programme the promotion of environmental protection by relevant external groups and organisations;
- include environmental issues in BT training programmes and encourage the implementation by all BT people of sound environmental practices;
- monitor progress and publish an environmental performance report on an annual basis.

Management of environmental performance

In attempting to improve an organisation's environmental performance it is possible to construct elaborate and comprehensive management systems to undertake monitoring and control activities. These structures, with clear lines of responsibility for the implementation and control of environmental programmes and procedures, may introduce a system which runs parallel to the management of the main business activities of the organisation. BT has chosen an alternative approach. The environmental management system within BT is restricted to the role of strategy development, co-ordination, monitoring and reporting. No executive powers of control rest within this structure rather, responsibility for implementation of environmental programmes has been integrated as fully as possible into the main business functions.

Although no formal decision has yet been taken to seek accreditation with the BS7750 environmental quality standard, BT has begun the development and implementation of its own system which is consistent with the latter standard (see Figure 4.1). The first stage of this programme involves representatives from 'functional units' within the company attending a training course on environmental management. The organisation is currently involved in

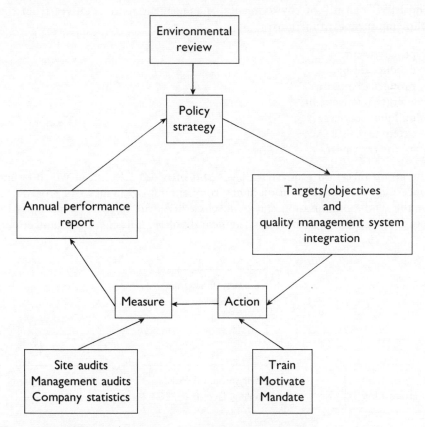

Figure 4.1 BT's environmental management system

undertaking environmental reviews for each unit, with the results being documented in an 'effects register' as required by BS7750 . Targets for the individual units can then be drawn up, based on the information contained within these registers, in the context of the company's strategic objectives.

The targets, together with actual achievements, are to be recorded in the annual Quality Plan and Budget. This documented system is BT's primary mechanism for recording and reporting fiscal and quality targets. The inclusion of environmental targets in the Quality Plan and Budget, therefore, represents an acceptance of one of Sustainability's principal recommendations that formal recognition of the link between quality issues and environmental improvement be made within the company.

As illustrated in Figure 4.2, the activities and responsibilities associated directly with environmental management development within BT as a whole are assigned between three groups. These are as follows:

1. Environmental Policy Steering Group (EPSG)

The EPSG consists of environmental management representatives from the following business functions:

- procurement;
- product design;
- product disposal;
- energy management;
- building services;
- external plant;
- motor transport.

The group meets on a quarterly basis and provides a forum in which issues concerning the implementation of environmental programmes and procedures for the whole organisation can be discussed. As the role of this group is to coordinate and endorse BT's environmental policy, it has neither a budget nor

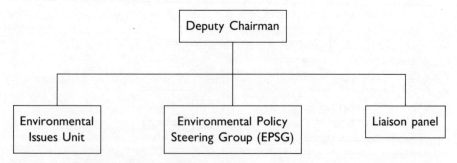

Figure 4.2 BT's environmental management structure

formal executive powers to control the implementation of programmes. The presence of BT's Deputy Chairman as the chairman of this group, underlines the commitment of senior management to a process of environmental improvement and, in reality, enables the EPSG to influence the adoption of environmental programmes and procedures.

2. Environmental Issues Unit (EIU)

Although not involved in the actual implementation of BT's environmental programme, the EIU has a key role in ensuring its success. The primary function of this unit is to act as coordinating body for the programme on a day-to-day basis. Its other responsibilities and activities involve it in: monitoring and reporting on trends and changes in environmental legislation; acting as a company 'think-tank' and providing a pool of expertise to develop new environmental strategies consistent with BT's activities. It undertakes environmental auditing of company sites and provides a communications channel between the company, stakeholders and the general public.

3. Environmental Liaison Panel

The Environmental Liaison Panel was established in 1990 to provide an independent forum to discuss differing views on the potential environmental impact of industry, and presents an opportunity for a variety of opinions regarding environmental priorities and strategies to be voiced and assessed.

The panel is chaired by an independent environmental consultant, with members being drawn from a variety of backgrounds including representatives from: the voluntary sector; organisations involved in energy policy, waste management and environmental auditing; those involved in undertaking and assessing research into climate change; sectors involved in teaching environmental skills; those concerned with the development and implementation of corporate environmental strategies; organisations involved in community programmes; those concerned with the development and implementation of local government policy; and organisations representing youth.

Previous members of the Environmental Liaison Panel have included representatives from waste regulation authorities, local government and even school children. It should be noted that representation on the Environmental Liaison Panel is voluntary, with all members appearing in a purely private capacity rather than representing any particular organisations. The company has actively approached the panel for opinions concerning the development of programmes within the organisation. To date issues raised and discussed by the panel have included policy statements and management systems, energy efficiency, waste management, environmental procurement standards, telephone directory recycling, environmental training needs and visual amenity.

Monitoring environmental performance

Effective monitoring mechanisms are critical to ensuring continuous environmental improvement. BT plans to meet this key need through the introduction of a comprehensive environmental auditing system communicated through its Annual Performance Report. Auditing of sites is necessary to assess the extent to which the company's environmental aims and objectives are being achieved. 1992 saw a series of environmental reviews throughout BT's operations, with the intention of providing an initial assessment of the company's environmental impact and current operating procedures. Current policy is to assess the environmental status of the organisation through site-specific and management-systems audits.

A significant problem facing BT is the practical one of effectively auditing its activities, when the company operates from approximately 9,000 sites. In an attempt to deal with this issue the company has introduced a system which identifies a statistically representative sample of its site operations; on-site audits are then undertaken. From the results of these audits the company draws conclusions regarding the overall environmental performance of the company. The audits are currently designed to address the following key performance areas:

- legislative compliance;
- compliance with BT policies;
- comparison of environmental performance against stated objectives and targets;
- assessment of operational activities, to determine whether environmental procedures are being fully and correctly implemented;
- review of management systems to determine their adequacy in supporting BT's environmental policies and objectives;
- identify examples of best environmental practice which could be implemented throughout the organisation to promote and improve environmental performance.

In addition to the site audits, BT undertakes management systems audits of its environmental programmes. This activity has been allocated to the company's internal audit function which is also responsible for auditing financial activities and systems and is consistent with, and re-enforces, the company's commitment to establishing environmental performance as a core strategic issue within the business.

A mechanism for reporting BT's environmental performance to the general public has been introduced with the company's commitment to publishing an annual Environmental Performance Report. The first such document was published in 1992 and therefore represented a baseline against which future performance could be assessed in the public arena.

EMPLOYEE TRAINING AND COMMUNICATIONS

Appropriate training of staff to raise environmental awareness and enable environmental programmes to be successfully implemented is formally accepted in BT's environmental policy. Moreover, it is recognised that training is a key form of communication which spreads and reinforces commitment to environmental improvement.

By early 1993 the company had completed a full review of its environmental training requirements. Although a special course on broad environmental strategies has been developed for key personnel from each of the functional units, and other courses are provided which address specific issues such as waste disposal and energy management, the company intends that training involving the majority of staff will be integrated into the company's general training programmes. BT's intention to focus on environmental performance as a quality issue, has resulted in the incorporation of training activities associated with environmental issues within the company's Total Quality Management training programme entitled 'Involving Everyone', attendance of which is mandatory for all non-managerial staff. The need to raise employee awareness early in their career with the organisation, and to gain their commitment to future programmes, has therefore been recognised within the company and BT is including an introduction on the company environmental policy in its induction pack for new graduates.

In addition to its training programme, an internal communications strategy has been adopted aimed at raising the environmental awareness of BT staff. A variety of channels have been harnessed, including articles in the company's internal newspaper and campaigns aimed at specific issues such as waste reduction and energy conservation.

WASTE MINIMISATION AND RECYCLING

Waste disposal has received greater attention recently with the introduction in the UK of the Environmental Protection Act. A key feature of this legislation is the requirement of a 'Duty of Care' on all those involved in the waste disposal chain, to ensure all material is handled and disposed of safely. BT has responded to the introduction of the new regulations by implementing new, more rigorous, procedures, defining clear areas of managerial responsibility and requiring environmental audits of all contractors involved in the disposal of hazardous and semi-hazardous waste.

A feature of the new legislation, with considerable implications for BT, is the requirement that all those involved in transporting controlled waste must be registered for the role. As any material being discarded as scrap is classified as controlled waste, the regulations directly affect many of BT's activities. For this reason the company has found it necessary to become registered.

In addition to its responsibilities under the Environmental Protection Act, BT is also actively seeking alternative means to minimise the environmental impact of its waste by reductions in consumption, and by materials-recovery and recycling. With approximately 2.9 million rental telephones recovered in 1992, recycling and materials-recovery from old telephones has had considerable implications for BT's environmental impact. However with the introduction of push-button technology this task has become more difficult. Unlike the previous dial phones, where dialling mechanisms could be recovered and inserted into a new body, refurbishing push-button phones was not economically feasible. Wishing to identify an innovative solution to this problem, which would avoid the implications (and expense) of having to landfill its redundant stock of telephones, BT invited contractors to tender for the opportunity to undertake the recovery process. The contract was won by Mayer Cohen Industries which is currently able to recover 85 per cent, by weight, of material from each phone. The recovery process initially involves dismantling each phone and isolating any toxic material. The different plastics are then sorted, a process now made easier by the requirement that every type is clearly labelled. Once separated, the plastics can then be granulated and re-formulated for use in injection moulding. Precious metals are also recovered. Although present in only small quantities in any one phone, the economies of scale involved in handling BT's supply of redundant phones, now make the process financially viable. BT has stated that for the year 1992/93 the total operating cost covering the disposal of hazardous materials from telephones and the recycling scheme was £600,000 and this figure is projected to rise to £1m for the year 1993/94.

The company also plans to improve materials recovery from telephones by incorporating environmental issues into the design stage of its products. Although materials standardisation and simplified construction will make disassembly easier, thus speeding up the process, the reduction in the use of certain materials, particularly precious metals, may reduce the potential value associated with the recovery of each phone. The economic gains associated with the process may not therefore be as great as originally anticipated.

However, one area of telephone disposal still representing a significant cost to BT, relates to the handling of old Trimphones. At present the company uses a licensed facility for the storage of the tritium gas, used to provide these devices' luminescent glow. This service, combined with the costs of developing a safe disposal route for the stored tritium, currently costs approximately £0.5 million per annum. The final disposal process is not expected to be available until the end of the 1990s.

At approximately 80,000 tonnes per annum, paper consumption at BT is considerable, representing 1.7 per cent of the newsprint, printing and writing paper consumed in the UK. The company is determined to improve its environmental performance in this area and – during 1992 – enlisted the help of a specialist environmental paper consultant to aid in the identification of the most effective means to achieve this. This work has now resulted in the development and publication of purchasing specifications for the major paper materials used within the organisation. Furthermore, guidance notes for managers on achieving paper consumption reductions, were distributed in May 1993.

A key feature of BT's drive to reduce the environmental impact associated with its paper consumption is the use of environmentally-responsible suppliers, with the company now setting the following procurement requirements:

● virgin paper must be sourced from forests managed in a sustainable manner;
● recycled paper must contain at least 50 per cent post-consumer waste;
● paper is produced using chlorine-free bleaching;
● paper mills are energy-efficient.

As paper is supplied to BT through several routes, the company has developed its environmental quality purchasing standards. Figure 4.3 indicates the nature of this standard. Virgin pulp must be sourced from a sustainably-managed forest and is pulped using a chemical or mechanical process. Recycled material must also be used in the production of BT's paper requirement.

With improving technology, BT is currently investigating the feasibility of increasing the recycled paper content of its telephone directories. However, as with its other paper products, the selection of the type and extent of recycled paper to be used must be both economic and consistent with the company's quality standards. In 1992, trials began in Hemel Hempstead, of a directory produced from 65 per cent recycled paper, while all remaining phone books

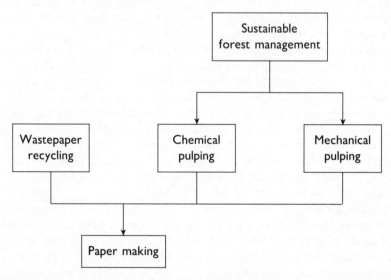

Figure 4.3 Environmental quality standard modules for the purchase of paper

contain a minimum 20 per cent pcw (post-consumer waste). With the publication of the company's 1993 Environmental Performance Report, BT committed itself to attempting to increase the minimum pcw content to 25 per cent.

As yet, the recycling of directories after use has not proved feasible as paper mills are currently unable to separate the pulp from the binding glues currently used. The company has investigated an alternative water-soluble glue; however, this has still failed to meet the requirements of the paper-recycling plants and has been abandoned. The company intends to continue work on identifying suitable technologies which will enable phone books to be recycled economically, but it is likely that the introduction of such techniques would be costly in terms of capital expenditure and, with the current over-supply of recovered paper, there is little incentive for paper mills to accept this material. In spite of these difficulties, alternative solutions for the productive use of some old phone directories have been identified. One solution offered by the animal-bedding supplier Fullstore, which has been purchasing such material and shredding, is to use it primarily for bedding in stables.

Further reductions in paper consumption for directories have been made through the introduction of a new ordering system, which enables the company to reduce the production run, thus reducing the number of excess directories produced. Modifications in directory layout have also enabled the company to reduce the paper content of each book by 10 per cent.

The current standards defined by the clearing banks, to enable their automatic character-reading machines to process payments, has meant that the scope for applying recycled paper to telephone bills is, as yet, limited. In theory, however, this constraint only applies to the bill's payment slip and the company is continuing to investigate the feasibility of using recycled paper for the remainder of the bill, envelopes and reminders.

Several schemes have been introduced within the company to promote recycling. The 'Big-Bin Collection Programme' for recycling confidential and general office waste is currently undergoing trials at several offices in Wales and the South of England, and the initial success of the scheme has prompted BT to commit itself to establishing a national contract for recycling this form of waste by October 1993. Other schemes, such as the collection of drinks cans, underwent trails in 1992 and by March 1993 BT had established aluminium collection points at every main building. To facilitate the recycling process, BT had insisted that, by September 1993, the company will purchase only aluminium cans for its drinks machines.

BT is a leading player in the IT industry and is therefore well placed to take advantage of advances in new technology to reduce its environmental impact. The introduction of electronic mail, while increasing energy use within the company, can significantly reduce paper consumption. Promoting the use of such technology can therefore lead to a net reduction in resource use, in addition to enhancing communication and information flow within the organisation.

Packaging is becoming an area of increasing focus for environmental legis-lation. In 1992 the company introduced a packaging policy and currently stipulates that all contracts regarding packaging must specify CFC-free materials. BT has supplemented its policy statement with a series of packaging guidelines for managers, which provide guidance on packaging materials and design, labelling, and the use of inks and adhesives. BT had intended to pro-vide more information concerning the selection, recycling and disposal of packaging materials, but this process was hampered during 1992 by the lack of agreed labels and standards. The company is committed to making further progress in this area and the establishment of the EC eco-labelling scheme will now facilitate this process.

OZONE-DEPLETING CHEMICALS

BT's activities have traditionally resulted in the emission of chemicals now known to contribute to ozone-depletion in the atmosphere. The largest single source of CFC emissions within BT has been from its cold-fusion laser printers, used to produce phone bills. BT intends to remove all these devices from service over time.

Solvents are also used extensively in the company, particularly in the cleaning and degreasing of electrical assemblies. A programme has now been introduced aimed at removing all CFC-based solvents from use. To date, con-siderable progress has been made in reducing the reliance on such chemicals, with major milestones, such as the requirement to identify and use alternatives for manual operations, already achieved. Aerosol cans are also used exten-sively by BT in the maintenance of plant and the cleaning of payphones. In both cases non-CFC solutions have now been identified and BT no longer uses CFC-based propellants in aerosols.

CFCs are used extensively in BT's refrigeration systems. The company is aware that alternative solutions are now under development and HCFCs are used in all new installations. However, until the effectiveness of new technolo-gies has been satisfactorily demonstrated, BT intends to retain its CFC-based technology where it has already been installed. In spite of this, the company believes it can significantly reduce CFC emissions in this area through the introduction of new procedures and improvements in the integrity of its systems.

As with many other electronics companies, BT employs halon fire extin-guishers extensively. Like CFCs, halons are an ozone-depleting chemical. As yet no viable alternative has been developed to replace this chemical in extin-guishers for fighting electrical fires. Until such time as viable alternatives have been identified, BT has stated that it will reduce emissions from those halon systems it currently owns, through improvements in procedures, and will pur-chase no new halon systems. Furthermore, the company is supporting the establishment of a national halon bank currently being coordinated by the

Department of the Environment. BT is currently unhappy about returning surplus halon stocks to manufacturers, as the company has little control over the disposal route chosen by these suppliers. For this reason the company has established its own storage facilities for halons until the national bank is operational.

BT's extensive commercial vehicle fleet presents a considerable environmental impact. Minimising this impact has resulted in the company switching to diesel power for many of its vehicles. Although more expensive initially, the company believes it can recover its investment through cheaper fuel and less maintenance, in addition to the environmental advantages. For those remaining purchases of petrol-engined vehicles, a catalytic converter has been included in the specification.

BT'S ENERGY POLICY

It is estimated that BT uses approximately 0.2 per cent of the UK's total energy consumption. More efficient and effective utilisation of this resource would therefore significantly affect the company's environmental impact. Energy efficiency within the company is coordinated by eighteen dedicated energy managers, appointed in different locations around the country. These managers are responsible for promoting and implementing energy-saving programmes at the company's sites. The decision-making process is supported by a comprehensive computerised monitoring system, which provides data on the total energy consumption patterns within the company and thus enables the energy managers to identify and focus on areas of greatest energy wastage.

Energy consumption at BT has grown steadily in spite of the company's energy efficiency drive and is now double the figure of ten years ago. This growth is largely a result of increases in telecommunications traffic and the greater energy requirements associated with modern digital exchanges. The company predicts that consumption will continue to rise until 1995 when growth rates will be matched by savings associated with the implementation of more energy-efficient equipment.

ENVIRONMENTAL POLICY AND THE SUPPLY CHAIN

With an annual purchasing budget of approximately £4bn or around 1 per cent of UK GDP, it is in the area of procurement that BT sees one of the greatest potentials for environmental improvement. Specifically the following factors have been identified as reasons for ensuring the development and implementation of an effective environmental procurement policy:

● Comprehensive life-cycle assessment is required to ensure effective product stewardship.

- Long-term benefits to the organisation can be achieved through the minimisation of environmental risk at the procurement stage.
- Product quality is likely to be higher from those suppliers who operate environmental programmes.
- The scale of BT's procurement budget enables it to influence the activities of its suppliers. The implementation of an effective environmental procurement policy, and its impact on these organisations, therefore enables it to produce a reduction in environmental impact considerably greater than that which could be achieved solely within the company itself.

Commitment to environmental improvement therefore requires BT to focus heavily on its procurement policy. BT has begun the process of assessing the environmental performance of its suppliers by requesting that these organisations supply copies of their environmental policy, if they have one. In addition, the company has provided copies of its own generic purchasing policy to all its suppliers, demonstrating BT's own commitment and indicating the increasing importance environmental performance must play if suppliers are to maintain BT as a customer.

The Generic Purchasing Policy Standard (GS13)

The cornerstone of BT's policy to promote environmental improvement from suppliers is the development of a generic purchasing standard, which has been added to the list of other generic standards covering safety and quality issues, which were already in place. GS13 will be mandatory for all tenders exceeding £750,000, or for purchases which represent a potentially high environmental impact.

The environmental purchasing policy states that BT's buyers are committed to:

1. Purchasing goods and services which can be manufactured, used and disposed of in an environmentally responsible way.
2. Meeting, and where appropriate exceeding, the standards required by environmental legislation.
3. Specifying and purchasing items which can be recycled and re-used.
4. Specifying and purchasing items which can be operated in an energy-efficient manner.
5. Selecting suppliers who are committed to sustainable environmental improvement.
6. Requiring all BT suppliers to identify any harmful processes and materials they currently use and, where feasible, securing their commitment to a phased elimination.
7. Enabling disposal of a good in a way that minimises its environmental impact and, progressively, requiring suppliers to take responsibility for disposal.

Consistent with the company's policy of integrating environmental issues into the decision-making process of the business units, no clear definition of a significant environmental impact is made. Rather, it has been decided that this judgement should be made by the individual purchasing manager. It is therefore clear from this policy position that, for the standard to be successful in meeting its objectives, it is essential for the company to ensure that management is fully committed to environmental improvement.

To meet the requirements of GS13, suppliers are requested to provide a statement indicating the cradle-to-grave environmental impact of their products/services, and their organisation's capability of complying both with legislation and with industry codes of practice. BT assesses each statement against a template, using weightings which vary, depending upon the environmental impact of the product, for each issue. For example, for paper suppliers, recycling and re-use would be heavily weighted. A limitation to this approach, and acknowledged by BT, is that although the system is effective in comparing similar products from different suppliers, the standard is likely to prove less useful for different types of product capable of performing the same task. In the former case, a decision can be made simply by comparing environmental product data from differing suppliers. However, where there are different solutions for the same task, a comparison will have to be made between products or services which may have radically different life cycles. Under these circumstances assessing the relative environmental impacts of the differing options may prove extremely difficult.

An important feature of GS13 is the importance placed on the development and implementation of environmental programmes. The issues incorporated into GS13 are weighted such that organisations committed to an on-going process of continuous environmental improvement will score higher than those with superior initial targets but little or no commitment to improvement over time.

The scale of BT's purchasing programmes would prove a considerable burden, in terms of overheads, if the company found it necessary to assess the environmental performance of potential suppliers for each contract. To overcome this problem BT is establishing a list of 'approved suppliers'. To qualify for inclusion on this list the supplier must satisfy the company that adequate insurance is maintained; that its directors have been free of any legal action for at least three years; and that specified quality standards will be adhered to by suppliers/contractors providing products and services. As yet inclusion on the list does not require suppliers to provide a copy of an environmental policy statement, although it has been indicated that 'BT will select progressively suppliers that are committed to sustainable environmental performance'.

COMMUNICATING WITH STAKEHOLDERS

The keystone to BT's external communication strategy is the company's commitment to the publication of its annual Environmental Performance Report.

The first such document was produced in April 1992 and received a positive response from many quarters for its level of openness and the inclusion of specific targets for the future. The company felt that in some respects publication of this report represented a high-risk strategy, as consumer research, undertaken by MORI in 1991, indicated that consumers perceived BT's activities to have little environmental impact. Under such circumstances, releasing a detailed environmental performance report could raise consumer awareness of the company's environmental impact and thus produce a negative response. In fact the survey did highlight one area of concern for the company: many people felt that those organisations most active in environmental improvement were those with the greatest environmental impact, while others, such as BT, were regarded as making little effort to improve their performance.

In addition to the positive response from shareholders and the wider community, the production of the report has proved beneficial to the organisation in promoting its environmental improvement programmes. Managers found that the act of collating information for the report focused their minds on the environmental impact of their activities, resulting in the identification of new areas for improvement. Furthermore the publication of the document provides a highly visible reminder both to employees and suppliers of the company's commitment to the continuous process of environmental improvement.

CONCLUSIONS

BT is the largest company in the UK and the publication of its environmental policy statement, together with the programmes it is currently running, indicate that the company is committed to environmental improvement. BT has chosen not to introduce environmental policy through an environmental management structure independent of the primary activities of the organisation; instead the company is integrating environmental decision making into the decision-making process of the individual business units. On the positive side this approach should lead to:

- recognition that environmental performance is a core business issue;
- recognition of the link between environmental improvement and quality issues;
- greater acceptance by management of environmental programmes, as it will be necessary to persuade them of the benefits of such programmes, rather than enforcing them from above;
- staff accepting greater ownership of environmental performance.

The decision not to establish an independent environmental management structure, with executive power vested in a central body, has other implications:

- it may make it difficult to overcome managerial resistance in the individual business units;

- it may result in slower implementation of programmes;
- it may result in increased problems associated with coordinating a common environmental performance across the company;
- it may result in different business units progressing at different rates, depending upon the commitment of management. This may lead to confusion on the part of customers, suppliers and stakeholders, and may make marketing the environmental performance of the company more complex and less effective.

BT's activities impact on the environment in many ways, however it is through its influence on its suppliers' activities that the company is likely to have the greatest scope for reducing the environmental impact of its products. Consistent with this, the company should continue to make the effective implementation of the GS13 procurement standard a priority.

At the centre of BT's philosophy is commitment towards environmental improvement. Through its publications, management structure, and training and communications strategies, it is trying to demonstrate that although BT is not a major polluter, it takes its responsibilities to the environment seriously. Commitment is at the centre of both its TQM and environmental initiatives, and the maintenance and strengthening of that commitment is of paramount importance. Pushing that message along BT's extensive supply chain is likely to be even more productive in achieving global environmental improvements than BT's own internal strategy, and that represents the challenge for BT in the 1990s.

Questions for discussion

1 Commitment is at the centre of BT's environmental strategy. Why do you consider this to be important?

2 Outline how BT manages to ensure ongoing commitment to both its TQM and environment programmes.

3 Why has BT focused heavily on the links between quality management and environmental management in its business strategy?

4 Why do you consider promoting BT's environmental management strategy to the public is actually considered by the company as being risky?

5 Why are procurement strategies of central importance to BT, and what sorts of systems does it have in place to improve the environmental performance of its suppliers?

6 Which areas of BT's activities do you consider need further attention if BT is to continue to improve its environmental performance?

Note: For further information on the topics raised in this chapter, please refer to Chapters 4 and 5 of *Environmental Management and Business Strategy* by Richard Welford and Andrew Gouldson (Pitman Publishing, 1993).

CHAPTER 5

Life-cycle environmental management and product innovation: the case of the Volkswagen Audi Group

Andy Gouldson

INTRODUCTION

> One of the most crucial tasks facing us in the future will be to design both industrial processes and products in such a way that the possibility of undesirable impacts on the environment is precluded – insofar as is technically possible – from the very outset. It is vital that we should not place undue strain on our natural resources, for only then can we safeguard the company's long-term prospects.

This statement, taken from Volkswagen Audi Group's 1992 Annual Report, could come from the environmental policy of any company. It recognises that continued economic viability relies on continued environmental viability, and in a very broad sense it commits the company to some level of environmental innovation and development.

However, many environmentalists suggest that the car, the core product of VW, has a greater impact on global sustainability than any other consumer product manufactured on this planet (Ekins *et al*, 1992). Is it possible therefore that a company which manufactures such a damaging product can ever come close to realising the goal of precluding environmental damage from the outset?

The very essence of the environmental debate is reflected in the polemic surrounding the environmental impacts of the automobile industry. In terms of sustainability at least, the ideal remains that society avoids environmental damage by demanding and being supplied with products which are compatible with the goals of sustainability. Clearly this ideal requires fundamental changes in societal thought and economic structure. In relation to sustainable mobility, it will require a change in the reliance that society places on the car, and a strategic U-turn in the operations of the oil and automotive industries, two of the most powerful multi-national industries in the world. While we are waiting to arrive at this utopia, companies such as VW, based on the drive for competitive advantage, are taking steps to improve the environmental performance of both their products and processes.

PRODUCT ENVIRONMENTAL IMPACT

The world now has more than 400 million cars, consuming over 200 billion gallons of oil each year and contributing 17 per cent of global CO_2 emissions (Ekins *et al*, 1992). In the UK, motor vehicles account for 80 per cent of lead emissions, 85 per cent of carbon monoxide, 45 per cent of nitrous oxides and 28 per cent of hydrocarbons (Rees, 1991). In all, cars produce over 1,000 types of chemical emission (Friends of the Earth, 1988).

In addition to their direct environmental impact, motor vehicles and their supporting infrastructure are responsible for significant land use, habitat destruction and loss of amenity. Cars are also associated with significant health and safety impacts. In the UK, for example, 6,000 people are killed and 300,000 injured each year on the roads (Rees, 1991).

The key environmental impacts in the life cycle of a motor vehicle relate to the use of the product because of the massive amount of environmental damage done through the burning of non-renewable fossil fuel and the consequent output of pollutants from that process. But there are also significant areas of environmental impact in product manufacture. As a major manufacturing industry, the automotive industry faces the common issues of resource consumption and waste generation. The market size, structure and product complexity of the automotive industry dictate that automotive manufacturers are also partially responsible for the environmental impact of their suppliers, and for all those impacts associated with servicing the product throughout its lifetime. The post-consumer disposal of automobiles also contributes significantly to the waste disposal problems which are now ubiquitous throughout the industrial world.

Therefore, as manufacturers of a product which generates an onerous environmental impact throughout much of its life, the automotive industry is beginning to be held responsible for the environmental impact of its product from cradle to grave.

CONSUMER PRESSURES

Clearly, governments and individuals are concerned about the impact that motor vehicles have on the environment. However, despite the level of the impact, the scale of the public response in relation to consumption and voting patterns has as yet been minimal. In the UK, notwithstanding increases in the cost of cars, fuel, tax, or congestion, car ownership and use have doubled between 1968 and 1988 (Ekins *et al*, 1992), and are predicted to increase by between 83 per cent and 142 per cent by 2025 (Rees, 1991). Therefore, irrespective of the growth in environmental awareness and concern amongst its customers, the automotive industry as a whole has not been subjected to significant degrees of green consumerism.

While the environmental concern of consumers does not impact on the apparently unrelenting demand for cars, it does drive companies such as VW to develop and maintain an innovative lead in the environmental performance of their product. Competition is intense to supply the characteristics that consumers demand from the increasingly homogenised products of the automotive industry. These characteristics include functionality, comfort, style, safety, efficiency and environmental friendliness. However, to date, environmental considerations remain a relatively minor component of the purchasing decision for automobiles. It is not only the producer which holds responsibility for the environmental impact of the product, the environmental concerns of society are evidently not impacting on the demand that the individual offers to the automotive industry.

Nevertheless, regarding their environmental performance, individual companies and products are subjected to more intense scrutiny than the industry as a whole. Substitutability is greater between automotive brands and models, than between private vehicles and alternative forms of transport. The amount of 'product loyalty' awarded to road transport has therefore offered significant market power to the industry as a whole, while individual manufacturers strive to develop the aspects of environmental performance which may form one of the many ingredients of competitive advantage.

GOVERNMENT PRESSURES

The reticence or inability of the consumer to substitute the use of cars for other forms of transport has had a profound influence on the transport policies which governments have adopted. In many countries, in the absence of an effective and affordable public transport network, there is little public, and hence governmental, support for measures which seek to lessen the use of cars. Furthermore, governments throughout the world have been reluctant to impose extra costs or regulations on the use of road transport due to its economic and social significance. Governments have also been effectively lobbied in many instances by the combined economic power of the oil, automotive and construction industries. As a result, the automotive industry has escaped the major controls which the life-cycle impact of its product would appear to warrant.

As with any major industry, however, automotive manufacturers are subject to the range of health, safety and environmental regulations that now face all industries in the Western world. Their productive efficiency relies on their ability to develop meaningful strategies to address issues of environmental compliance, stakeholder pressure and competitiveness.

For the purposes of this study, however, emphasis will be placed on the efforts of the Volkswagen Audi Group in the field of product development and life-cycle environmental management. While mention will be made of the internal environmental management strategies that VW are developing, VW are currently implementing environmental auditing pilot studies for internal production processes, the detailed results of which are not yet known. As a result, a broad overview of the environmental management strategies applied in VW's production processes will be offered, while greater emphasis will be placed on the responses developed by VW to the complex life cycle of the car, particularly in relation to product design and disposal.

THE BACKGROUND TO VOLKSWAGEN

Volkswagen was established in 1938 and, since then, through the Volkswagen Audi Group, which includes Volkswagen, Audi, SEAT and SKODA, the company has grown to control 9 per cent of the world market and 17.5 per cent of the Western European markets for automobile production. The Volkswagen Group now produces 3.4 million vehicles per year, around 65 per cent of which are manufactured in Germany. The group manufactures in 12 countries throughout the world and employs 273,000 people directly. Prior to its review of its suppliers in 1993, VW purchased from around 3,000 suppliers, and has an annual turnover of DM 53.2 billion.

EARLY INITIATIVES IN ENVIRONMENTAL PROTECTION AT VOLKSWAGEN

Due to water shortages in the region surrounding VW's major manufacturing facility in Wolfsburg, Germany, environmental considerations have played a central role in the production process since the plant's construction in 1938. Since this time, production processes have been based on the minimisation of water use through the development of water recycling processes. An ethos of efficient resource use has therefore been present since the company's founding.

However, environmental considerations in the production process were not widely recognised as an operational concern until the late 1980s. As in many companies prior to the advent of widespread environmental awareness, environmental management issues were implicitly monitored and controlled through day-to-day production and health and safety management practices. Similarly, efforts to improve product environmental performance through vehicle fuel efficiency were motivated by economic rather than environmental concerns. Therefore to state that environmental management strategies are only now emerging throughout VW's activities would be a misrepresentation. The inherent links between economic efficiency and environmental performance have ensured that, where environmental costs and benefits are internal to the firm, the environmental performance of both production and the product have been optimised for many years but have only recently been recognised and communicated as such.

As with most other companies, environmental issues emerged as critical strategic issues in their own right in the late 1980s. At this time, the first public pressure was exerted on VW in relation to the proposed development of a new vehicle paint shop in Wolfsburg. Although all employees are assigned environmental obligations, VW now employs a department of over 100 staff with explicit environmental responsibilities. Aside from the advance of public pressure, VW recognises that its environmental performance inherently relates to both its operational efficiency, for instance through waste management, and to its public relations record.

MINIMISING THE OVERALL ENVIRONMENTAL IMPACT

VW's environmental management strategies implicitly seek to minimise the overall impact of both the product and the process of its manufacture. In theory, some form of life-cycle assessment (LCA) should be utilised to collect and analyse the information with which decision makers can address the impact of a product (including its manufacture) from cradle to grave. While a formal framework of LCA has not been applied, VW are seeking to address the environmental impact of the main areas of their supply chain and product life cycle. Thus, strategies of varying intensity are in place to improve environmental performance in each of the major stages of the life cycle as illustrated in Figure 5.1. An assessment of the initiatives that have been or are being developed in each of these stages follows.

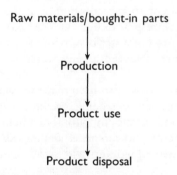

Figure 5.1 Stages of the product life cycle

DIFFUSION OF ENVIRONMENTAL COMMITMENT TO SUPPLIERS

VW has recently established a framework for the assessment of the environmental performance of its 3,600 dealers in Germany. VW Audi partners have access to the VW Audi Environmental Consultancy Service which offers advice on environmental performance, particularly in relation to the technologies and techniques available to VW Audi dealers and their workshops suppliers which can reduce their environmental impact.

Another initiative also seeks to recognise those suppliers which maintain high environmental standards through the incorporation of environmental criteria into the quality assessment of suppliers. Suppliers and dealers are assessed in relation to both internal (VW) and external (legislative) standards to ensure that they comply both with the law and with VW's own policies. However, as yet, no supplier or dealer has been refused a contract as a result of poor environmental performance alone.

Further, in line with its policy of waste avoidance before reduction, reduction before re-use and re-use before disposal, VW actively seeks to use material inputs which are both recycled and upon disposal will be recyclable. The selection of material inputs clearly relates to the strategies that are being developed by VW to design recyclability into the product and to set up the necessary infrastructure to collect and recycle its used products. Analysis of these initiatives is offered below.

ENVIRONMENTAL MANAGEMENT IN THE PRODUCTION PROCESS

Initiatives which today would be given an environmental label have been under way within the main production facility since its inception in 1938. The main focus of early environmental initiatives in the production process related to water usage. Since 1973 VW has reduced its consumption of mains water by 40 per cent. Of a total consumption at the Wolfsburg plant of 27.67 million m^3 in 1990 (the equivalent to the consumption of 7 million people), only 3.5 million m^3 came from fresh drinking water. As part of this system of water recycling, each unit of drinking water is subsequently used six times as process water. The plant has now achieved a total water recycling rate of 87.3 per cent.

Notable process changes have also been made in relation to energy use and its associated air emissions. The extruding, casting, welding, grinding, sticking and painting of metals and plastics in automobile manufacture consume considerable amounts of energy and can generate air pollution problems relating both to the health and safety of workers within the plant and to the community outside it.

The production plants within Wolfsburg, Hanover and Kassel in Germany together have energy-generating capacity of 691 MW of electricity and 1,265 MW of heat. In total, production in VW consumes 740,000 tonnes of coal, 10,000 tonnes of heating oil and 260,000 tonnes of natural gas each year. Therefore, it goes without saying that energy efficiency initiatives within VW are well established. In Wolfsburg, VW's combined heat and energy generation, which is economically and environmentally more efficient, also supplies electricity and community heat to the surrounding populations. Within the plant, at all external temperatures above − 5°C, the factory is sufficiently heated through heat exchangers driven by surplus process heat. Clearly, such a scheme has both economic and environmental benefits, and fits in with VW's policy to apply the best available technologies at all points, which, in the long run, are seen to be more efficient.

To improve the environmental performance of its energy demand, low sulphur content fuels are used, and traditional coal-burning furnaces are being replaced with fluidised bed coal burners which are considerably more efficient and less polluting. Additionally, flue gas desulphurisation and catalytic conversion are used to reduce sulphur dioxide and nitric oxide emissions. Air emissions are also electrostatically precipitated to reduce dust emissions, the collected dust is then used within the construction industry. Sulphur dioxide emissions have been reduced by 72 per cent in the last 20 years, and dust emissions have fallen by 59 per cent. The investment of time and money which has enabled the development of better technologies in the production process has ensured that VW exceeds many of the relevant emissions standards. Air emissions are constantly monitored and controlled to assure continued compliance.

The development of environmental auditing methodologies

On a wider level, day-to-day operational management has also included regular auditing of quality, waste management, and health and safety. A variety of initiatives have been, and continue to be, developed, and VW is currently formulating an environmental audit methodology for use in all of its sites. At present the environmental audit programme only covers German facilities, although once the pilot project is concluded and the audit methodology is refined, it is planned that the scheme will be extended to apply to other sites.

Rather than seeking to fine-tune existing systems, the audit methodology seeks to address information gaps in areas of poor performance and to uncover integrated solutions to efficiency, quality and environmental management issues within VW. Due to the early stages of the environmental audit programme, as yet no new technologies or management practices have been implemented as a result of its findings, but VW is clearly willing to act on these issues in the future.

Although the environmental audit programme could eventually have external benefits, it is essentially driven by internal motivations for information-gathering and dissemination. It is important to recognise, however, that in its main facility VW employs some 55,000 staff, so the networking of information is not a simple task. Nevertheless, the results of the audit will be disseminated throughout the company. This will reinforce the company-wide environmental protection training programme that has been established in order to develop the attitudes which VW recognises as a vital component of efficient environmental protection. Indeed, VW views its training programme as a more efficient strategy for environmental protection than the application of new technologies. While currently there are no schemes to recognise and reward environmental initiatives within the company, VW is considering introducing such a scheme to foster commitment to environmental performance amongst the whole workforce.

In relation to the external communication of the audit programme, it is envisaged that the audit results will be verified by external consultants, and that VW will eventually register some of its facilities under the EC eco-management and auditing registration scheme.

ADDRESSING THE ENVIRONMENTAL IMPACT OF THE PRODUCT

As outlined above, the major area of environmental impact for the automotive industry is the impact of the product in use. It is quite possible that the entire future of the automotive industry depends on its response to this issue, particularly as any advances in the environmental efficiency of each individual product will be offset by the rapid growth in the overall number of cars on the road throughout the world.

Governmental responses to the threat of global warming alone are therefore likely to be a fundamental strategic issue for the automotive industry, although to date the powerful lobbying activities of the world's fossil-fuel-dependent industries to slow down global responses to the threat of global warming, have been severely criticised (Leggett, 1993). Obviously, few companies would reveal any support that they might offer to such lobbying activities.

While VW does not accept that the phenomenon of global warming is as yet proven, it is committed to improving the fuel efficiency of its products as rapidly as possible. As VW perceives the traditional characteristics of product differentiation to be diminishing in its market, competitive edge through technical standards of environmental performance will become a more significant selling point. For the industry as a whole, its commitment to the advancement of product efficiency may well determine the extent to which it is regulated in the future. As self-regulation rather than government regulation is the preferred option, this gives an added incentive for the automotive industry to continue its efforts to improve product efficiency.

It is fortunate that the automotive industry can respond to the combined threats of global warming and intense government regulation by harnessing the economic self-interest of its customer. Product fuel efficiency, economic efficiency and environmental efficiency are synonymous for the industry's consumers, and the forces of competition will dictate that every major automotive manufacturer implements meaningful research and development programmes to address these common issues. It is doubtful whether this scale of commitment into the research and development of clean technologies would be afforded under any system other than the capitalistic structure of the multinational automotive industry.

VW has prided itself on its position as a leader of product innovation in the industry. Environmental management strategies in this respect are two-pronged. Firstly, initiatives relating to the fuel efficiency of its cars, and secondly, developments to design-in product recyclability and to encourage the necessary infrastructures to allow product recycling. Each of these issues will now be addressed in turn.

FUEL EFFICIENCY

VW states that its central aim in developing technologies for environment-friendly products is to reduce fuel consumption in order to conserve fossil-fuel energy sources and to cut CO_2 emissions. The drive for improved product efficiency is supported by a research and development programme which, in 1992, had a budget of DM 3 billion and employed some 14,000 staff. VW has been able to reduce the average fuel consumption of its motor vehicles by 25 per cent over the last ten years and, largely as a result of the adoption of catalytic converters, hydrocarbons and nitrogen oxide emissions have been reduced by 90 per cent.

VW accepts that increases in the price of oil, for instance, as a result of the implementation of a carbon/energy tax, would increase the incentives to develop alternative fuel sources, although it suggests that significant increases in the price of fossil fuels would be necessary to sever the strong bond between consumers and their cars. In the absence of such changes in the relative prices of different fuels, VW is developing alternative technologies for use in particular circumstances. In Brazil, for example, in the early 1970s, VW developed engines powered by ethanol fuels derived from sugar cane, and has since built over 2 million cars to run on this alternative fuel source. Although the life-cycle carbon balance of ethanol fuel is better than that of petrol (that is, in aggregate it contributes less to the greenhouse effect) the wider adoption of bio-fuels is restricted by both climatic and land-use considerations.

VW is also cooperating with various other companies, including electricity utilities, battery manufacturers and other vehicle manufacturers to develop technologies for the use of electrical energy in transport, particularly in relation to public transport in inner city areas where local air quality is a significant environmental problem. Once more, the automotive industry is in an ideal position to resource and undertake research into the technologies which will be needed in the future to develop truly sustainable patterns of mobility.

There is evidence to suggest that legislative and regulatory standards are driving technical innovation in the motor industry in this respect. In California, for example, where local air quality is a significant problem, 2 per cent of all vehicles must be 'zero-emissions vehicles' (ZEVs) by 1998, and 10 per cent by 2003. Although these targets may force the development of more efficient technologies, a central problem associated with electrically-powered transport remains. Specifically, the electricity must be generated and this in turn has associated environmental impacts. Nevertheless if, in the future, energy-generating capacity shifts towards more renewable sources of electricity, the potential for sustainable mobility will be considerably enhanced by the technology-forcing standards adopted in areas such as California. Furthermore, as the USA has driven product standards in the automotive industry in the past, for instance in relation to catalytic converters, these targets may provide a strategic insight into the future of product standards for the car industry. Some commitment to research and development in this field is therefore wise.

At present, however, VW does not foresee a time when the focus of its product moves away from fossil fuels and towards bio-fuel sources or electrically-powered cars. Rather, VW is striving to increase the fuel efficiency of traditional fossil-fuel-driven engines. Indeed, VW has been responsible for a number of milestones in the advancement of fuel-efficient technologies in the automotive industry. VW was the first manufacturer to develop and market small diesel engines for cars, and has developed the diesel catalyst and the turbo diesel engine which, with low emissions, can now provide fuel efficiencies of 46.2 miles per gallon at a speed of 103 mph. More generally, technological developments in standard production engines have enabled an average 25 per cent reduction in fuel consumption over the last ten years.

Besides more environmentally-friendly engines, which are already in full-scale production, VW has developed a number of other technologies which are currently being market-tested. The main advance has been the development of the 'Automatic Momentum Gearbox' (AMG). The AMG, which is being tested on the Eco-Golf, automatically disengages the transmission and cuts off the engine whenever the drive power from the engine is not used, so the car only continues to roll under the force of its own momentum. This enables zero fuel consumption and zero emissions over long periods of day-to-day use, particularly within urban areas. The AMG only re-engages and restarts the engine when the accelerator pedal is pressed again. In daily operation, the Eco-Golf requires 20 per cent less diesel fuel and emits 10 per cent to 20 per cent less pollutants in its exhaust.

The market success of product innovations such as these depends very much on the reaction of the consumer. There is intense discussion within VW on the likely response of consumers to the AMG. VW is also considering a programme of customer education to encourage the successful introduction of the product to the market. Nevertheless, unless there is a favourable reaction from the consumer, the diffusion of cleaner technologies, such as this, will be curtailed for economic reasons. Clearly it is vital that VW adopts both a market-led and market-leading strategy in the development of new product technology and educate the consumer about its new product innovations.

The patenting and successful introduction of technologies such as the AMG into the market will afford VW a considerable competitive advantage through protected product differentiation. Should technologies such as the AMG be rejected by the consumer, the automotive industry can rightly claim that it has developed cleaner technologies and that the barrier to the improved environmental performance of its product is the consumer. Potentially this is a powerful argument to dispel the prospect of future regulation for the automotive industry, suggesting that the emphasis of regulation should be placed on the consumer rather than the producer.

PRODUCT RECYCLING

One of the major life-cycle environmental impacts of the car is in its final disposal. Indeed, the automotive industry could be criticised for the planned obsolescence of its product, whereby motor vehicles are designed to last for a limited period only, thereby assuring regularly renewed market demand for the industry. Clearly such a policy, whether explicit or implicit, would contribute significantly to the waste disposal problems associated with the industry and its product.

However, there is growing evidence that VW, and the automotive industry more generally, are developing the products, technologies and infrastructure necessary for effective recycling of the industry's product waste. The partial recycling of scrap cars has been under way for many years through vehicle dismantlers and scrap metal dealers. More recently, issues of life-cycle assessment, product stewardship and legislative developments such as the German Packaging Ordinance, which demands that suppliers of packaging materials arrange for their re-collection and recycling, have encouraged industry to develop strategies for recycling. As a result of the German legislative framework for waste recycling, German automotive manufacturers, including VW, are emerging as the market leaders in the global automotive industry in product innovation to encourage recycling. It is important to stress however that recycling initiatives are not only being developed in response to legislative pressure, they are also due to the adoption of product stewardship policies in the automotive industry and the effects of increased stakeholder pressure.

Traditionally, there is a range of factors which impede the development of recycling initiatives. These factors include the lack of economies of scale in collection and recycling for many products (particularly for mixed or contaminated waste streams), the instability of market prices for waste materials, the low and variable quality of recycled products, and hence the lack of an endmarket. In combination, these factors combine to discourage recycling activity. However, for a range of reasons, the automotive industry is in a very strong position to overcome these barriers and to develop successful recycling initiatives.

Firstly, the industry and individual producers within it are of a sufficient scale to allow economically viable collection, dismantling and recycling facilities. Further, the size and nature of the product ensures that the industry's product waste is not contaminated through mixing with other materials from other waste streams. In the case of many waste streams, this is a situation which normally increases recycling costs and reduces the quality of the recycled product. While the size and nature of the product favours recycling in the automotive industry, it should be noted that, traditionally, motor vehicles are made up of a wide range of components and materials and are therefore difficult to dismantle, separate and recycle. Nevertheless, scale economies and product reformulation can counteract the difficulties associated with the collection, dismantling and recycling of complex products. VW have undertaken feasibility studies to analyse the possibilities for a regional or supra-regional waste collection association. They have also been developing technologies and techniques for dismantling, cleaning and recycling waste materials in order to generate the highest possible quality of recycled product.

Secondly, car manufacturers are increasingly utilising recycled materials in vehicles which are designed to be easily dismantled and recycled upon disposal. Clearly, the automotive industry could ultimately be both the supplier and consumer of the waste material through recycling and re-using its own product waste. As a result, it is in a possibly unique position to ensure that the materials selected, and the methods of recycling, meet the necessary specifications to make vehicle recycling a feasible option. VW recognises that the success of vehicle recycling depends on the design of the product. This relates to the ease of dismantling, cleaning and reprocessing, considerations which benefit from a reduced number of raw materials used in manufacture. VW has responded to this issue in a number of ways, notably by increasing the proportion of polypropylene in the total amount of plastics used in each vehicle from 25 per cent to 50 per cent, thereby simplifying dismantling, unifying waste streams and generating a recycled product of a relatively higher quality than that which might be achieved if a greater mixture of plastics were used.

Thirdly, the industry is able to ensure that an effective and assured demand is generated for the waste product, potentially enabling the materials life cycle for the car to be closed (see Fig. 5.2), although in reality it is unlikely that 100 per cent recycling rates will be achieved. By buying back its recycled product waste, the industry is able to avoid a major obstacle to recycling that is experienced in many other industries, namely the lack of a stable market for recycled materials. As the leader of a number of recycling initiatives, VW is able to cooperate with other companies downstream in the life cycle of its product, to encourage them to recycle. Without this vertical cooperation in the market, the prospects for growth in the automotive recycling sector would be greatly diminished.

Fourthly, deliberate and planned obsolescence followed by efficient waste

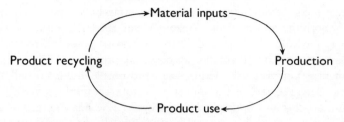

Figure 5.2 Materials life cycle for the car

collection and recycling effectively encourages car manufacturers to 'lease' materials to consumers for the life cycle of the product. Given the rapid advances in fuel efficiency, this allows the industry to periodically re-instal the best available technologies and hence to address one of the most significant environmental impacts of the car, namely its consumption of fossil fuels. Conveniently, this also provides a regularly renewed source of demand for the industry. Companies such as VW are therefore seeking to encourage waste minimisation and the continual application of the best available technologies by extending the life cycle of the materials used rather than the product itself. VW for example is seeking to develop the use of aluminium in vehicle manufacture, not only to reduce weight and hence increase fuel efficiency, but also to facilitate more efficient recycling which would eventually offset the extra raw materials costs associated with aluminium in the first cycle of its use.

The development of recycling activities such as those developed by VW can be seen to have a range of underlying motives. Firstly, they respond to the growing problem of waste disposal and may therefore be seen to be a proactive response to impending environmental legislation. Secondly, they offer a response to increased stakeholder pressure to adhere to the principles of product stewardship by accepting responsibility for the product from cradle to grave. Thirdly, they allow the automotive industry access to valuable recycled material inputs. Fourthly, they address potential criticism relating to the disposability and limited life cycle of the car. By offering to regularly update the road transport stock with the best available economic and environmental technologies, the automotive industry can be seen to be addressing key environmental concerns while assuring the future of its market. Recycling strategies such as those of VW have therefore translated a potentially significant market threat into a potentially equally significant opportunity through the development of proactive environmental management strategies.

CONCLUSIONS

It is clear that companies such as VW are committed to improving the environmental performance of both their products and the process of their manufacture. The potential for the wider adoption of environmental management strategies is enhanced in many cases by the overlap between the economic self-interest of both the producer and consumer, and the environmental imperative that society has collectively placed on the automotive industry to lead the way in developing sustainable modes of personal mobility. High standards of environmental performance within the automotive industry will therefore become an integral part of the industry's future economic success. Through innovation at all stages in its product life cycle, VW has emerged as a market leader in the field of environmental performance in the automotive industry.

Arguably, given current economic structures, harnessing the forces of self-interest and capitalism to drive environmental improvement is the only way society can develop the scale of response needed if we are to achieve sustainability. While undoubtedly companies such as VW are committed to environmental improvement for altruistic as well as commercial reasons, it is far from clear whether the products of the automotive industry are compatible with the long-term goal of sustainability. Given time, it is clear that VW and the automotive industry more generally will build, and should be encouraged to build, on the significant progress made to date, and continue to move towards sustainability. The question that remains is whether such an industry could ever arrive at the elusive goal of sustainability, and how much time it should be given in which to try.

Questions for discussion

1 Why is it important to examine the design of industrial processes and products if a company is committed to environmental improvement?

2 To what extent is VW using life-cycle assessment in evaluating the environmental impact of its products?

3 How is VW pushing environmental improvement up and down the supply chain?

4 Outline VW's audit methodology.

5 VW has put a lot of emphasis on the recyclability of their cars. Explain how they have improved this. Do you consider that recyclability in itself is a sufficient measure to improve the environmental performance of cars?

6 Do you consider that the car industry can ever arrive at the goal of sustainability?

Note: For further information on the topics raised in this chapter, please refer to Chapters 7 and 8 of *Environmental Management and Business Strategy* by Richard Welford and Andrew Gouldson (Pitman Publishing, 1993).

References

Ekins, P., Hillman, M. and Hutchison, R. (1992) *Wealth Beyond Measure*, Gaia Books, London.

Rees, A. (1991) *The Pocket Green Book*, Zed Books, London.

Friends of the Earth (1988) *The Environment – The Government's Record*, Friends of the Earth, London.

Leggett, J. (1993) 'Climate Change and the Insurance Industry', *European Environment*, Volume 3, Part 3, June.

CHAPTER 6

Pushing forward the frontiers: environmental strategies at The Body Shop International

Richard Welford

BACKGROUND

The Body Shop was founded in March 1976 when Anita Roddick opened her first shop in Brighton. Before 1976, working for the United Nations, she had travelled around the world and met people from a number of different cultures. Observing how people treated their skins and hair, she learned that certain things cleansed, polished and protected the skin without having to be formulated into a cream or shampoo. When she started The Body Shop, Anita Roddick aimed to utilise these raw ingredients such as plants, herbs and roots, in products which would be acceptable to consumers. Only sixteen years later she was described by the International Chamber of Commerce as 'the inventor of sustainable retailing' (Williams and Goliike, 1992).

The first shop was basic and at first sold only fifteen lines. They were packed in different sizes to fill up the shelves and to give the customer an opportunity to try a product without buying a large bottle – a principle which remains today. A refill service operated which allowed customers to refill their empty bottles instead of throwing them away. Although this was clearly an environmentally-friendly strategy, it was also initially implemented to cut down the costs of packaging.

Today, The Body Shop's principal activities are to formulate, manufacture and retail products which are primarily associated with cleansing, polishing and protecting the skin and hair. The underlying aims are to conduct that business ethically, with a minimum of hype, and to promote health rather than glamour. Naturally based, close-to-source ingredients are used wherever possible, and ingredients and final products are not tested on animals (Wheeler, 1994). Packaging is kept to a minimum and refill services are offered in all shops. Packaging, in the form of plastic bottles, can be returned to shops and is recycled into various accessory items.

The Body Shop's full range now contains nearly 400 products. The organisation trades in over 40 countries and employs around 6,000 people, either directly or in franchises. Senior management in the organisation is committed to the encouragement of positive change. The aim is to establish a new work ethic that will enable business to thrive without causing adverse damage to the environment, at both the local and the global level. There is an emphasis placed on not selling products which have an adverse effect on sustainability. That is, those which consume a disproportionate amount of energy during manufacture or disposal, generate excessive wastes, use ingredients from threatened habitats, which are obtained by cruelty, or which adversely affect other countries, especially the developing countries.

It is claimed that the company is not a major polluter, nor a major user of energy and raw materials (Wheeler, 1994). Manufacturing at its principal site, Watersmead, in West Sussex, produces no airborne emissions and only 23 m^3 of waste water per day. Energy consumption by the entire UK operation (including distribution and retail outlets) is responsible for only 0.003 per cent of total UK emissions of CO_2 (around 18,000 tonnes per annum). And the use of plastics in packaging represents only 0.01 per cent of total EC demand (Wheeler, 1992). Nevertheless environmental strategies are at the centre of The Body Shop's approach to business. Moreover, the organisation has been so successful in raising the profile of the environment both within and outside the business that it is endlessly cited as being the leading business, world wide, in this field. Even though the organisation itself would argue that there is still more to be achieved, this case study examines the practices and systems which have enabled The Body Shop to reach this leading position.

COMMITMENT AND POLICY

One of the most apparent characteristics of The Body Shop is its commitment to environmental and social excellence. This is often attributed to Anita Roddick herself and while many of the principles are hers, the truth is that commitment in the organisation exists not only at board level but throughout the whole organisation. Everybody is encouraged to contribute to environmental improvement. The ultimate aim of The Body Shop is to include environmental issues in every area of its operations but, at the same time, the organisation rejects environmental opportunism which has often paralleled the green marketing strategies of more cynical firms.

At first, The Body Shop did not commit itself to a formal strategy or programme of environmental improvements. Action was taken when environmental problems were identified. This approach tended to increase employee involvement and reduce bureaucracy. However, with the continued growth of the organisation, it has been necessary to move to a more systematic approach, setting targets and planning for environmental improvement.

The overriding factor for The Body Shop is the perception of a moral obligation to drive towards sustainability in business (Roddick, 1991). It is impossible to measure progress towards this ideal without a detailed policy statement, followed by a systematic process of data-gathering and public reporting. Hence, auditing activities are considered absolutely essential to the company's long-term mission to become a truly sustainable operation; in other words, aiming to replace as many of the planet's resources as are utilised. That fundamental aim translates into a wish to play a full part in handing on a safer and more equitable world to future generations. The fundamental basis of this goal is a commitment to the broader concept of sustainable development which considers not only concepts associated with the environment, but also equity and futurity. It is the strong belief of The Body Shop that the moral burden of achieving sustainability in business should become the principal driving force behind business in the future. These fundamental commitments are highlighted in The Body Shop's environmental policy which is divided into the following ten areas:

I. Thinking globally

The Body Shop's international business is the manufacture and retailing of skin and hair care preparations and cosmetics. Our business policies are defined by our core values: care for the environment, concern for human rights and opposition to the exploitation of animals.

We have developed this policy as a constant reminder of our responsibilities to act in order to protect the environment both globally and locally. We want to do things better than they have been done before, and we want to include our staff, franchisees, subsidiaries and suppliers in making that happen.

2. Achieving excellence

Sound environmental management is both good housekeeping and good sense. Through regular reviews and assessments of our operations around the world, we will set ourselves clear targets and time-scales within which to meet those targets. These will provide us with positive incentives to achieve best environmental practice because each target we hit will be proof of progress.

3. Searching for sustainability

Sustainable development is about achieving a fairer and safer world for future generations. At all levels of operation – in our head office, in our manufacturing facilities, in our subsidiaries and franchises, and in our retail outlets around the world – we will use renewable resources wherever possible, and we will conserve natural resources where renewable options are not available. This will apply in particular to our purchasing which will be supported by a comprehensive system of product stewardship including life-cycle assessments of our products and packaging.

4. Managing growth

The quest for economic growth, as demanded by national and international financial institutions, is the cause of much environmental and human exploitation. Our future planning will be guided as much by the environmental implications of our business decisions as by economics. We will devote increasing efforts to establishing non-exploitative trading arrangements with communities in less developed countries as a means of protecting their cultures and their environments. The relationship between our commercial success and our principles got us where we are – it will take us where we are going.

5. Managing energy

Global warming, acid rain, nuclear waste – problems caused by the misuse and abuse of energy resources – provide urgent reason to achieve the highest possible energy efficiency in our operations. We will use the absolute minimum, and work towards replacing what we must use with renewable resources.

6. Managing waste

We believe that wealthy societies have an urgent and overwhelming moral obligation to avoid waste. As a responsible business, we will adopt a four-tier approach: first, reduce; next, re-use; then, recycle; and finally, as a last resort, we will dispose of waste using the safest and most responsible means available.

7. Controlling pollution

Pollution is a special form of environmental abuse – it is more than exploitation, it involves degradation and despoliation. Environmental damage is an inevitability of much business practice, but we are committed to protecting the quality of the land, air and water on which we depend. We will avoid contamination and reduce polluting emissions to negligible levels. We will adopt a cautionary approach to all processes and products which might involve environmental damage.

8. Operating safely

The reputation of a service-based business rests on safety – for staff, for customers and for the community in which the business operates. We will minimise risk in every one of our operations, from ensuring the safety and quality of our products to good neighbour policies in the communities where we work. We will be on constant alert for the unexpected, and will maintain emergency plans to safeguard the environment in the event of fires, floods and other natural disasters.

9. Obeying the law

The minimum requirement for any responsible business is to observe legal requirements and regulations wherever the company operates. We will ensure that environmental laws are complied with at all times and in the event of difficulties these will be reported to the regulatory authorities without delay.

10. Raising awareness

Our mission is nothing less than to forge a new and more sustainable ethic for business. We want our efforts to set a precedent for others. We are committed to continuous education for our staff on environmental issues. We are committed to freedom of information and full, honest public disclosure of the results of our environmental assessments. Meanwhile we will continue to educate, enthuse, campaign and inspire. This goal – taking our internal efforts into the public arena – is the culmination of all that has come before. (The Body Shop, 1993).

Such a comprehensive policy speaks for itself. It reflects commitment to change and improvement and it also sets out goals for the organisation to strive towards. Adopting such a detailed, comprehensive and public policy does mean that it has to be adhered to and deviation from it will inevitably lead to accusations of dishonesty. Indeed those sorts of accusations have caused The Body Shop problems in the past. For example, when it was highlighted that some of The Body Shop's ingredients had, in fact, been tested on animals by other companies at some time in the past, this created a media furore. What had not been properly understood was that the policy on animal testing stated that only ingredients which had not been tested on animals in the last five years would be used. This stance (developed in concert with the BUAV) was justified since it was seen as providing an incentive for suppliers, that is, if they ceased animal testing today there may be an increased demand for their products five years into the future. If there is a lesson to be learned here, it is that communicating a clear message is of paramount importance to any overt business strategy. It also highlights rather cynical attempts in some quarters to 'rubbish' what The Body Shop is trying to achieve and therefore, in turn, to devalue the whole concept of sustainable development for industry. The Body Shop would never claim that it is a 100 per cent environmentally-friendly organisation (it is not and never could be). It would claim, however, that it is campaigning, educating and setting examples of what is achievable if companies really are committed to environmental improvement.

It seems that there are those who will always wish to criticise those with high ideals, and a healthy cynicism towards business and the environment is probably a positive attribute. Much of what has been said and done in the name of environmental management, by so many other firms, has turned out to be dishonest and destructive, and environmental claims have so often been misleading. However, what The Body Shop sets out to do in its policy must be applauded. Indeed The Body Shop goes further than simply having a policy, it translates this into targets for action. For example, past targets have included the end to purchases of products and packaging containing PVC, identifying a site for a suitable wind farm, improving energy efficiency at the Watersmead site by 15 per cent and including all suppliers of any significance in the company's Environmental Accreditation Scheme. These had all been achieved by 1993 and further targets were then set to continue the push forward.

ENVIRONMENTAL MANAGEMENT AND ENVIRONMENTAL AUDITING

The only real way to achieve the aims of an environmental policy, which is as comprehensive as the one outlined above, is to take a systematic approach to achieving its aims through an appropriate management structure and to periodically assess or audit progress, measuring the extent to which targets and basic objectives are being met. For that reason environmental auditing has a very high profile at The Body Shop. On the main site, it involves all staff and managers in continuous data collection, frequent reviews of priorities and targets (on a department-by-department basis) and an annual process of public reporting of results. The process extends to all retail outlets in the UK, and during 1993/94 it was being replicated in all overseas franchise operations.

In parallel with the need for environmental auditing, there is a need to put in place management systems capable of achieving targets and adhering to environmental policy. The Body Shop maintains a very decentralised system of environmental management. A corporate team of Environment, Health and Safety (EHS) specialists acts as a central resource for networks of environmental 'advisers' and coordinators in headquarters departments, subsidiaries, retail outlets and international markets. Environmental advisers and coordinators are usually part-time, fulfilling their role in environmental communications and auditing alongside normal duties.

In headquarters departments, there is approximately one adviser for every twenty members of staff. Every individual department has at least one adviser as does every retail outlet in the UK. Internationally, each country has one or more environmental coordinator. A number of these are full-time positions. In every case, environmental advisers and representatives have specific environmental training, usually via a combination of annual educational events and monthly or bimonthly updates and training notes. In addition there is a wide range of general sources of environmental information circulating within The Body Shop.

The corporate EHS team serves the networks of environmental advisers and representatives, ensures that policies and guidelines are disseminated effectively, coordinates terms of reference for auditing and environmental management, and receives and collates data on environmental indicators relevant to each part of the operation. The corporate EHS department also coordinates environmental policy development in direct contact with the main Board of The Body Shop and liaises with senior managers on a regular basis to ensure constant support for the environmental management system. On an annual basis (during the formal audit process) liaison with the Board and senior managers includes the setting of targets and objectives at corporate and departmental levels.

In line with the flexible and non-hierarchical management structure of The Body Shop, it is common for environmental advisers, managers and representatives of the EHS department to convene *ad hoc* task groups to address issues of broad interest. In 1992 these task groups included waste management, energy efficiency, product stewardship/life-cycle analysis, environmental statistics, environmental emergencies and environmental communications.

One of the most interesting aspects of the environmental strategy of The Body Shop is revealed when one examines the incentives to undertake an environmental audit process. We have outlined the general incentives to undertake the audit earlier in this book, but the reason why all this effort on auditing is expended at The Body Shop has almost nothing to do with external pressure (legal or otherwise). Where they exist, such pressures are relatively undemanding compared with internal policy commitments and targets. Equally, environmental auditing at The Body Shop has little to do with cost saving – most efficiencies have already been gained. And the activity is certainly not driven by the more cynical commercial considerations too often seen elsewhere. The fundamental reason for adopting an environmental auditing methodology is that there is simply no choice but to carry that out in an ethical organisation committed to environmental improvement. How else is an organisation going to identify progress?

In The Body Shop's (first) *The Green Book* (The Body Shop, 1992) the organisation makes it clear that it is 'outraged that environmental auditing is not yet compulsory in business' (page 9). It regrets the fact that initial drafts of the EC eco-management and audit scheme, which may have led to compulsory auditing in some industries in the Community, have been lost, and it intends to campaign for mandatory auditing and public disclosure of environmental information. The Body Shop itself undertook its last audit in line with the draft EC regulation on eco-auditing which existed at that time. It sees that as generally compatible with BS7750, but where they differ, precedence is given to the EC scheme because of its tougher requirements for verification and disclosure. The Body Shop views both the EC and British standards on auditing as blueprints which any committed organisation should follow to achieve a high standard of environmental excellence.

In addition to adopting auditing as a tool of measurement for, perhaps, subtly different reasons than we might see elsewhere, the approach taken to auditing is also different. In order to assess those differences, we need to examine audit methodologies which have developed to date. David Wheeler, General Manager for Environment, Health and Safety at The Body Shop, identifies a staged progression in auditing methodologies, culminating in the need to audit for sustainability (Wheeler, 1994).

The methodology with the longest track record is that based on safety auditing. The recognition that industrial processes which go wrong can lead to injury to both workers and the surrounding community has been understood since the advent of the chemical industry. Today, managing and reducing the risk of such occurrences have become standard practice in responsible companies dealing with oil, petrochemicals, chemicals, mining and power generation. So, with the development of environmental concerns in the 1960s and 1970s, it was natural for companies in those industries to extend their concern for the local community to a broader concern for the local environment. The industries developed internal procedures which were aimed at measuring and reducing risks to the health and safety of workers as well as to neighbouring communities and local environments. Environment, health and safety auditing was the technique, and in the chemical industry it eventually became known as 'responsible care.' It was all about measuring management effectiveness, legal compliance and reducing risks and liabilities. Environmental and safety audits were no more than common sense for high-risk businesses wishing to protect their bottom lines.

The 'second wave' of environmental audits which are prevalent at the moment have tended to focus on management systems: issues of policy, internal resources, purchasing, product or service design, communications and education. Of course, questions like impacts on air and water, energy and waste management, and legal compliance are still examined. But in many cases greater emphasis is placed on the effectiveness of systems to manage and control a diverse range of issues of environmental consequence. This management systems approach which mirrors the quality systems approach emerging in the 1980s, led to proposals for the development of frameworks for comprehensive audits at national, European and international level, and is embodied in BS7750 and the European Community eco-management and audit scheme.

When, in 1991, The Body Shop carried out its environmental auditing, it did so in line with the draft version of this scheme, publishing *The Green Book* in 1992, laying out its report to the public on its environmental performance. Early on it was decided that the most important areas of environmental concern at The Body Shop were energy efficiency, waste management and product life-cycle assessment. Although the retail outlets fell outside the scope of the formal auditing procedure, other assessments have been or are being conducted in these areas. All UK shops, for example, were given an 'eco-audit' checklist covering their most important environmental issues. This was supplemented by training programmes on environmental improvement for Shop Environmental Advisers (SEAs).

During 1992/93 The Body Shop updated its policies and procedures for environmental management, taking into account the results of the 1991/92 audit process and developments in best environmental practice world wide. In addition to developing a new general policy on the environment, specific policies were developed for purchasing, packaging and wastes. These actions and policies were laid out in *The Green Book 2* which was published in May 1993.

Recently, however, The Body Shop has started to think about progressing the environmental auditing methodology still further. This relatively new approach is based on the process of auditing for sustainability. It is a holistic approach predicated on a clear world view and an understanding of the need for a 'paradigm shift' in business culture (Commoner, 1990; Wheeler, 1993). Organisations auditing for sustainability should be committed to integrating environmental performance to wider issues of global ecology. Thus energy efficiency should be focused on the need to minimise NOx, SOx and CO_2 emissions and avoid nuclear waste. Waste minimisation, re-use and recycling should be driven by the need to conserve non-renewable resources. Product design should prioritise the use of renewable resources. Sourcing of raw materials should have no negative impacts on global biodiversity, endangered habitats or the rights of indigenous peoples (Wheeler, 1994).

Companies are faced with a challenge of integrating considerations based on the three elements of sustainable development (environment, equity and futurity) into their production and marketing plans. There is always an incentive, however, for profit-maximising firms seeking short-term rewards, to opt out and become a free rider (assuming that everyone else will be so environmentally conscious that their own pollution will become negligible). European Community environmental legislation is increasingly plugging the gaps which allow this to happen, and firms attempting to hide their illegal pollution are now subject to severe penalties. What is really required, though, is a shift in paradigms towards an acceptance by industry of its ethical and social responsibilities. If that is an insufficient reason for change in a profit-driven world, then businesses should recognise that it is not only ethical to be environmentally friendly, but with the growth of consumer awareness in the environmental area, it will also be good for sales. Such an approach continues to leave aside the key concepts of futurity and equity, however, and The Body Shop is one of the very few organisations worldwide which is addressing these issues as well.

Firms clearly have a role to play in the development of substitutes for non-renewable resources and innovations which reduce waste and use energy more efficiently. They also have a role in processing those materials in a way which brings about environmental improvements. For many products (e.g., cars and washing machines), the major area of environmental damage occurs in their usage. Firms often have the opportunity of reducing this damage at the design stage, and when new products are being developed there is a whole new opportunity for considering both the use and disposal of the product. But this all ought to be done in the context of ensuring that operations do not exploit the developing world and its peoples. Moreover, environmental costs ought to be properly accounted, that is, they ought to be measured on a time-scale which has not to date been considered. The real cost of using non-renewable resources when measured over time therefore approaches infinity since, once used, they are lost forever. The Body Shop is moving forward on this front as well, especially as it is now putting increasing emphasis on life-cycle assessment and product stewardship within its environmental management and auditing framework. To some extent, therefore, The Body Shop is breaking down the traditional links between quality management and environmental management (Welford, 1992), which is becoming an accepted (but somewhat flawed) ideology (Welford, 1994), and pushing on further to the real measurement of sustainability, stressing ecology and not quality-based management systems.

This sort of approach inevitably leads on to the question as to whether ecological performance can be measured quantitatively. The Body Shop's view is that some environmental inputs and outputs to and from the organisation may be amenable to full cost accounting. Some of the costs of environmental impacts (usually externalised by industry) might then be included in the annual reports and financial statements of the company (Wheeler, 1994). The full cost accounting option remains speculative and highly controversial, and there are many ecologists and environmental managers who doubt both the wisdom and practicality of attempting to reconcile all ecological impacts with conventional financial indicators. The Body Shop shares this concern. Firstly, it is not possible to make realistic financial estimates of the intrinsic value of numerous important ecological assets, e.g., unique habitats, endangered species, the ozone layer or the homelands of indigenous peoples. Secondly, it is not possible to predict what value would be placed on these assets by future generations.

Thus it is impossible to envisage all key indices of sustainability emerging from cost accountancy. For this reason, The Body Shop's approach to environmental auditing and reporting is never likely to be more than passing attention to financial indicators. However, it is committed to devoting increasing efforts to the definition of ecological impacts with respect to true indices of sustainability (Wheeler, 1994).

The Body Shop's approach to many environmental issues has been to focus on particular areas of concern, to set itself clear targets and to put into place programmes and actions which improve environmental performance in these areas. It is therefore worth turning our attention to these key areas of activity where significant progress has been made.

ENERGY EFFICIENCY

Energy is central to many of the world's key environmental issues. Global warming, acidification, nuclear waste and the consumption of non-renewable fossil fuels are all the result of growing energy demands. In playing its part, The Body Shop has committed itself to generating as much electricity from renewable resources as it consumes, and over the last two years has been introducing wind and solar energy sources at its Watersmead site, and has been exploring possibilities for the establishment of a wind farm which will feed as much energy into the national grid as The Body Shop takes out.

The Body Shop also undertook an energy audit and strategy review of its Watersmead site in 1991. The audit found that savings of £23,000 out of a total energy bill of £405,000 were immediately obtainable through small investments in 19 energy-efficiency projects in the warehouse, manufacturing and office buildings. As a result of the review The Body Shop also set itself a two-year target of a 15 per cent improvement in energy efficiency. This target was met after only one year.

Even more significantly, The Body Shop has made a commitment to energy self-sufficiency in the UK using wind power. An agreement has been signed with National Wind Power to develop a wind farm which would eventually match the energy requirements of The Body Shop throughout the UK. During 1992, The Body Shop also signed the Energy Efficiency Office Declaration of Commitment to responsible energy management.

WASTE MANAGEMENT

In The Body Shop's 1989 Environmental Review, waste was highlighted as an area in need of improvement. Recycling schemes and a wastewater recycling system have been improved and a Waste Management Taskforce has been established in order to develop a strategy for handling the waste from the Watersmead site. The approach to waste management is simple: reduce, re-use and recycle (in that order). Thus the most important thrust of the waste management strategy has been to produce less.

At the centre of the waste management strategy has been the documentation and recording of both sources of waste and outputs of waste. All sources have been identified and characterised as being hazardous or non-hazardous. Procedures check to see that the management and handling of all sources comply with current regulations and detailed records are kept of all materials leaving the Watersmead site: their quantities, who the disposal contractor is, and how the waste is treated and disposed. Staff who handle waste are trained to carry out their job and to comply with regulatory requirements.

At present wastewater is processed in an ultrafiltration wastewater treatment facility which removes approximately 90 per cent of the organic load. What is left goes to the sewer, and the concentrated sludge is taken away by tanker for secondary treatment. The view taken by The Body Shop's management is that this is still not good enough and an ecologically engineered system of wastewater treatment is currently under development which could reduce burdens to zero. The system creates numerous micro-habitats which promote the breakdown of organic material in the effluent. The breakdown products are then used as nutrient by plant species which grow and can be harvested for composting.

In May 1992, The Body Shop set itself the target of a 25 per cent reduction in the organic content of its effluent stream. The deadline for this target was the end of February 1994. The target was met in November, 1992.

PACKAGING AND PACKAGING WASTE

The most important step taken to reduce waste is to reduce packaging. The strategy here is to avoid excess packaging, refill empty product containers and make packaging out of readily recycled materials. A recycling system exists for all plastic containers but this relies on customers bringing back their empties and placing them in 'dump bins' located in every shop. Although there have been campaigns to encourage consumers so to do, only a minority currently take advantage of this facility (around 4 per cent of bottle sales in the UK). Customers are also encouraged to refill their containers and, again, have been encouraged so to do by price reductions on refilling larger bottles.

The Body Shop sells many of its products together in the form of gift baskets. This involves an extra layer of packaging materials and might therefore be considered by some to be excessive. However, strong consumer demand for this service means that gift-basket sales continue to increase. In 1991, 600,000 gift baskets were produced for sale in UK company-owned shops alone. The emphasis has therefore been on reducing the environmental impact of gift-basket packaging. The use of PVC in boxes and drawstring bags has been phased out and more educational messages are inserted into the baskets themselves. This encourages customers to re-use gift baskets given as presents.

In 1992 The Body Shop set a target ensuring that by 28 February 1994, 80 per cent of products (excluding colour cosmetics) would be packaged in its most readily recycled materials or have no packaging at all. By February 1993, the total stood at 72 per cent, which includes 12 per cent which have no packaging at all (The Body Shop, 1993).

PRODUCT STEWARDSHIP AND LIFE-CYCLE ASSESSMENT

The whole business of The Body Shop is very product-driven and there needs, therefore, to be considerable emphasis placed not only on processes but also on the environmental performance of the product itself. The traditional cradle-to-grave approach is therefore vital and The Body Shop concentrated a lot of effort on life-cycle assessment (LCA). Central to the LCA approach is therefore the sourcing of product ingredients and packaging and The Body Shop has a five-point policy in this area (The Body Shop, 1992):

● We are committed to using renewable resources and conserving non-renewable ones.

- We strive to obtain raw materials from communities who want to use trade to protect their culture and who practise traditional systems of sustainable land use.
- We only use product ingredients that have not been tested on animals in the past five years and suppliers must provide reassurance on this.
- Natural ingredients from renewable resources are favoured by the Research and Development Department whenever new product formulations are tested.
- Where ingredients and packaging come from non-renewable resources, for example, from synthetic chemicals, we make sure we minimise quantities and maximise biodegradability (for ingredients) and recyclability (for packaging).

Life-cycle assessment at The Body Shop therefore involves tracking product ingredients and packaging to assess their impact on the environment from sourcing, and on to re-use, recycling and disposal. Every item is given a numerical score based on approximately 100 environmental criteria. This means that the environmental characteristics of ingredients can be rated which will, in turn, influence day-to-day decisions in relation to formulations and purchasing decisions.

One area of environmental verification which is central to providing a reliable picture of the activities of The Body Shop is the assessment of suppliers and their environmental performance. It is important in the evaluation of the environmental impact of any organisation to ensure that no unacceptable indirect impacts are occurring in the procurement and supply chain for raw materials and finished goods used by that organisation. In order to ensure due environmental diligence in The Body Shop's supply chain, the Company has set up a programme of product stewardship which takes a life-cycle, or cradle-to-grave, approach to the sourcing, manufacture and use of products. The programme has four elements.

1. Environmental accreditation scheme for suppliers

The scheme is run centrally by the materials control function within The Body Shop and it involves a star rating (0–5 stars) which grades suppliers according to predetermined criteria. Positive responses to questions on a general first-stage questionnaire relating to environmental management and auditing enable a supplier to achieve one or two stars depending on their overall score. This gains the supplier a certificate and encouragement to do more. Two-star suppliers are requested to complete a further, more detailed, questionnaire relating to compliance, emissions and waste management. Satisfactory progress with this questionnaire and provision of other, more detailed, information leads to the award of a three-star certificate or higher.

2. Life-cycle assessment (LCA)

This process is necessarily quite complex and detailed. It requires the active cooperation of suppliers, and satisfactory collaboration is a prerequisite for progression to higher levels in the accreditation scheme. However, The Body Shop is increasingly concerned that LCA may become a non-ecological activity. It is clearly in the interest of suppliers of bulk commodities to draw the boundaries of LCA quite tightly in order to focus attention on those factors which are most easily controlled: wastes, polluting emissions and energy consumption. However, for The Body Shop, a full ecological consideration of product life cycles also has to take into account the impact of raw material procurement on biodiversity, endangered habitats, human and animal rights and non-renewable resources. Ignoring these issues may be convenient (especially to the agrochemical, petrochemical, chemical and mining industries), but it is not tolerable from an ecological perspective.

3. Risk assessment

This involves consideration of raw materials used in the greatest quantity and those where there may be toxicity or biodegradability issues to address. The Body Shop takes care in the specification of raw materials in order to minimise any unwanted impacts of this nature.

4. Guidance notes

Specific guidance notes on commodities and products used by The Body Shop in its operations world wide are available for use by all the company's buyers. They are simple 'aides-memoires' which a buyer can refer to when renewing an order or placing new business with a supplier. The guidance notes include a black list of substances and processes which should be avoided in all cases.

TRANSPORTATION AND DISTRIBUTION

The approach to transport at The Body Shop covers not only how products are transported and distributed but also the behaviour of the organisation's staff. For all staff, subsidised bicycle schemes exist where employees and their families can purchase bicycles at reduced rates. To make them more affordable, employees can pay for their bicycles over a twelve-month period. At the Watersmead site, staff are encouraged to use the train and a minibus service is provided between the train station and the Watersmead site.

During 1992 The Body Shop stopped its practice of giving cars to senior executives who did not necessarily need them for their jobs. As a result the company car fleet has declined from 111 to 96, of which 23 are pool cars.

ENVIRONMENTAL REPORTING

The EC eco-management and auditing scheme requires publication of all relevant data on environmental impacts. This places the regulation alongside measures such as the US Toxic Releases Inventory – a procedure which has clearly had an enormous effect on US industry and its relations with the wider community. Although the EC regulation is not mandatory at the present time, it may become binding on the most important sectors of industry in due course. This should lead to the systematic and periodic public disclosure of all relevant environmental impacts by a very large number of industries based in the EC. It is The Body Shop's view that the importance of public disclosure of environmental information cannot be overstated (Wheeler, 1994). But whatever the proportion of companies engaged in environmental auditing in the UK, only a very small proportion publish the type of independently verified statements of their environmental impacts required by the EC regulation and undertaken by The Body Shop.

The European Community auditing regulation is only one part of a much wider set of demands for transparency in environmental reporting. The Fifth Environmental Action Programme of the European Community requires that the public must have access to environmentally-relevant data to enable them to monitor the performance of industry and regulators alike. The Body Shop's position on environmental reporting is that comprehensive environmental statements verified by a third party should be available to the public of right.

MARKETING STRATEGY

The growth of The Body Shop is fundamentally based on its decision, early in its corporate history, to adopt a system of franchising as its dominant growth strategy. Those franchises use a common corporate image covering the exterior of the premises through to the ways in which products are displayed, and even the way in which staff dress. This strong and consistent external image provides the framework for the innovative marketing strategy adopted by the company.

The Body Shop does not have a traditional marketing department, but Anita Roddick spends most of her time on widely-defined marketing activities. Some of the most powerful of these are associated with the campaigns run by the organisation, and the presence of Anita Roddick at conferences and in the press, often making unconventional and challenging demands of industry as a whole. The company does, however, have a department responsible for preparing written material about The Body Shop's principles and practices, and this is distributed widely.

The Body Shop has never advertised in newspapers or on television. Its focus has been to use its shops and its staff to spread its various messages. The rationale for this approach is that advertising is very costly and would increase the price of the company's products. In addition, short messages made in media advertising are seen as too likely to be interpreted as frivolous and meaningless. The stated aim is to sell quality products at reasonable prices, not to give customers a false belief that certain products will make them look more attractive or younger. Explanations of the benefits of using certain products are often printed on labels but absolute claims are never made. For many people there is a feel-good factor associated with products which have not been tested on animals and which have less of an impact on the environment, and The Body Shop's continued campaigns in these areas reinforce that as a marketing strategy.

If imitation is seen as the best form of flattery then The Body Shop certainly has its admirers. As well as a range of companies starting up their 'green line' or natural products there have been a number of direct imitators. One of the biggest is the Irish company Nectar. Their shops look very similar to The Body Shop's outlets, but their colour is red instead of green. Nectar has also imitated the use of plastic bottles in different sizes labelled with 'Not Tested on Animals' and 'Friends of the Environment'. Nectar does not mount its own campaigns although in Sweden it has been involved in a number of Community Campaigns in conjunction with environmental organisations. Such competition led The Body Shop to employ a lawyer in 1990 with a specific responsibility for looking after the company's interests, trademarks and patents, and monitoring the activities of competitors.

The Body Shop is very well known in the UK and that gives it competitive strength. Overseas, the company is less well known and customers are often much less aware of The Body Shop's tradition and commitment. Pushing The Body Shop message internationally is therefore a key task for the organisation. Nevertheless, from experience, the company knows that once it has committed customers they tend to stay with The Body Shop's range of products and word-of-mouth becomes a powerful marketing tool in its own right.

ECO-LABELLING

In 1994, eco-labels began to be seen in high street shops which had been accredited through the EC eco-labelling scheme. In theory, this gave consumers an authoritative guide as to which consumer products cause the least ecological damage. The Body Shop's view of the scheme mirrored that of many people who thought that the EC eco-labelling regulation, while good in principle, overlooked crucial ecological criteria when guidelines were produced for some product groups. For example, the protection of indigenous peoples and their habitats, conservation of non-renewable resources, animal rights and biodiversity, had not been considered in the guidelines drawn up by the UK Eco-labelling Board (Wheeler, 1993).

The basis of the eco-labelling scheme, life-cycle assessment, has been interpreted narrowly in the UK and was seen by The Body Shop as inadequate because of the emphasis put on physical and material inputs and outputs from a manufacturing process, rather than assessing the impact of raw-material procurement on biodiversity and the sustainability of resources. Together with environmental and consumer groups, The Body Shop is preparing to challenge the implementation of the scheme in the UK, although it has been working closely with the French eco-labelling authorities in trying to identify much stricter criteria for the award of eco-labels for shampoos.

COMMUNICATION AND EDUCATION

Since 1985, The Body Shop has collaborated with environmental organisations and others on a wide variety of single-issue campaigns. These have included opposition to commercial whaling, demands for action on ozone depletion, global warming and acid rain, petitions against rainforest destruction, and promotion of the re-use and recycling of post-consumer waste. In each case considerable resources have been devoted to the campaigns. Shop windows have run posters, members have been recruited for environmental organisations, cash has been collected to help in clean-ups from pollution incidents, thousands of letters have been written and millions of signatures have been collected.

The knowledge that The Body Shop is prepared to campaign as a corporation at public and political levels has a profoundly energising effect on the environmental management and auditing process. And constant contact between the corporate EHS department and environmental campaign groups ensures that The Body Shop remains at the cutting edge of best environmental practice in industry.

CONCLUSIONS

The key concept of sustainable development is at the heart of The Body Shop's philosophy of business. It requires a new approach to business but we have seen little evidence of such a radical paradigm shift either in the eco-management and auditing, eco-labelling, or BS7750 standards. Indeed current approaches are suboptimal and inappropriate but they are still likely to be adopted widely because they will become part of a dominant ideology (Welford, 1994). A responsible and proactive approach to the environment requires us to examine new and radical approaches to doing business and The Body Shop has provided us with a model which challenges many aspects of traditional business practices.

Rethinking business strategy along the lines of sustainable development does require a change in corporate cultures and it therefore opens up new opportunities to reassess other aspects of business. Issues that need to be addressed in line with environmental demands include worker participation, democracy in the workplace, the treatment of women and minority groups, animal testing, public accountability, and the impact on the Third World and indigenous populations. Indeed, these issues should not be seen as separate entities but as part of a new overall strategy to doing business ethically and holistically. Moreover, the very power which endorses the currently common piecemeal approach to environmental improvement is the same power which continues to deny rights to workers and to the less developed countries. Many of these issues will necessarily challenge the very foundations of the system which we have too often seen as immovable, and will therefore be opposed by vested interests. Nevertheless, such ideas are achievable and indeed fundamental to the very existence of the planet on which we live.

There is little doubt that The Body Shop leads the business community in coming to terms with many of these issues and delivering workable strategies which can make a difference to the world in which they live. Moreover in an on-going and developing programme of environmental improvement, widely defined, The Body Shop is pushing forward the frontiers of doing business ethically and sustainedly. Environmental management is not a 'pipe-dream', it is not an added extra, it is not a luxury, it is fundamental to the future of our planet. The Body Shop has proved that we can reshape the way in which we do business and that we do not have to continue to degrade the planet, be cruel to animals and exploit people with less power than they deserve. The Body Shop provides us with a path along which we should expect other businesses to tread.

Questions for discussion

1 What sort of positive change and new work ethic do you think the directors of The Body Shop are trying to achieve?

2 Assess the coverage of The Body Shop's environmental policy. Do you accept that it is based on the fundamental needs of a sustainable society?

3 What are The Body Shop's reasons for undertaking environmental audits? Do you consider that they are different compared with the justification given by other companies?

4 Why are communications and education campaigns central to the corporate strategy of The Body Shop?

5 Outline The Body Shop's marketing strategy and compare this with the more commonly adopted strategies of other companies.

6 To what extent do you think it is ethical to incorporate social issues other than environmental management into the corporate strategy of leading businesses? What issues are The Body Shop also keen to promote?

Note: For further information on the topics raised in this chapter, please refer to Chapters 4, 6, 7 and 8 of *Environmental Management and Business Strategy* by Richard Welford and Andrew Gouldson (Pitman Publishing, 1993).

References

Commoner, B. (1990) 'Can Capitalists be Environmentalists?' *Business and Society Review*, Vol. 75, pp. 31–35.

Roddick, A. (1991) 'In Search of the Sustainable Business,' *Ecodecision*, 7.

The Body Shop (1992) *The Green Book*, The Body Shop, Watersmead.

The Body Shop (1993) *The Green Book 2*, The Body Shop, Watersmead.

Welford, R. J. (1992) 'Linking Quality and the Environment: A Strategy for the Implementation of Environmental Management Systems', *Business Strategy and the Environment*, 1, 1, pp. 25–34.

Welford, R. J. (1994) 'Breaking the Link between Quality and the Environment: Auditing for Sustainability and Life-Cycle Assessment', *Business Strategy and the Environment*, 2, 4.

Wheeler, D. (1992) 'Environmental Management as an Opportunity for Sustainability in Business–Economic Forces as a Constraint', *Business Strategy and the Environment*, 1, 4, 37–40.

Wheeler, D. (1993) 'Eco-labels or Eco-alibis?', *Chemistry and Industry*, April, p. 260.

Wheeler, D. (1994) 'Auditing for Sustainability: Philosophy and Practice of The Body Shop International' in '*Environmental, Health and Safety Auditing Handbook*', McGraw-Hill, Mass., USA.

Williams, J. O. and Goliike, U. (1992) 'From Ideas to Action, Business and Sustainable Development', ICC Report on the Greening of Enterprise, International Chamber of Commerce, London.

PART 3

Case Studies of Environmental Issues

Management systems and environmental disasters: the cases of the Bhopal catastrophe and the Alaskan oil spill

Richard Welford

INTRODUCTION

There are dozens of accidents reported every year involving the activities of firms. Perhaps however, two key accidents stick in the mind of environmentalists and the public alike. Although different in their nature, the accidents at Bhopal and in Alaska both had huge impacts on the environment. When an accident occurs, key questions revolve around corporate responsibility (no matter who in particular was to blame) and whether the organisation involved acted ethically. The issue is often complex and goes far beyond the question of legal responsibility. Legally-based damage claims on behalf of victims abound, regardless of how culpable the deep-pocketed defendant is. But ethics and legality are not always synonymous. The ethics issue hinges on carelessness, negligence, responses to the accident, and bad judgement. It also relates to the design of production or distribution processes, standards being maintained, and the treatment of workers. The issue becomes more complicated when several parties are negligent or have acted unethically.

It is management's responsibility to control what happens in any company, and the finger of blame often comes to rest on ineffective management systems and information flows. The investigations into many accidents and disasters have concluded that the event could have been avoided had there been an effective system in place which could adequately deal with the event or, alternatively, that although there was a system in place, there were gaps in it which allowed the event to happen. Moreover it is often the lack of a comprehensive and effective management system which has caused accidental damage and has cost firms and organisations heavily in terms of clean-up costs and damaged reputations. When we think of key disasters such as the Exxon Valdez oil spill, Bhopal, the Three Mile Island explosion and the chemical spills in Tours, France, it was the environment which became irreparably damaged due, at least in part, to inadequacies in systems which were supposed to prevent such disasters.

Management systems aim to pull a potentially disparate system into an integrated and organised one. To that end the system covers not only management's responsibilities but the responsibility and tasks of every individual in an organisation. An integrated system which covers the totality of operations helps management and workers clearly to see their place in the organisation, and to recognise the interdependence of all aspects of an organisation. Through establishing clear communications and reporting channels it should pull a potentially tangled web of structures and tasks into a clearly-defined matrix of relationships with clear horizontal and vertical links. This means that functions are less likely to be lost in a maze of mini-organisations and that key aspects of an organisation's tasks are not forever lost in a black box labelled 'nobody's responsibility' until it is revealed by a mistake, accident or disaster (Welford, 1993).

THE BHOPAL CATASTROPHE

On the night of 3 December 1984, a Union Carbide chemical plant located near Bhopal, India, was involved in a disaster, the ramifications of which have stayed with the company some ten years. Shortly after 11.00 p.m., a worker in the plant noticed that the temperature of a tank, which stored methyl isocyanate (MIC), a toxic chemical used in the production of pesticides, was dangerously high. Sometime after midnight, after attempts at bringing the tank's temperature under control had failed, the concrete over the tank began cracking. Suddenly, 40 tons of MIC escaped, forming a dense fog of toxic gas that began to drift toward Bhopal.

Bhopal is located 350 miles south of New Delhi. It is the capital of the Indian state of Madhya Pradesh which is one of the poorest and least developed states. Bhopal's population is more than 750,000 people. The chemical plant was operated by Union Carbide of India Ltd, and was 51 per cent owned by Union Carbide and 49 per cent by Indians. Management links between the Indian subsidiary and Carbide's corporate headquarters in Danbury, Connecticut, were few. Though Carbide was the majority owner, the plant was essentially an Indian operation. At the time, Union Carbide was the third-largest US chemical company, operating plants in thirty-eight countries and manufacturing a wide range of products, from industrial chemicals and powerful pesticides to such consumer goods as plastic bags and automotive products. Of Union Carbide's 1984 sales of $9.5 billion, over 14 per cent came from international operations which contributed 21.6 per cent of total profits.

On the night of the accident, the air was cool and the wind was calm, and these conditions added to the disaster, preventing the fog from dispersing and scattering. Gradually, the fog made its way across the town leaving behind it animal and human corpses, and panic. An estimated 2,500 deaths occurred, with as many as 350,000 people injured. Even worse was the way in which the people died. There were crowds of men, women, and children dying painfully. Thousands struggled to hospitals for treatment, resulting in medical chaos. Severe environmental damage also occurred to land and livestock, with an estimated 20,000 cattle killed. Longer-term repercussions followed with thousands of people who, afterwards, were no longer able to put in a full day's work. People suffered from breathing problems and some experienced months of severe vomiting. The numbers of premature or disfigured babies grew rapidly.

As well as the physical disaster, there were also severe economic consequences. In the year following the leak, the Indian government spent about $40 million on the victims. This included food, medical attention, new hospitals, research projects, and individual payments of $835 to the 1,500 families who lost relatives in the disaster, and $125 to the 12,000 families with incomes below $40 a month (Dobrzynski, 1985). The economy of Bhopal was devastated, with spending falling and a consequent negative multiplier effect on the whole region.

The exact details of how the disaster occurred are still, to this day, somewhat uncertain. Union Carbide and the Indian government do agree that the cause of the accident was the entry of up to 2,000 gallons of water into the MIC storage tank resulting in a chemical reaction. The resulting rapid rise in pressure caused a relief-valve to open, releasing the poisonous gas for about two hours. During the release, pressure probably averaged 180 psig (pounds per square inch gauge), and maximum temperature probably exceeded 200 degrees Celsius. MIC is normally stored at 0 degrees Celsius and at a pressure of between 2 and 25 psig. The relief valve was supposed to open at 40 psig to avoid excessive pressure build-up. Further investigation revealed that a number of problems existed.

Firstly, the MIC unit's refrigeration system had been shut down for five months. As a result, the MIC temperature in the tank was significantly higher than it should have been. Secondly, the unit's vent-gas scrubber was on standby for over a month and had to be restarted manually after the release was discovered. The scrubber should have worked by releasing caustic material designed to destroy the escaping gas automatically as it is sensed entering the containment area. Thirdly, the tank temperature alarm had not been reset when the refrigeration unit was shut down. When the water reacted with the MIC, temperature and pressure rose, but there was no alarm to signal the change. Lastly, the flare tower, which is intended to incinerate any of the highly flammable gas that escapes past the scrubber, was out of service.

Union Carbide's management was at first sceptical about the accuracy of the estimates of dead and injured. The organisation sent medical supplies and equipment to India along with a doctor with extensive knowledge of the effects of the chemical. But the company was operating with a lack of detailed information, and a team of technical experts was sent to examine the plant. On the evening of 4 December, with the death toll still rising, the

Chairman of Union Carbide took the company jet and followed the technical team. But Indian officials arrested him upon arrival. They held him briefly before releasing him on bail, then sent him to New Delhi. There, he was advised to leave the country for his own good. Government officials refused his offer of $1 million in immediate aid, and the use of the company's guest-house in the hills above Bhopal for orphans of the victims. The technical team was refused access to the Bhopal plant, and the Indian government seized all of the plant's records and arrested the plant supervisors. As a result, information was difficult to obtain and Union Carbide was reduced to relying on Indian news reports relayed by phone from employees at its subsidiary in Bombay.

On the Stock Exchange, Union Carbide stock prices fell, causing a total loss in market value of nearly $900 million. This plunge in Union Carbide stock led the company to begin affirming its financial soundness in press releases. However, these actions had the unwanted side-effect of making the company seem financially oriented rather than compassionate. According to a Harris poll taken a few weeks after the event, 44 per cent of Americans who had heard of the accident believed that Union Carbide had done only a 'fair' or 'poor' job of telling the truth about what happened, as opposed to 36 per cent who judged it to have done an 'excellent' or 'good' job. Of those surveyed, 31 per cent declared that they would be 'less likely' to buy Union Carbide products if it turned out that either company or employee negligence was responsible (Hartley, 1993).

Because of the litigious nature of US society, lawyers flocked to India. They saw an excellent opportunity for financial gain in representing the victims. Five lawyers filed a $15 billion law suit for negligence and defects in the company's design and construction of the Bhopal MIC storage facility. The complaint also alleged that Carbide failed to warn the citizens of Bhopal and the Indian government about the dangerous nature of MIC and MIC storage, and stated that Carbide did these things knowingly, wilfully, and wantonly, or with utter disregard for the safety of the residents of Bhopal, India. The American lawyers thought the trial should be held in the United States because the victims could win more money. Union Carbide argued that since the accident occurred in India, the trial should be held there. Some of the Indian attorneys also maintained that the case should be tried in their country. The stakes were high and the whole company even at risk because of the multibillion dollar awards US juries were likely to dispense.

In May 1986, a year and a half after the actual accident, all claims in US federal courts against Union Carbide were dismissed, and the trial was kept in India. This effectively put an end to the involvement of American lawyers, and preserved Union Carbide. In February 1989, the company paid $425 million to settle all litigation arising from the 1984 leak. Union Carbide of India Ltd also paid $45 million.

THE ALASKAN OIL SPILL

At just after midnight on 24 March 1989, in the cold of an Alaskan night, a huge oil tanker, the Exxon Valdez, came to an unexpected and sudden halt, and one of the worst oil spills in history commenced. The damage done to the natural environment, to fish, and to wildlife in the area of the Prince William Sound, and to the people who depended on it, was to become profound. Exxon, the world's largest petroleum firm, would in due course spend 2.5 billion US dollars in clean-up efforts, but the damage done to the environmental image of the company was profound and lives on.

The captain of the Exxon Valdez was Joseph Hazelwood, who had worked for Exxon for twenty years. At the age of forty-two, he was seen as quite young to be captaining such a vessel, although he was regarded as a very able seaman. However there were rumours that he was an excessive drinker, with a reputation for alcohol abuse, although it was never proven that Hazelwood was drunk when he captained the Exxon Valdez. Hazelwood had twice been convicted of drunk driving in the preceding five years and had had his driver's licence suspended three times. At the time of the accident, though, he had retained his licence to command a super tanker, although he was not permitted to drive a car. After the accident, Exxon fired Hazelwood, not for his drunkenness, but for not being on the bridge of the ship as company regulations required.

At the time of the accident, the Exxon Valdez was reported to be the newest and best-equipped ship in Exxon's fleet. It had a collision-avoidance radar, satellite navigational aids, and depth-finders (Rempel, 1989). At 987 feet long, it drew 33 feet of water when loaded. On this particular trip from the port of Valdez to Long Beach, California, it was loaded with 52 million gallons of crude oil. Because of its sheer size and mass the ship required one minute to respond to any steering changes. There was no particular reason to expect any trouble as 8,548 tankers had previously made the rather routine trip up to the disaster day. The local pilot left the tanker at 11.24 p.m. and Captain Hazelwood took command. However, very soon after this he left the bridge and went below to his cabin, against company policy which stated that a captain should stay on the bridge until the ship reaches open water.

Shortly before the accident, the tanker contacted the Coast Guard for permission to steer a course down the empty incoming-ship lane to avoid icebergs in the outgoing lane. Permission was granted, and the Valdez altered course. The Coast Guard lost radar contact with the tanker as the Exxon Valdez ran aground on Bligh Reef in Prince William Sound. By 5.40 a.m. the Valdez had lost more than 8.8 million gallons of oil. By 7.30 a.m. the oil slick was more than 100 feet wide and around five miles long. Eventually, 10.1 million gallons of oil were spilled. The oil slick continued to spread, soon covering more than 1,000 square miles and contaminating hundreds of miles of beaches. The slick eventually moved 100 miles out into the Gulf of Alaska. For a spill of such a magnitude, the clean-up technology was initially inadequate. In addition, the timing of the disaster could hardly have been worse. Millions of fish were headed towards Prince William Sound for spawning and millions of birds were migrating north.

Oil spills can be controlled in four ways: containment, collection, dispersion, and burn-off. The first priority should be containment. If the slick is prevented from spreading over a wide area, it is obviously easier to collect. But, in this instance, containment efforts largely failed. Containment booms that could have been used to surround the oil spill at the very earliest stages of a leak were not aboard the Exxon Valdez and the nearest booms were back in the town of Valdez. The barge which could have been used for transporting the booms was damaged and in dry dock for repairs. It therefore took fourteen hours for the first booms to arrive at the site, and by that time the slick was beyond containment. Once an oil spill is contained, various methods can be used to collect the oil. For example, ships can travel through a slick and 'skim' off the thicker, lighter oil on the water surface and place it into storage barges. But the problem with the Exxon oil slick was that, given its wide distribution and magnitude, it was difficult to find enough barges to hold the collected oil. Chemical dispersants are another possibility. These react with the oil in the same way as soap does with grease. However, these chemicals do not actually remove the oil, and they are themselves toxic. Finally, it is possible to set the oil on fire, which has obvious drawbacks because of air pollution and ash fall-out. This alternative also requires calm waters. But although the weather cooperated at first during the Exxon oil spill, bureaucratic bungling and disagreement impeded early burn-off efforts. Then the weather worsened.

A number of organisations were involved in cleaning up the spill. They all had the same objective but there was a lack of coordination and they disagreed on how best to cope with the problem. Despite Exxon eventually coordinating efforts, debate surrounding the most appropriate clean-up strategy raged for four days, while the problem escalated. By the time permission was granted to use dispersants, and a permit was issued for burning, the calm weather conditions had changed and there was a blizzard, also twenty-foot waves. Planes scheduled to spray the chemicals were grounded, boats to be used for sea operations could not leave their harbours, and the spill went unchecked. Before long, virtually every island in Prince William Sound was surrounded by oil, and over 800 miles of beaches were covered. Since any attempt at mitigating the impact of the spill had failed, emphasis was then placed on protecting the fisheries and cleaning up the beaches.

After a sixteen-month investigation into the accident, the National Transportation Safety Board issued a report on 31 July 1990. The report concluded that Captain Hazelwood was not able to supervise the tanker at the time of the accident because he was impaired from alcohol, and that the Third Mate Cousins who was steering the ship at the time of the accident was unable to avoid the accident because of fatigue and overwork. Exxon was blamed for failing to provide a fit Master and a rested and sufficient crew, and for failing to monitor Hazelwood's drinking problems. The US Coast Guard was criticised for inadequately tracking ships and icebergs in the area, and the State of Alaska was criticised for not having a pilot aboard past the dangerous reef. On 8 October 1991, a federal judge in Anchorage, Alaska, approved a settlement reached between Exxon, the Alaskan government, and the US Justice Department over criminal charges arising from the accident. The judge's approval effectively ended all state and federal lawsuits resulting from the spill. Exxon agreed to pay over $1 billion in fines and restitution payments through to the year 2001. However, the settlement still gave rights to native Alaskans and other private litigants to continue to bring separate private lawsuits against Exxon.

The spill's immediate destruction of fish, wildlife, and unspoiled beaches shocked the world. Pictures of dead birds and fish, and of oil-covered beaches, became common in the media. All of these scenes were linked with the name Exxon. In time, and at vast expense, Exxon employed thousands of temporary workers in a massive clean-up operation. Unfortunately, these clean-up operations were not without their downside themselves. Beaches were often left sterilised and unable to support life. Thousands of people came to collect the $16.67 an hour Exxon paid for clean-up labour, but unsanitary conditions, crime, and litter were by-products of these efforts. By early May 1989, Exxon had revised its clean-up plan, leaving some of the clean-up work largely to wave action and nature. By the end of the summer, much of the surface pollution had been eradicated, though there was still the question of how much oil had sunk to the ocean floor. Efforts continued in the following summer, with the company spending over $2 billion in clean-up efforts. By the autumn of 1990, little oil remained on beaches, although below the surface it was still a problem. Estimates suggested that up to 2,000 otters and some 35,000 birds may have died. More worrying was what the long-term effects might be, especially the effects of the oil deposits that had sunk to the sea bed. It was suggested that these might release harmful hydrocarbons for several years, contaminating the food chain and ruining the catches of fish, shrimp and crabs.

In retrospect the spill itself and Exxon's crisis management of the aftermath had a profound effect on the firms's reputation. In general, the media, environmentalists and the public were hostile to the company. Customers were urged to boycott Exxon products. Even some business executives were critical. Responding to a survey, 200 North American managers said that Exxon was slow to react, attempted to shift blame on others, ducked its responsibility, lacked preparation, seemed arrogant, was negligent, lost control of information processes, and ignored opportunities to build public support (Lukaszewski, 1989 and Small, 1991). Exxon responded with an apology, taking up full-page advertisements in many newspapers nationwide, a week after the accident, with a statement from its Chief Executive that the company was sorry and that it would meet all of its obligations.

Exxon also spent a lot of money, in addition to the $2 billion it spent on the clean-up itself. It reimbursed the city of Valdez, the State of Alaska, and the federal government, for direct expenses, wildlife rescue, and rehabilitation. What it failed to do, of course, was immediate containment and clean-up. Perhaps most important, it failed to convey a public image of sufficient concern, openness, and repentance (Hartley, 1993).

DISASTER-PREVENTION AND MANAGEMENT

The Exxon Valdez and Bhopal accidents have much in common. Many events led to the shipwreck, and to the chemical spill, and to the poor handling of the situations that followed. The businesses, governments, and societies involved all contributed to the disasters. The finger of blame cannot realistically point to just one person or one organisation; the responsibility for the disasters must ultimately rest with the companies involved. One common denominator was a degree of complacency and poor management systems. But another issue of pertinence to both situations was the role of regulation. In India regulations and standards were low, and those in place went largely unmonitored. Even in the Alaskan case though, where regulations were tighter, the Reagan administration can be faulted for creating a climate of less regulatory action and placing more reliance on businesses to govern themselves. What is evident, however, is that left to govern themselves, businesses find it difficult to balance short-run profit motives against adopting a precautionary principle in relation to long-term environmental impacts.

In the case of the Exxon Valdez, no serious mishaps had occurred for over ten years, despite thousands of trips and millions of tanker miles. But a combination of circumstances came together which caused a major environmental catastrophe. The accident was not an 'Act of God'; it occurred because insufficient attention was paid to potential risks and hazards. Management had a role to play which was neglected. Better safeguards should have been established, controls needed to be tighter, and more resources were needed for the training and management of personnel. Manager and worker incompetence at Bhopal showed up both in the build-up to the disaster and in the mishandling of the crisis itself. Their training and monitoring by the parent company left something to be desired.

In the case of the Bhopal disaster, we know that, due to the backward state of the Indian economy, much of the technology of the Bhopal plant was imported. Union Carbide of India paid a technical service fee to the parent for its technology, patents, and training. Consequently, Union Carbide of India was dependent on the parent to provide the information necessary to use this technology effectively. The employees' low educational level and poor technical ability (again, due to low levels of training), coupled with a lack of attention to safety, greatly contributed to the accident. But insufficient technical competence among both managers and workers is by no means unique to India. It is a problem many multinational firms face as they export advanced technologies to less developed countries. A major incentive for building manufacturing facilities in underdeveloped countries is the high rate of return on investment due in many cases to low wages, low land prices and low regulatory costs. It is the profit motive which therefore drives so many companies to adopt differing health, safety and environmental standards in different locations.

Attitudes among more forward-thinking business executives, and public opinion are moving strongly towards protecting the environment. Barriers to that objective, nevertheless, still revolve round the need to ensure that profits are made in the short run to satisfy shareholders and stock markets. New, environmentally-conscious attitudes also pose new constraints on business; they lead to less public tolerance, new consumer demands, and strong pressure on governmental bodies to take punitive and restrictive measures. The management of Exxon and Union Carbide may have been surprised at the strength of public criticism over the accidents. The public were unwilling to accept excuses and were quick to blame 'insensitive corporations'. Such a stance was fuelled by the media and by politicians eager to gain publicity as 'defenders of the environment'.

One of the harshest criticisms levied at both firms was that they were uncaring and arrogant. No amount of company institutional advertising and public relations activities achieved what might have been gained by more prompt and effective action. An accident saddles any firm with major public image problems and tends to denigrate a firm's reputation. Although a serious environmental accident is about the worst scenario any corporate executive can envision, what is usually overlooked is that such scenarios present an opportunity to enhance the firm's reputation as a caring and concerned organisation (Hartley, 1993). To convert catastrophe into some gain is very difficult to accomplish. It certainly requires a significant sacrifice of short-term profits, a real commitment to correcting the situation and to helping the victims, regardless of cost, and an attitude of openness and caring in all public actions and statements. Even then, of course, the efforts may be misunderstood and condemned. But there is far greater risk of a destroyed reputation if a more negligent stance is taken.

THE NEED FOR SCENARIO PLANNING

One of the key roles of management in an ethical and environmentally aware company is to ensure that their firm plans for worst-case scenarios. So often, because of competing demands or pure negligence, the worst-case possibilities are not considered, not planned for, and not even given any thought. Yet the lesson from these cases is clear: the worst-case scenario, by some combination of events and/or human error, is always a possibility, even though the probability seems remote. Such planning requires commitment and should be based on an effective and comprehensive management system. Once again however, the immediate barrier to doing this is that short-run profits may be somewhat curbed. But expecting and preparing for the worst has much to commend it, since a person or a firm is then better able to cope with adversity, not be overwhelmed, and therefore make prudent decisions (Hartley, 1993). We know from the Bhopal case that some industrial activities carry with them a potential risk so large as to threaten the organisation's very survival. Had the chemical spill occurred in the USA then the outcome for the future existence of Union Carbide could have been very different. An important part of worst-case scenario planning is that managers, employees, and communities near to locations of possible accidents need to be informed about such possibilities and advised on safety procedures in the event of an accident. Local governmental bodies need to be kept informed, and hospitals should be well prepared to treat any local industrial accident victims, keeping a stock of appropriate drugs and equipment. Mock accident drills need to be conducted from time to time.

ENVIRONMENTAL STANDARDS AND LOCATION

One of the key principles of environmental management is that the highest environmental standards should be enforced by companies irrespective of location. In the Bhopal case, Union Carbide was, in general, adhering to local laws and requirements for health, safety and the environment. But the lax regulation of occupational safety and environmental laws was of great embarrassment to India when the accident occurred. However, we are also left with the question as to why Union Carbide, since it was a US firm, was not operating US standards in all of its plants world wide.

It is common practice for multinational firms to locate plants within developing countries, such as India. Labour costs are lower and usually industrial safety standards are lower than those in more industrialised economies. Often governments of the developing economies, eager for the economic benefits of such plants, new technology, employment and renewed infrastructure, provide incentives, including development costs, natural resources and tax holidays. Profits can therefore be greater than with domestic operations. But in the production of hazardous substances, the dangers at these plants are extremely high. Although many multinational firms now contend that the plants they build abroad are identical to those built in their home countries, the management systems and operations existing 'on the ground' are often far more lax and imprudent. According to Thatcher (1987), you have to assume that in a developing country, people will not be as careful in terms of inspection, quality control, and maintenance. And you must assume that if a problem occurs, it will be more difficult to cope with. So, the multinational, in its quest for higher profits and fewer restrictions on worker safety and environmental protection, faces the risk of accidents occurring unless it exercises systematic care and monitoring. But these important systems them-selves add to costs.

CONCLUSIONS

In both of the cases reviewed here, terrible accidents happened. Moreover, they need not have happened. The companies involved did not deliberately dis-regard health, safety and environmental measures. But they did not exercise the close controls needed, and there was a fundamental failure of management systems to foresee and act upon worst-case scenarios.

One positive outcome of both disasters is that they emphasised the need for more care with respect to the environment. They shocked people into action and made businesses world-wide think about their own possible environ-mental impacts. It is puzzling, therefore, to see that more is not being done. It has to be said that it is a minority of firms who are now taking the environ-ment seriously and one wonders how many more disasters of this nature we have to experience before every individual and every company takes the action which the world needs to save the environment.

Questions for discussion

1 Outline the steps which Union Carbide and Exxon could have taken to reduce the likelihood of the accidents happening.

2 Explain why comprehensive management systems are at the heart of proper environmental management strategies.

3 What is meant by worst-case scenario planning, and how might this have reduced the impact of the accidents outlined above?

4 Best environmental practice would suggest that firms should adopt the highest environmental standards regardless of location. Why does this commonly not happen in practice?

5 Do you consider that the companies were uncaring and showed negligence towards the environment in their attempts to rectify the situations caused by accidents?

References

Dobrzynski, J. H. (1985) 'Bhopal, a Year Later: Union Carbide Takes a Tougher Line', *Business Week*, 25 November, p. 96.

Hartley, R. F. (1993) *Business Ethics: Violations of the Public Trust*, John Wiley, New York.

Lukaszewski, J. E. (1989) 'How Vulnerable Are You? The Lessons from Valdez', *Public Relations Quarterly*, Vol. 34, Fall.

Rempel, W. C. (1989) 'Disaster at Valdez: Promises Unkept', *Los Angeles Times*, 2 April, pp. 1–20.

Small, W. J. (1991) 'Exxon Valdez: How to Spend Billions and Still Get a Black Eye', *Public Relations Review*, No. 17, Spring.

Thatcher, P. (1987) 'The Lesson of Bhopal: The Lure of Foreign Capital Is Stronger than Environmental Worries', *Atlantic*, March.

Welford, R. J. (1993) 'The Implementation of Environmental Management Systems and BS7750: A TQM Approach', *Disaster Prevention and Management*, Vol. 2, No. 2, pp. 14–30.

CHAPTER 8

Environmental strategies of leading UK supermarket chains

Geoff Taylor and Richard Welford

INTRODUCTION

Arguably it was the major supermarkets who were the first commercial organisations to respond to the growth in green consumerism. In the early days, some accused them of jumping onto the green bandwagon for short-term economic advantage but over time we have seen increasing commitment to genuine, longer-term environmental improvement. We now see nationally-based strategies which encompass not only the supermarkets' own activities but those of their suppliers as well and, although we will argue that there is still a lot more to do, the three chains chosen for this study (Sainsbury's, Tesco and Safeway) have shown that environmental change can benefit not only companies themselves but also the buying public.

From a marketing perspective there is a need to recognise the potential gains which can be achieved by being proactive. Such benefits have already been recognised by companies like Sainsbury's, Tesco and Safeway who have successfully integrated environmental considerations into many of their activities. It has also been suggested that consumers do not expect their favourite brands and favoured companies merely to jump on the green bandwagon, they expect them to be at the forefront, so successful companies will need to push forward on environmental themes if they are to retain their market shares.

In the 1980s, as a range of environmental issues became of increasing importance, concern spread beyond the bounds of those groups traditionally committed to reducing the environmental impact of human activity, to encompass a broader range of consumer groups. The emergence and success of 'dolphin friendly' tuna, and the Ecover range of household products, are typical examples of the increasing demand at that time for products which claimed environmental considerations had played a role in their production.

Aware of this new and growing market, the large retail multiples introduced both branded and own-label products with claims such as 'environmentally friendly' or 'ozone free'. However, as the recession of the early 1990s cut into consumer expenditure, cost became of increasing importance in the purchasing decision. This, together with growing consumer sophistication and a more cynical attitude to environmental claims, has seen interest in many of these environmentally-oriented products decline. These market changes indicate that simply stacking shelves with products making environmental claims is no longer sufficient for retailers wishing to indicate a commitment to environmental improvement. Such organisations increasingly recognise that they need to consider environmental issues as a key element in their overall corporate strategy if they are to obtain measurable benefits.

As yet, none of the major retail multiples operating primarily in the grocery trade can be considered as having committed themselves to making environmental improvement the central issue in strategic planning. However, Sainsbury's, Tesco and Safeway have made progress in this area with the introduction of environmental policy statements and programmes, and the assignment of responsibility for environmental affairs to a senior member of management.

THE ROLE OF THE SUPERMARKET CHAINS

At first glance, the activities of the major multiples would not appear to represent a major environmental impact. As a result of their position in the customer/supply chain however, these organisations have considerable buying power. Manufacturers of both own-label and branded products cannot afford to be de-listed by such powerful buyers and must therefore meet their demands. Traditionally this position has been used to gain competitive advantage by obtaining discounts from suppliers, and controlling delivery rates, volumes and credit arrangements. The introduction of new environmental strategies by the supermarket chains, with stated environmental policies with regard to their suppliers' activities, can therefore have a huge impact on the behaviour of everybody involved in the production and distribution of final goods. This has the potential of leading to a much greater reduction in the overall environmental impact of the industry than could be achieved within the limited bounds of the supermarket's own activities.

To date, the major grocery multiples have been driven largely by the marketing opportunities presented by the growth in consumer concern over the environment. Although this is likely to remain their major 'driver', these organisations are increasingly looking to improvements in financial performance from the cost savings associated with some environmental programmes (i.e., reappraisal of energy usage within the company). Environmental legislation is also likely to have a greater impact on the activities of these companies, with the introduction of EC legislation on packaging and waste expected in the near future.

ENVIRONMENTAL STRATEGY

The major grocery multiples have adopted somewhat different strategies in addressing environmental matters within their organisations. The approach adopted by both Sainsbury's and Safeway has a clear corporate orientation, while Tesco has focused to a greater extent upon individual products and the activities of stores. It is therefore worth briefly reviewing the individual objectives and strategies of these companies.

Sainsbury's

None of the multiples has adopted a comprehensive environmental policy with clear and well-defined goals, however Sainsbury's corporate objectives do indicate that the company's activities should provide a contribution to the quality of life in the community, therefore environmental performance is regarded as a key issue in the organisation. Sainsbury's currently has the most comprehensive environmental policy of the grocery multiples, which states:

> Sainsbury's seeks to maintain the highest standards of the environmental management in all areas of business, to reduce its detrimental impact on the environment, and to improve on these standards at all times. Equally, Sainsbury's expects all its suppliers to reflect these standards in their business.

Sainsbury's has recognised the need to approach environmental issues at both a corporate and product level. However, it has recognised that it is unable to address all issues at once and has therefore chosen to focus upon those areas where it feels it is in a position to achieve the greatest impact. Its priorities have therefore been in the area of:

- energy usage and conservation;
- pollution and CFCs;
- waste resulting from Sainsbury's own activities;
- waste resulting from the production of products sold by Sainsbury's;
- waste resulting from the disposal of products sold by Sainsbury's.

In each of these areas, the company has developed clear strategies with targets, in order to achieve a more acceptable level of environmental performance. Sainsbury's environmental marketing is low key, being confined to the labelling of shelves to enable consumers more readily to differentiate 'environmentally-friendly' products, and to the provision within its stores of leaflets on environmental issues. To ensure that environmental issues are represented at senior management level, and to facilitate the development and implementation of environmental programmes, the company has appointed both an Associate Director with responsibilities for environmental affairs and a Senior Environmental Manager. Sainsbury's was awarded joint first place in the 1988 *Green Consumer Guide* and received four stars in the 1989 *Green Consumer's Supermarket Shopping Guide*. It has since won a number of environmental awards.

Tesco

Tesco began looking at the environmental implications of its activities in 1987. Although environmental considerations are not referred to explicitly in the company's stated objectives, they are regarded as an integral part of Tesco's corporate strategy. Richard Pugh, Tesco's Technical Director has stated the following:

> We knew that we could offer the consumer opportunities to be better behaved – but we had to look at our own activities first. Environmental considerations should not be just something that is added on. It should be a part of business practice. (Quoted in Hill, 1992.)

In its approach to reducing environmental impact, the company has developed differing strategies for dealing with its food and non-food products. Key considerations in the assessment of food products are:

● the amount of chemicals used in growing a food crop;
● the types and extent to which veterinary medicines are used with animals;
● the conditions under which animals are kept.

After assessing the results of a research programme, undertaking internal consultations, and evaluating the evidence presented by pressure groups and politicians, Tesco developed a framework for assessing the environmental impact of non-food products, based on the following six criteria:

● contribution to ozone depletion;
● contribution to global warming;
● contribution to air pollution;
● contribution to water pollution;
● contribution to land pollution;
● the extent to which non-renewable resources are used.

Each product is assessed against these criteria and a judgement is made as to whether its impact is none, low, medium or high. The company readily acknowledges that at present this approach is pragmatic and lacks technical rigour, however it has provided a 'yardstick' to assess products and has enabled the company to move forward rapidly in assessing the environmental impact of the products it offers. In 1989, Tesco came joint first in the *Green Consumer's Supermarket Shopping Guide*.

Safeway

Safeway is the principal part of the activities of the Argyll Group plc. To date, Safeway makes no reference to environmental issues in its overall corporate objectives, however the company has produced an environmental policy which states that:

> Safeway will operate in harmony with the global environment and promote environmental protection as part of its business activities.

and has appointed a Director for the Environment.

Safeway has chosen to give its environmental improvement programmes a corporate focus and has identified the following specific areas to address, where it feels it can achieve the greatest impact:

● energy conservation;
● sustainable use of raw materials;
● waste management;
● development and implementation of effective environmental audit systems;
● environmentally responsible marketing;
● the education and training of staff in environmental issues.

Safeway initiatives are based on a long-term vision that environmental protection has an important role to play in business activity and, consistent with this vision, has set specific targets, with time-scales, for a range of initiatives. Furthermore through its links with a variety of educational establishments, and by emphasising the green consumer awards it received in the late 1980s, Safeway has adopted a high-profile marketing approach to the environment.

Safeway is the leader in the organic produce market, with products first introduced in 1981. The company sponsors organic farming in Scotland and in 1989 won 'The Grocer' award for the 'Greenest Own-Label Product'. In February 1989, Safeway announced a ban on all raw materials from tropical rainforests or other areas of the world which do not have a recognised forest management policy. It won the joint top rating in the *Green Consumer's Supermarket Shopping Guide*.

PRODUCT AND PACKAGING DEVELOPMENT

All three of the retail multiples reviewed provide an alternative range of products for which environmental considerations have represented a greater influence in their design, development or production. Furthermore with the advent of packaging legislation, such as the German Packaging Ordinance, in several European countries, and the imminent introduction of an EC Packaging Directive, the environmental impact of packaging is becoming of increasing importance to a range of organisations and industries. All three retailers have addressed the issue of packaging.

Sainsbury's 'Greencare' and 'Revive' own-label ranges of non-food products have been specially formulated with sustainability and environmental priorities in mind. All aerosols are now CFC-free although only non-aerosol sprays are labelled 'environment-friendlier', while the company's household cleaning products use vegetable-based ingredients, which are renewable and biodegradable. In addition to the 'environment-friendlier' label, consumers may also find that Sainsbury's products are marked with a recycling logo, depending upon the nature of the packaging and any agreements made with the manufacturers. A range of own-label cosmetics, which are not tested on animals, have also been produced, and the tuna sold is caught using preferred methods.

With respect to packaging, as an approach to minimising resource usage Sainsbury's has moved to using lighter materials and introducing refill packs and concentrated products in its detergent and fabric-conditioner ranges. The company is also working with the British Retail Consortium on a uniform code of practice for packaging, while a series of guidelines for its own suppliers and buyers have now been introduced, with the following objectives:

- to minimise the amount of packaging, while still ensuring the packaging function is met;
- to use recycled materials in packaging wherever possible to ease the problems of waste disposal;
- to help recycling through the proper choice of materials.

Sainsbury's has introduced a range of recycling initiatives in association with many local authorities, with most supermarkets now having collection facilities. The company now produces a range of products, also bags made from recycled material, and supports the recycling of office paper, cups and cans. As a result of the programmes running at Sainsbury's, 90 per cent of its transit packaging is re-used or recycled. Within the stores, cardboard outer cartons are compacted and baled and sent for recycling wherever possible.

Tesco's environmental programme is the most product-oriented of the stores reviewed. The company has produced a 'Green Choice' range of products which it claims are 'greener' than other equivalent products on sale. The following key criteria have been set to which all products must adhere if they wish to be sold by Tesco as a 'greener' option:

- the amount of raw materials and the volume of packaging must be reduced;
- only vital ingredients are allowed;
- packaging should be recyclable;
- where possible, products and packaging should be made from material that has already been recycled;
- where it is practical, packaging will be made either to be re-usable or refillable;
- materials that could have a harmful effect on the environment are to be removed;
- any materials from non-renewable resources should be replaced where possible.

In addition to the above requirements for its 'Green Choice' products, all recycled products and packaging, in both standard and 'Green Choice' ranges, are labelled with a green heart symbol, while all UK suppliers of organic foods are required to adhere to the standards of the Soil Association of the UK Register of Organic Food Standards.

Tesco has introduced a range of recycling initiatives at its stores, with recycling collection facilities existing at most outlets and ongoing pilot schemes for other products such as mixed plastics and aluminium and steel cans. The former programme is of particular importance as it enables effective monitoring of the levels and mix of materials presented for recycling. With respect to transit packaging, the company has ensured, since January 1989, that most outer packaging, pallet separators and dividers, are produced from recycled cardboard. In addition to undertaking recycling activities itself, Tesco, through its involvement in the DTI/DoE Recycling Strategy Advisory Group and Wastewatch (the organisation run by the National Council for Voluntary Organisations to promote recycling in the UK), is supporting other groups and organisations to become more active in recycling programmes.

Tesco stock tuna fish caught only by acceptable methods, while the range of 'Green Choice' toiletries have a 'rabbit' symbol depicting the lack of animal testing on the product. The cruelty-free cosmetics range is labelled 'Nature's Choice'.

Safeway was the first retailer to introduce its own label 'Ecologic' range of environmentally-caring products, and organic produce is available in all stores, including organic wines, meat and bread. For own-label products the aim has been to achieve the most effective reduction, re-use and recycling of packaging materials without affecting the safety of the product. The company believes that all materials used should reflect a cradle-to-grave approach and recycling logos can only be used where proper systems for recycling the materials exist.

The introduction of the EC eco-labelling scheme has only limited value to the retail supermarkets, as food items will not be eligible for the award of such a label. However, all the companies sell a range of non-food products in their stores and are investigating ways to capitalise on this marketing opportunity. Although Tesco, with its product-oriented environmental strategy, would seem to be best positioned to benefit from the scheme, it is Sainsbury's which is currently the scheme's most active advocate. Through the appointment of its Director of Non-Foods Buying to the National Advisory Group on Eco-labelling, Sainsbury's has ensured that it is in a position to actively influence developments in the scheme within the UK.

SITE DEVELOPMENT AND ENERGY USAGE

The development of new superstores represents one of the most controversial aspects of the major retailers' activities, with several cases of high-profile public opposition to the development of new sites. All the retailers reviewed claim that environmental considerations now play a part in the design and development of any proposed store.

Sainsbury's claim that particular consideration is now given to developments resulting in environmental improvement, such as the use of derelict land, under-utilised land or land utilised in a piecemeal or haphazard way. The company states that over half its new stores built in the last five years fall into this category.

In addition to location, environmental considerations have also played their part in store design. Sainsbury's states that store design should be appropriate to local building styles and materials where these project a strong and attractive existing character. Where possible the company also uses building materials from buildings previously located on a site, to provide fill and foundation substance, and where appropriate, for walling and roofing material. In addition to store construction, Sainsbury's also attempts to use existing vegetation where possible, while undertaking to re-plant where existing trees and shrubbery are removed.

Tesco also includes environmental considerations in its architects' brief to ensure that store design is in keeping with location and the surrounding environment. Furthermore, the company employs environmental consultants to provide advice and ensure that environmental attributes of a site are maintained once a store is completed.

Energy conservation has been an area of particular focus for the major retailers. Over the last fifteen years Sainsbury's has systematically reviewed store design, introducing computer-controlled systems for cabinets, cold stores and central plant, and it sets energy targets which are reviewed on a four-weekly basis. The introduction of the company's energy management system has resulted in a reduction in electricity usage by around 40 per cent. Furthermore, by integrating lighting and ventilation systems, the life span of the lamps has been extended and waste heat from their use is now being recycled in the winter months. As a result of its investment in technology and the introduction of energy programmes, Sainsbury's modern supermarkets use only 60 per cent of the energy used by stores ten years ago, and the company saves £10 million per annum in energy costs.

Tesco has introduced a number of energy efficiency programmes with energy surveys and audits being undertaken at its sites. Furthermore, the company has its own Tesco Energy and Management Awards, given every year to encourage inter-store energy reduction. The company estimates that its energy-saving measures result in savings of approximately £2,250,000 per annum. As with the other retailers, Safeway has also invested heavily in energy efficiency programmes, with the introduction of energy monitoring, control and recovery systems to conserve energy consumption.

In addition to addressing the issue of CFCs in aerosols, all the retailers reviewed here have introduced measures to reduce the impact of ozone-depleting refrigerants. At Sainsbury's this has involved switching to a refrigerant (R22) with a lower ozone-depleting potential. The new chemical has been a fixture at all new stores constructed since 1989, while its introduction at older stores occurs during refurbishment. For intermediate temperature systems such as cold cabinets, an ozone-benign refrigerant is used. Sainsbury's intends to ensure that by 1996 all systems employed within the group use only R22 or an ozone-benign refrigerant.

As with Sainsbury's, Tesco and Safeway now use refrigerants which are ozone-benign or represent low damage potential. Further reductions in the environmental impact of these activities have been achieved through improving maintenance procedures and thus reducing leakages of ozone-depleting gases to the atmosphere.

COMMUNICATION STRATEGIES

Communicating policies, programmes and targets both to employees and to customers is of vital importance if the retailers are to achieve their environmental objectives. Sainsbury's ensures that all staff receive bulletins on environmental progress and policy along with other company information. Particular emphasis is placed upon ensuring that staff in the Customer Services Department are fully briefed so that customer queries can be dealt with efficiently. Information is also supplied to customers at the point of sale.

Tesco has introduced a number of measures to support the communication of environmental issues within the organisation. These include:

- a Managers' Briefing Pack to explain the rationale behind environmental claims;
- a training pack and store training video;
- assigning to training officers within each store responsibility for keeping staff informed of current environmental initiatives.

Tesco provides in-store leaflets to help explain environmental issues to customers and the company's position with respect to these. Tesco was a pioneer in the introduction of nutritional labelling, and incorporates Braille on selected own-label products. The education of consumers with regard to environmental issues plays a central role with Safeway, particularly with regard to children, students and teachers. Consistent with this policy, the company's Environment Director is member of the Open University Environmental Education Task Force which identifies environmental educational and training needs. The commitment of Safeway to investing in education is also evident from its sponsorship of the degree of Environmental Policy and Management at London Guildhall University.

ROOM FOR IMPROVEMENT?

Increasing consumer demands in the 1980s for organisations to be more proactive in response to environmental issues resulted in several of the major grocery multiples introducing a range of environmental programmes and 'green products'. As yet, their environmental initiatives cannot be regarded as being as comprehensive as those of companies operating in more environmentally-sensitive industries, such as the chemical industry. The environmental policies of the organisations reviewed here are still general in nature and do not commit them to sustainable development or the introduction of a comprehensive environmental audit programme; however Sainsbury's, Tesco and

Safeway have made some progress in the development and introduction of environmental programmes and products.

As yet the importance of the large retail multiples investing in environmentally-sensitive products and programmes cannot be underestimated. The position of these organisations as the point of contact for consumers places them in an ideal position to influence the decision-making process through the range and mix of environmental products sold, and by raising environmental awareness through the provision of information. Furthermore these large retail outlets represent considerable buying power, therefore placing them in a position to heavily influence the activities of the producers of both branded and own-label products.

Although the retailers reviewed here have reaffirmed their continued commitment to improved environmental performance, there is some doubt as to whether environmental issues will, in fact, continue to be viewed as such an important strategic issue as it was in the late 1980s. Although programmes such as the energy-saving drives have produced visible cost savings, retailers are finding it increasingly difficult to market products based upon environmental factors. To some extent this is the industry's fault. In the 1980s many products were launched which made false, exaggerated, or misleading claims. This has resulted in increasing cynicism on the part of consumers, who are less likely to accept environmental statements associated with products. The launch of the eco-label scheme is of particular importance in addressing this problem, as consumers have indicated that they would give far more weight to an independent environmental label than those produced by manufacturers or retailers.

The uptake of environmental products has also been adversely affected by economic recession in the early 1990s. This has resulted in consumers becoming far more price-sensitive and less willing to pay the premium prices associated with some 'green' products. As yet, it is unclear whether the end of the recession will again see consumers willing to pay a premium for such products. One issue of particular concern to manufacturers and retailers is the growth in the perception that some 'green' products, such as detergents, perform less well than standard products. Increasing demands from consumers for quality of performance, suggest that unless this perception can be addressed effectively the growth in the 'green' product market will be weak. Also worrying to the major multiples is the emergence of the discount stores such as Netto and Aldi which are taking an increasing share of the market. These organisations are putting an increasing pressure on the margins of the established retail grocery chains, who may, as a result, have fewer resources to allocate to the development of environmental products and programmes.

An area of particular importance, and one recognised by the major grocery retailers, is that of education. Research has indicated that consumers continue to be confused by environmental issues and the claims associated with various products and organisations. The retailers with their ready access to consumers can raise environmental awareness across a large cross-section of the population. They can also influence the behaviour of consumers as individuals, in terms of recycling materials and minimising the use of resources. Education will be particularly important if the EC eco-label is to be successful, as consumers need to be aware of its independent nature and of how products are to be assessed. The supermarkets can make a major contribution here.

CONCLUSIONS

Although the three organisations reviewed here have stated their commitment to environmental issues, and their belief that they will be of increasing strategic importance in the future, it is clear that these issues are still not fully integrated into the decision-making process, resulting in failure to develop a co-ordinated environmental strategy. This is evident from the statements of commitment to the environment and the marketing of 'green' products, yet the stores continue to build new outlets on out-of-town, green-field sites. These developments have considerable environmental impact and are sometimes built in opposition to local wishes. Furthermore such sites encourage bulk buying and the use of cars for shopping.

Questions for discussion

1 From a marketing perspective, outline the potential gains which can be achieved by being proactive.

2 How have the companies discussed minimised resource use with respect to packaging?

3 Why are education and communications strategies and programmes important to the companies?

4 How has industry itself contributed to declining public confidence in the purchase of green products? How could this situation be rectified?

5 Outline the environmental impacts of building more out-of-town supermarkets.

Note: For further information on the topics raised in this chapter, please refer to Chapter 8 of *Environmental Management and Business Strategy* by Richard Welford and Andrew Gouldson (Pitman Publishing, 1993).

Reference

Hill, J. (1992) *Towards Good Environmental Practice*, Institute of Business Ethics, London.

CHAPTER 9

Environmental policy, legislation and business strategy: the case of the transport sector

Peter Hopkinson, Mark Shayler and Richard Welford

INTRODUCTION

The topic of the car and its use is increasingly becoming an emotive issue when discussing environmental management at the level of economic planning. The extensive press coverage given to the furore over damage to various sites of national and international nature conservation, landscape and archaeological designation by new road schemes illustrates the unpopularity of further road expansion. Invariably the automobile industry is blamed at some point for this state of affairs. It is often suggested that this is a simplistic argument which fails to recognise the many complex factors which have led to spiralling traffic growth and decline in public transport; but the car manufacturers are only too aware of the public perception that it is they who cause the damage. They are therefore actively looking at ways in which they can improve the environmental performance of their products. The motor car is a major consumer of resources and source of significant environmental impact, and the motor industry recognises that it has a key role to play in helping to address these issues. Environmentalists would argue, however, the industry is addressing the issue without questioning the central problem: the reduction of car use and the role of the car in a sustainable lifestyle.

Car manufacturers recognise the major role of the media in influencing the environmental requirements of customers. They are beginning to use environmental benefits explicitly to sell cars although some companies are sceptical about how much weight customers really attach to environmental buying criteria. This suspicion is reinforced by the fact that to date few customers, with the exception of those in Germany, are currently willing to pay a price premium for environmental improvements. Indeed, Vaughan and Mickle (1993) suggest that the overwhelming view of car producers is that few customers would be willing to pay a higher price for environmental qualities, and that the market is saying that manufacturers must produce greener products at the same price as before. Therefore, manufacturers do not feel able to treat environmental performance in the same way as other parameters: they feel unable to offer environmental quality at the expense of other traditional qualities such as luxury and road performance.

Reducing the environmental impact of transport is one of the most important policy issues in the 1990s. The management of transport is recognised as one of the key requirements of sustainability and is regarded as one of the critical sectors for co-ordinated action in the EC Fifth Environmental Action Programme. In the UK however, it has led to some open disagreement between the Department of Transport (DoT) and the Department of the Environment (DoE). The DoE want to reduce car use by improved land use planning, while the DoT has an ambitious plan to build more roads. Arguments like this have meant that the concerns about the direct and indirect environmental impacts of transport have prompted action on a number of fronts. Many of these measures have been initiated by the automotive industry itself, often in response to real or threatened legislative pressures. Other measures impact on the wider business community. This case survey presents a brief overview of the legislative and policy pressures being developed or implemented to deal with the environmental impact of the motor car and discusses the consequent responses from the automobile industry.

THE IMPACT OF THE PRIVATE MOTOR VEHICLE ON THE ENVIRONMENT

The automobile sector, in particular, has a huge impact on international environmental problems like global warming and air pollution, and local problems such as public health and safety in urban areas. Car manufacturers make products for sale directly to the general public. Changing public perceptions of environmental issues are therefore likely to affect the sales of such products in the future. However, the environmental motivation of car buyers is volatile, making long-term environmental planning difficult. Almost all vehicle manufacturers are selling their products on global markets and are therefore faced with differing regulations in a number of countries. All of these issues combined are providing uncertainty with respect to how the manufacturers themselves ought to respond.

Concern about the impact of road transport on the environment has a recent history and has risen as car ownership and travel have increased. Until relatively recently the policy response to this apparent demand for private mobility has been to increase the supply of road space, usually through new road construction but also through a wide range of traffic management measures aimed at improving the efficiency of existing road space. The announcement by the Department of Transport in 1989 that it predicted road traffic levels to approximately double over the next thirty years, followed by the White Paper 'Roads for Prosperity' which set out a major £16 billion expansion of the roads programme, shocked many observers. This policy direction forms the basis of considerable debate surrounding transport policy and the environment at the current time.

What is clear is that the UK Government is unlikely, in the foreseeable future (other than as a result of some external shock), to modify its transport policies. These cater for future traffic growth, further deregulate the public transport sector, and offer no concrete plans to improve the safety of pedestrians and other road users. Despite the considerable literature on the subject, the main elements of the transport debate can be summarised as follows.

On the one side there are those who argue against the expansion of the roads programme and policies to allow continued growth in road traffic. The critical elements of these arguments are:

Firstly, the direction of transport policy is inconsistent with the commitment to sustainability which the Government has set out in its White Paper 'This Common Inheritance' and in various Planning Policy Guidance notes (PPGs). Unfortunately those arguing this line are in the difficult position of being unable to define, in any coherent way, what sustainability means for the transport sector. One of its likely requirements is a reduction in levels of various air pollutants and exhaustible resource depletion. Beyond this there is much confusion and muddled thinking. In the case of CO_2 emissions, the transport sector is now the largest single energy end-use sector and the fastest growing major source of CO_2 in the UK. A commitment to sustainability requires a reduction in the levels of pollution emissions to a level within the carrying capacity of the environment; in this case the global atmospheric system. It appears that in the future, critical loads will have to be defined for each environmental impact. It is argued that reductions in environmental impact via technical fix approaches alone are likely to be inadequate. Critical loads for NOx, ground level ozone and sulphur are currently exceeded in the UK and elsewhere in Europe. Car use contributes to all of these.

Secondly, the ground rules for investment decisions in road transport are different from those used in public transport appraisal and are systematically biased against the latter (Nash *et al*, 1991). Road transport investment decisions are based upon a social cost-benefit analysis whereas public transport projects are assessed using financial appraisal with the view that public transport operations are run on a commercial basis. This leads to a difference in the way the benefits of investment in private and public transport are calculated. Where public transport schemes have been assessed using cost-benefit analysis, they produce higher rates of return and therefore appear more favourable than under the financial rules. This has been one of the major factors inhibiting investment in major public transport schemes in the UK. The strength of this argument is such that the UK Department of Transport is now introducing investment procedures which allow private and public transport projects to be assessed on a common footing (MVA and Institute for Transport Studies, 1993). This is likely to see increased investment in public transport projects.

On the other side are those who argue that traffic growth and road construction is both necessary and desirable. The key arguments of this debate focus on the contribution that transport and vehicle manufacturing make to the UK economy.

Firstly, in 1989, the CBI estimated that traffic delays and congestion cost the UK economy approximately £15 billion per annum (CBI, 1989). This argument rests on the assumption that traffic delays and congestion result in direct monetary losses rather than causing inconvenience and frustration. While there is some evidence to show that scheduling constraints resulting from longer journey times do restrict some commercial operations, and small increases in fuel consumption occur as a result of slower driving conditions, this tends to be a small proportion of the traffic affected by traffic congestion. Placing a precise value on direct economic losses from traffic congestion is therefore an inexact science. However, most evidence suggests that where there is already an extensive road network, reduced transport costs, arising from new infrastructure provision, has little effect on economic growth. The main effect is on industrial location.

Secondly, the UK motor industry is a major manufacturing sector and employer. It is indicated that the UK is set to be the fastest growing centre for car production in Europe during the 1990s. The prospects are for a rise from 1.3 million in 1992 to between 2.5 and 2.8 million by the turn of the century, with exports rising from 600,000 in 1992 to 1.2–1.5 million. Predictions suggest a trade surplus in automotive products by 1996. The industry employs around 315,000 people. In 1989 the motor industry accounted for around 28 per cent (£6.6 bn) of the UK visible trade deficit. The recovery in this sector has been driven by investment totalling £2.1 billion by the Japanese companies Nissan, Toyota and Honda. Japanese components suppliers such as Nippondenso, Calsonic and Sumeto have located in the UK. These figures and projections illustrate the importance of vehicle and component manufacture to the UK economy and hence the political difficulty of introducing measures to constrain car ownership or use.

The motor industry also supports directly and indirectly a large number of activities which have a significant contribution to economic output and employment. The motor car is a major consumer of raw materials, for example. In the USA, motor vehicles consume, as a proportion of total US consumption, about 75 per cent of natural rubber, 50 per cent of the lead, 40 per cent of synthetic rubber, 40 per cent of the platinum, 20 per cent of the aluminium, 15 per cent of the steel, 10 per cent of the copper and large quantities of glass, wood and other materials. Add to this the employment and contribution to national output from the associated oil extraction and supply industry, road construction groups, quarrying, components retailers and scrap dealers and it becomes apparent that the motor industry still forms the backbone of many advanced economies. It must be noted however, that all of these associated industries have environmental impacts of their own.

On top of this, the influential role of service organisations such as the Automobile Association, trade groups such as the Motor Manufacturers Association and Freight Transport Association, means that attempts by government in recent years to introduce measures to curb the use and growth of the motor car have been vigorously and effectively opposed.

Thirdly, despite apparent concern about the environment, this concern is not sufficient for people to give up their motor cars. A major market research exercise found that in households with at least one car, nearly 90 per cent of those interviewed would not want to be without it (Hallet, 1990). Around half of those interviewed believed a car to be essential to their lifestyle. Despite a high level of awareness about environmental problems less than a third of the sample believed it to be the driver's fault. Reactions to measures to increase the costs of travel are viewed unfavourably.

These debating points indicate the dilemma which faces the Government in its attempts to deal with the environmental impact of the motor car. On the one hand there is growing evidence on the environmental impact of the motor vehicle and road construction. On the other there is the strength of the motor industry and public attitudes which make it difficult to curb the growth in car ownership and use. This has not prevented concerted effort being expended on finding ways of dealing with some of the problems. It is to these which we now turn.

TRAVEL SUBSTITUTION

Analysis of the rapid growth in road traffic (a virtual doubling in the past twenty-five years) has shown that 60 per cent of this increase is a result of people travelling further. The remainder comprises more frequent journeys and, less significantly, higher car ownership. The reasons for this phenomenon are many. More people, for example, now choose to commute long distances facilitated by improvements to the road network and car comfort. Changes in land-use, notably out-of-town shopping centres, means people are prepared, or by necessity have to travel further for certain types of retail purchases. The extent to which such trends will continue if traffic congestion increases, and the costs of travel increase, is open to debate but it should be noted that 62 per cent of car trips are under five miles in length (Department of Transport, 1988).

Developments in information technology and telecommunications, however, increasingly provide the means for travel substitution. The affordability of office technology such as the fax, portable computers, electronic mail and multimedia systems is providing a small but growing proportion of the working population, especially those involved in information or data processing, with the opportunity and choice of where to work and whether to travel to and from work on the conventional daily basis.

There are, of course, disadvantages and cost implications of tele-commuting and limited evidence to date shows a continued resistance by all but the most progressive companies to relax their control on the organisational structure. Moreover, evidence on the impact of telecommunication and information technology on travel patterns is limited. In some cases the amount of travel and trip length has fallen while in others the total amount of travel by private vehicles has actually risen. However, a recent report for the European Commission concludes that the effects of information systems and telecommunications can be considerable. It is suggested that substitution effects (fewer trips) will mainly occur in passenger transport rather than freight (Tanja and de Ligt, 1991). The complexity of the effects underlying the relationship between travel and telecommunications should therefore not be underestimated. In certain cases technical developments act as a complement to travel, enabling more contacts and travel opportunities to be made. The longer-term effects on land use and organisational structure add to this complexity.

Continued developments in tele-conferencing technology, video phones, optic fibre systems and other facilities will continue to enhance the prospect of a greater number of businesses looking seriously at the long-term potential of home working. Similarly developments in tele-shopping and tele-banking will provide the opportunity for greater control over travel decisions. Given the evidence to date, one suspects that the effects of such developments on car sales and the environmental effects of vehicles in use will be slight. The major effect will be on freedom to the individual in the amount, time and location of travel rather than car ownership.

PRODUCT SUBSTITUTION

Improvements to public transport are usually put forward as a means of reducing the dependence on the motor car. Proponents of public transport point to the fuel- and space-use efficiency of public transport over private transport although, of course, this depends on the loading of the vehicle. While various studies have provided different sets of figures based upon different assumptions, the general relationship between modes is the same. In general, rail is between two and four times more energy- or fuel-efficient than cars and between four and five times more fuel-efficient than air. This does not include energy use in manufacture or infrastructure construction and maintenance. Comparison of air emissions between modes is even more difficult, due to the different fuel mix and operating conditions. In general, though, rail and buses produce lower emission per passenger or tonne kilometre than road transport, although exact definition of the comparison being undertaken is needed to avoid misleading conclusions being drawn.

The environmental advantage of public transport over private transport requires medium to high loadings. An empty bus is equally, if not more, polluting and energy-intensive than a fully loaded car. But average car occupancy remains low. Bus operators and British Rail have appeared reluctant over the years to press home apparent environmental advantages in terms of marketing. This is probably due to there being scant evidence to show that environmental factors are influential in affecting consumer choice, although those who currently travel by rail or other forms of public transport may do so for environmental reasons. By and large, public transport has a quality, image and price problem. When Sheffield City Council was forced to drop its heavily subsidised bus fares, bus patronage fell dramatically. This indicates that if public transport was subsidised to the same degree as private transport then public transport use and quality of service would be likely to increase. Bus travel is also frequently perceived as second-rate and down-market. The absence of strong policies to improve bus priority measures reinforces this view. The bus industry sees little added value in improving service quality and provision, and under deregulation has entered a new phase of cost containment and service retrenchment.

Experience from France, with its high-speed rail network, indicates that the provision of a high-quality, high-frequency, fast, comfortable and relatively inexpensive service is able to compete with other modes. Rail traffic growth on the Paris–Lyon TGV service was found to increase during the first three years of operation at a time when inter-city rail traffic elsewhere in France was stagnating. About a third of the traffic had diverted from air, about 20 per cent from road and the remainder was generated traffic.

Elsewhere in Europe, and in many cities in the world, developments in new rail systems (light rapid transit) are part of the attempt to provide high-quality alternatives to the motor car. Such systems have high capital and running costs and there are few which operate without subsidy. Such initiatives appear successful in helping to stem the growth in traffic in urban areas but only as part of a coordinated transport strategy. Deregulation of public transport and the investment appraisal regime have inhibited the development of urban rail systems in the UK. In many countries where public transport and other modes have high patronage, car ownership rates are higher than they are in the UK, but cars are used less frequently and for longer, and therefore less polluting, journeys (TEST, 1991).

REDUCING THE DEMAND FOR TRAVEL

The third approach to dealing with the motor car relies on measures to deter travel or manage the internal efficiency of the system. One very effective measure for restraining travel may be to increase its cost. This is, however, politically unpopular. In the UK the Department of Transport is currently involved in a major study into the potential for introducing road pricing for London. Such a system would increase the marginal cost of travel. Motorists would be required to pay for using specific routes. The charge might vary by time of day. A variety of systems for administering the charge are being considered including smart cards, which are automatically debited when a vehicle passes a roadside beacon, to a much simpler toll and supplementary licensing systems. Such systems require little or no modification to conventional vehicle design. Companies such as Plessey, Siemens, GEC and Phillips are all involved in the development of technology for electronic road-pricing systems. A number of these are being trialled in major European cities.

The idea of taxing vehicles in use rather than ownership as a means of curbing congestion and environmental problems is fraught with difficulties. The technology is relatively straightforward. On the other hand, setting a pricing structure which achieves the necessary reduction in traffic without penalising certain sectors of society disproportionately, is immensely difficult. Demand for car travel is notoriously inelastic meaning that fairly steep price levels are needed to reduce traffic use. Figures equivalent to around £5 per gallon of petrol might be required to achieve significant reductions in traffic levels.

Experience from Stockholm, where electronic road pricing has been in operation for nearly two years, and the Randstadt in the Netherlands, indicate that technical systems are sufficiently developed to cope with most situations. But public attitude to road-pricing remains hostile. In the Netherlands for example, political and public reaction to the proposed road pricing cordon in the Randstadt were sufficiently adverse for the system to be postponed indefinitely. In Germany proposals to introduce electronic tolls on the German Autobahn by the ruling coalition received such a hostile reaction that they were forced to withdraw the proposals. In Britain political and public reaction to toll systems for motorways or road-pricing systems have been largely negative. Motorist organisations argue that the motorist already pays up to three times as much in motoring taxation per year as the Government spends on building and maintaining roads. On the other hand, environmental groups and independent bodies estimate that motoring is subsidised heavily, possibly by as much as £20 billion per year (Whitelegg 1992, Bray 1992 and CTC 1993). The Government currently collects around £14 billion per year in fuel tax and vehicle excise duty. Road user charges would add to this figure considerably. In Oslo the introduction of electronic road pricing was brought in on the promise that revenue raised by the system was earmarked for strategic highway improvements and public transport investment. Clear indication of how revenues from a system are to be spent appears to be crucial in their effective implementation.

Evidence from the few cities in the world (Oslo, Singapore, Stockholm), where some form of direct user charges have been introduced, show reductions in overall traffic levels but also many journeys are being re-timed (to avoid the periods when the toll charge is operating or at its maximum) or relocated (people choosing to shop/visit elsewhere). There is currently too little experience to assess the longer-term implications on businesses in terms of location and costs. The long-term impact of such systems on car ownership are unlikely to be significant. We should note however, that road pricing is likely to accentuate the present social class divisions with relation to access to transportation.

High purchase tax has been used in a number of countries as a way of reducing car ownership levels. In Denmark, for example, where all cars are imported, there is a high sales tax of at least 105 per cent of the car's value. On a *per capita* basis, ownership levels are now 20 per cent lower than in the UK although in 1978 they were higher. Successive UK governments have resisted any attempts to increase sales tax or measures designed to restrain car ownership.

Other technical developments which have been designed and promoted to improve the internal efficiency of the road transport system include computer assisted in-vehicle navigation and information systems. Progress in this area stems from the involvement of leading electronics firms and major EC research initiatives such as DRIVE and PROMETHEUS. In future it is likely that in-vehicle navigation systems will become more widespread but, as with the in-vehicle telephone, they are likely to appeal to, and be afforded by, a limited business and commercial target group.

REDUCING THE PRODUCT IMPACT: A ROLE FOR THE MANUFACTURERS

Many German car manufacturers believe that environmental pressures present them with a business opportunity while recognising that they have to spend money both to comply with environmental constraints and to exploit new market segments (Vaughan and Mickle, 1993). The links between the disposal or emission of the by-products of industrial production and environmental damage are fundamental; waste and environmental degradation are synonymous. The challenge to industry, as set out by mounting social and environmental pressures and ever more stringent legislation, is to minimise its impact on the environment through changes in its products and how they are produced.

The by-products of the production and use of a product which cause environmental damage can take many forms, whether as gaseous, liquid or solid wastes. However they have a wider dimension than the tangible measures of waste which are normally reported. It is not only the losses of materials and energy that occur as a result of production and use, but also the environmental damage which comes about through the inefficient utilisation of materials and energy.

Increases in efficiency and the associated decreases in waste output are key factors which conspire to encourage industry to minimise its environmental impact. Waste is not only an environmental problem but also a very significant business problem. Whether due to the inherent value of resources which may be under-utilised, sent up a chimney or down a pipe, or due to the costs and liabilities imposed by legislation seeking to address the environmental problem, the formulation of a company level environmental management strategy is central to efficient business management. Effective waste manage-ment, for example, not only avoids significant input and disposal costs and liabilities, but through the creation of new market opportunities can offer notable revenue-generating potential.

At the company level, companies can work to further break down the rela-tionship between the scale of their production and the environmental impact of their activities. In order to achieve sustainability, the emphasis of industrial activity must be directed towards providing the services that are demanded from their goods and not necessarily the goods themselves. When purchasing a car, the consumer demands a mode of transport with a combination of characteristics such as convenience, speed, safety and style. The consumer does not demand the car itself, but the services which it provides, and these services could be offered with a considerably lower environmental impact.

Such a subtle change in outlook would encourage the provision of the services demanded by the consumer with the minimum environmental impact at all stages in a product's life. Products and the ways in which they are produced must become environmentally benign through the application of waste-minimisation techniques. Such an approach to the waste problem has significant financial as well as environmental advantages. The challenge that faces industrialists, environmentalists and legislators alike is to ensure that such mutual interests are translated into action.

Chapter 5 of this book has reviewed a number of the ways in which the Volkswagen Audi Group, the German car manufacturer, is attempting to reduce the environmental impact of its manufacturing process and product. For VW one could read any number of car manufacturers. In the areas of product design, manufacturing process, waste management, fuel efficiency and recycling, there are points of convergence by many of the leading manufacturers. The industry is now in the midst of a huge increase in research and development activity to find improvements to existing car engines. This is driven by regulations and legislation, first introduced in California and now percolating through to Europe. The issues receiving most attention from busi-nesses operating in this industry are in the areas of fuel efficiency, emissions technology, waste management and product disposal.

Fuel efficiency and emissions technology

Penetration of fuel-efficient vehicles into the market place has been slow. Fol-lowing the oil price shock of 1973, considerable effort was put into improving the fuel efficiency of road vehicles so that improvements of more than 50 per cent for individual models were commonplace over the period 1973–1987. Between 1978 and 1987, average new car fuel economy improved by about 25 per cent. In recent years, however, average new car fuel economy has declined with the tendency towards higher powered performance cars and larger engine sizes. At the same time, a decline in the real price of petrol has meant that, despite considerable technical development in engine design/fuel efficiency, this has not penetrated through to the market.

Fuel efficiency still appears to be given low priority by consumers when choosing between vehicles. This is reinforced by the industry which promotes power and performance rather than fuel economy or environmental performance. Few manufacturers have yet tried to promote themselves or their products consistently in terms of environmental characteristics. Any reference to fuel economy tends to appear in the small print of adverts or as an aside. The residing television image of motor cars, other than the recent fashion for catalytic converters (now a statutory requirement on all new cars), is on speed, acceleration, power output and passenger safety. In any case, there have been many doubts surrounding some of the new technology used on cars including the catalytic converter which, in most cases, is ineffective for short journeys and increases CO_2 emissions. The recent increase in diesel sales indicates that economy and fuel efficiency may be beginning to attract a more discerning consumer, though this still represents a small fraction of the total market. Moreover diesel vehicles emit more CO_2 per vehicle kilometre than petrol equivalents (but lower levels of other pollutants).

This sluggishness looks set to change however. Concern about the effects of various air pollutants has been a much greater stimulant to technical innovation than simple fuel consumption. The curbing of motor vehicle emissions has been a major feature of legislation in the EC and USA, including tightening of standards for new vehicles, ambient air quality standards and control of fuel specification.

Companies such as VW, Volvo and many others are responding to these challenges. For example the Volvo ECC has been developed to comply with the Californian zero- and ultra-low-emission vehicle definitions sparked by the stringency of air pollution regulations in California. This development involves using power sources which have never been commercialised, such as electricity and methanol, and combining fuel sources in ways previously unimagined. The commercial advantage to those first to the market is likely to be great. Companies such as Volvo are not simply focusing on the product in use however. Adopting the cradle-to-grave assessment of the total environmental load of vehicles and fuels is well advanced. This work is in recognition of greater customer awareness and in anticipation of future legislation. Effort throughout the motor industry is being placed on developing cars which are energy-efficient and have high environmental specifications without sacrificing comfort, performance, passenger safety and economy.

In the long term, a recent report by the Rocky Mountain Institute (1993), suggests a more radical future for the motor industry. The future supercar comprising a lightweight carbon fibre shell able to run at 200–300 mpg and as simple to use as a computer is suggested to be just around the corner. There are a number of major advances that make this possible including braking systems with energy recovery, minimal tyre resistance and low weight, and aerodynamic drag. Of equal importance, the vehicle would be powered by small petrol, diesel or gas turbine engines which in turn drive an electric generator which then powers the car. Advanced fuel cell technology and energy-storing devices based on carbon fibre flywheels would enhance performance.

The supercar concept, it is argued, would dramatically alter the motor industry. Traditional assembly line processes would disappear. Labour and space requirements for manufacture would be cut. The Rocky Mountain Institute report likens this development to the stage that personal computers were at twenty years ago. Then it was felt that computer technology rested in the hands of a few major monopolies. A new generation of design engineers, however, found ways of combining and modifying the technology more innovatively and at lower cost. PCs are now assembled from standardised parts in numerous small businesses. The same pattern could occur for motor vehicles. Such a move, as the Rocky Mountain Institute report concludes, would challenge existing corporations and national economies. However, attaining a zero-emission car does not eradicate all the environmental impacts of private motorised transport. Impacts still remaining include land and ecology loss due to road building, loss of life, resource depletion, pollutant run-off, severance of communities and poor mobility levels for certain social groups.

Waste management and product disposal

The most efficient process design will facilitate the management of waste at all stages within the process. This will allow the optimal input mix and the integration of more efficient alternative technologies. It will also allow the segregation of wastes at source, thus avoiding the mixing of wastes and their subsequent contamination, and will aid the collection and treatment of all non-re-usable and recyclable wastes. This necessitates a move away from the conventional output-oriented (end of pipe) production process and toward the preventive input-oriented (along the pipe) production process which seeks to combine production goals with the minimisation of inputs into the process through the waste minimisation strategy. Such a waste-management strategy needs to be implemented, where possible, across the whole life cycle of a product in order to ensure maximum environmental benefits. At the heart of any such approach there needs to be increased emphasis placed on the recycling of the product after use.

On the issue of vehicle scrapping and disposal, companies like VW, Volvo, Rover and the Japanese manufacturers are all converging on the concept of the totally recyclable vehicle. This is being driven by a view that legislation will be introduced which will make it compulsory for car makers to take back their old cars when they are ready for scrap. In most cases when a vehicle is scrapped, valuable, re-usable and high-value components are salvaged. The vehicle is then crushed and shredded. Crushing rules out the ability to remove plastics or other non-metallic components in one piece. The metallic elements (about 75 per cent by weight) are recovered and recycled. The plastic and glass components are disposed to landfill. Vehicle fluids are often drained onto the ground, which creates potential water contamination or contamination of the shredded materials, which can lead to landfill site pollution.

In countries like Germany new waste legislation means shredder waste will, in future, be classified as hazardous waste which attracts a disposal charge between 5–10 times higher than standard household waste. Across the EC the increasing costs of landfill, driven by the shortage of available or acceptable sites and adverse public reaction to this method of waste management, mean that these costs are likely to rise sharply in the future.

In anticipation of these changes various manufacturers are developing products and cradle-to-grave assessment processes to improve the ability to recycle individual vehicles quickly and safely. The European Car Manufacturers Association (ACEA) is developing initiatives on vehicle scrapping processes. In Britain, a number of car manufacturers and the UK Society of Motor Manufacturers and Traders have formed a consortium on recycling and the disposal of vehicles. In 1991, Rover and the BIRD group, one of the largest materials reclaimer groups in the country, began a joint vehicle recycling project. This work examines ways of facilitating vehicle recoiling through vehicle design, components markings (virtually all plastics components in new Rover cars now carry basic materials markings in line with the European VDA 260 standard) and materials. One of the critical targets for the Rover recycling project is to be able to remove all fluids and at least half of the plastics material from a car within ten minutes. The overall objective is to achieve as near 100 per cent recyclability of a vehicle as possible. Such changes are driven not by any clear customer demand but by concern in the industry that, in the future, vehicles will be more difficult to scrap (perhaps meaning a reduced turnover of new vehicles) and that they will attract final liability for safe disposal. BMW at its pilot plant in Landshut, Germany, has procedures which enable two workers to strip all the re-usable parts from a late 1970s vehicle in 45 minutes. With its latest 3-series car, BMW manages to recycle more than 40 per cent of its non-metallic components.

BMW is the only company working with a network of recycling plants, including its most modern plant, Bolney Motors, in Sussex. The aim is to have an extensive network by 1995, including fifteen partner plants in the UK. At the current time there is no requirement for a vehicle owner to go to an authorised recycler. BMW are anticipating that such legislative changes in the future will give the company a leading advantage, and that those firms which make the effort to get involved with BMW early will obtain similar benefits.

The future is likely to see the demise of the local dismantler and scrap-vehicle merchant. Instead, small numbers of large, licensed, materials-disposal groupings, working closely with individual vehicle manufacturers, will emerge using rapid disassembly techniques to remove and separate the various liquids and solid materials components from individual vehicles in sequence.

CONCLUSIONS

The pattern of increasing traffic growth and new road construction seems likely to continue. Various measures to curb the worst traffic congestion in urban areas will be introduced, including improved public transport provision, limited road pricing or user charges, and some new road construction. Technical systems to reduce the need to travel may become more widespread though these are unlikely to have a major effect on traffic levels. There will be few if any attempts to curb car ownership. Innovation and responsiveness in the public transport sector is likely to remain sluggish because of insufficient investment.

Businesses themselves are often torn in different directions. They would like to see their car-based sales teams increasing productivity by visiting more customers. New communications technology, which was first designed to cut down on car mileage, is now increasingly put into the car so that personnel can make even more trips. Even the move towards Just-in-Time management methods is leading to more frequent deliveries of raw materials and components and increasing the number of trips made (often with less than full loads).

There are signs that environmental policy which affects the car industry will continue to increase, and therefore the main attack on environmental problems will (somewhat ironically) come from the motor industry itself, driven by legislative reform affecting product design and disposal. Indeed, many car manufacturers have complained about the inadequate enforcement of existing EC environmental Directives in countries like Italy and Spain, which leads to a competitive disadvantage in countries like Germany and the UK (Vaughan and Mickle, 1993). Increased competitiveness in the motor industry is likely to lead to increased availability of vehicles with high environmental specifications, though the market for such vehicles is not yet proven. All of these conclusions are based on the business-as-usual scenario. A sudden external shock or a major breakthrough in vehicle design could transform the market. However, given the evidence to date and current political and public attitudes, such transformations seem a long way off.

However, if we are to reduce the environmental impact of private car transport then it is not only the manufacturers of cars who have a role to play. As usual, individual consumers have a very important role but other companies need to think carefully about their policies towards company car incentives. Company-assisted car travel represents a major distortion of the transport market, influencing model choice, travel pattern and behaviour. A recent report by the Transport Research Laboratory (Kompfner et al, 1991) showed that 80 per cent of cars entering London during rush hour were either company cars or were receiving some form of financial assistance from their business. Current arrangements constitute a major incentive to travel by car and the removal of such perks is now being advocated by a wide range of bodies including the leading business organisation, the Advisory Committee on Business and the Environment (ACBE, 1992).

Questions for discussion

1 Outline the major areas for concern in relation to transport use in the economy.

2 How are the major manufacturers of cars attempting to reduce the overall environmental impact of their cars?

3 What economic or other policies do you consider are needed to tackle the pollution problem emanating from the transport sector?

4 How have modern management techniques (e.g., Just-in-Time systems) affected the transport of goods and the associated environmental impact?

5 Explain how consumer attitudes towards the environmental impact of cars is both acting as an incentive and a barrier to further environmental improvements in the car industry.

6 To what extent do changes in communications technology reduce the environmental impact of the transport sector?

Note: For further information on the topics raised in this chapter, please refer to Chapters 2 and 7 of *Environmental Management and Business Strategy* by Richard Welford and Andrew Gouldson (Pitman Publishing, 1993).

References

ACBE (1992) *First Progress Report*, Advisory Council for Business and the Environment, Department of Trade and Industry and Department of the Environment, London.

Bray, J. (1992) *The Push for Roads: a Programme for Economic Recovery?*, ALARM UK and Transport 2000, London.

CBI (1989) 'Trade Rates to the Future: Meeting the Transport Infrastructure Needs of the 1990s', Confederation of British Industry, London.

CTC (1993) *Costing the Benefits of Cycling*, Cyclists Touring Club (CTC), Godalming.

Department of Transport (1988) *National Travel Survey 1985/6*, HMSO, London.

Hallet, S. (1990) 'Drivers' Attitudes to Driving Cars and Traffic', analysis of the results of a National Survey. Report to the Rees Jeffrey Road Fund, Oxford.

Kompfner, P., Hudson, R. H. C., Shoarian-Sottari, K. and Todd, D. M. (1991) 'Company Travel Assistance in the London Area', Research Report 326, Transport and Research Laboratory, Crowthorne.

MVA and Institute for Transport Studies (1993) 'Common Investment Appraisal', Report to Birmingham City Council and CENTRO, University of Leeds.

Nash, C. A., Hopkinson, P. G., Preston J. and Tweddle, G. (1991) 'The Future of Railways and Roads'. Final Report to the Institute of Public Policy Research, London.

Rocky Mountain Institute (1993) *Super Cars – the Coming of the Light Vehicle Revolution*, Snowmass, Colorado.

Tanja, P. T. and de Ligt, T. J. (1991) 'Research and Technology Strategy to Help Overcome the

Environmental Problems in Relation to Transport: Transport Demand Study', Commission of the European Communities, Luxembourg.

TEST (1991) *Changed Travel, Better World?*, Transport and Environmental Studies (TEST), London.

Vaughan, D. and Mickle, C. (1993) *Environmental Profiles of European Business*, Earthscan, London.

Whitelegg, J, (1992) *Traffic Congestion: Is There Any Way Out?*, Leading Edge Press, Hawes.

CHAPTER 10

Barriers to the improvement of environmental performance: the case of the SME sector

Richard Welford

INTRODUCTION

It should be clear by now that in order to improve the world in which we live all businesses need to be serious about environmental management. Small- and medium-sized enterprises (SMEs) have an important role and although it might be argued that their individual contribution towards environmental degradation is small, taken together they have a very large impact. An obvious problem is that small-business managers do not have access to information concerning environmental management and, in addition, many small firms do not have the capital or the expertise to undertake the sort of strategies which larger, more cash-rich, firms are able to put into place. These barriers and others outlined in this case study of the SME sector indicate that we need to think very carefully about introducing innovative ways in which small- and medium-sized enterprises can be involved in the move towards sustainability.

In looking forward to the ways in which environmental management can be integrated into the small organisation, we need to consider wider aspects of small-firm development. Increasingly, small firms are being forced by the market to be more flexible and at the same time more specialised, producing high-quality goods. We know that quality standards and environmental standards are increasingly being forced along supply chains and that all firms are having to respond to the changes which the Single Market brings. However, those pressures often result in SMEs being reactive to change whereas the ideal situation would be to encourage them to be proactive.

Throughout this book we have stressed the need for an integrated approach and, in particular, we have identified important linkages between environmental improvement and quality, and between environmental management systems and the ethos of total quality management. These linkages are no different in the SME sector but are sometimes compounded by the developments which are occurring in the sector itself and the sorts of demands increasingly being made by the customers. SMEs are having to respond to a market where they have to be more flexible in their operations and produce goods which clearly satisfy the particular needs of their customers who are often large firms with their own environmental agendas. SMEs are therefore faced with a number of competing agendas and multiple demands. They are often drawn in different directions and managers of SMEs are often forced to push objectives which are not seen as urgent down their list of priorities. This has inevitably meant that even when managers have a personal commitment to environmental improvement their actions are more determined by short-term considerations of issues such as cash flow and short-term profitability.

The starting point for considering the environmental performance of SMEs and strategies for improving that performance must be to examine the barriers to environmental action in the SME sector. To this end this chapter reports on the results of an on-going survey of 102 small/medium-sized businesses (up to 100 employees) in West Yorkshire. All firms were in the manufacturing sector. The research on which this case study is based was conducted in 1992 and 1993. Since there is no reason to believe that SMEs in West Yorkshire would act in a different way from those in any other parts of the United Kingdom, or indeed Europe, it is argued that the results of this survey give us some idea about the impediments to environmental improvement.

SURVEY RESULTS

The starting point for any business committed to environmental strategies and environmental improvement is the publication of an environmental policy committing itself to targets and objectives which will improve the environmental performance of the company. Such policies are increasingly common in larger businesses but out of the 102 SMEs in the survey only 4 had an environmental policy in 1992 and this had increased to 5 in 1993. The extra firm developing its environmental policy in 1993 did so because of pressures put on it by one of its major retail customers, demonstrating that environmental issues are slowly being pushed down the supply chain.

The relative lack of action in this area seems to mirror the attitude amongst the SMEs surveyed towards environmental management. The general view is that that aspect of their business will become only marginally more important over the next five years. Only 6 firms in 1992 and 12 firms in 1993 saw environmental management as becoming very important, while 56 firms in 1992 and 55 firms in 1993 saw it as quite important. Nevertheless the recognition that there was at least some importance attached to environmental management should be seen as encouraging, and the doubling of firms considering environmental management as very important, between 1992 and 1993, seems to reflect the idea that environmental issues are being pushed up corporate agendas. Nevertheless there were 40 firms in 1992 and 35 firms in 1993 which saw environmental management as not important.

Action on the environmental front often occurs as firms see a demand for environmentally-friendly products from their customers. This often leads them to develop their product range in a way which reflects that growing demand. There were 20 firms in 1992 and 30 firms in 1993 who thought that their product profiles would increasingly integrate green issues; 33 firms and 27 firms in 1992 and 1993 respectively thought that there might be some change in their product profiles; while 49 firms and 45 firms in 1992 and 1993 decided that there would be no change at all. Such statistics are indeed encouraging, but again we see a hard core of businesses viewing green issues as irrelevant in terms of their own products. It must be stressed, however, that some of these firms viewed their product profiles as environmentally benign.

An active approach to environmental management will be reflected in a move towards environmental reviews and environmental audits in firms. One firm surveyed had already carried out an environmental review and was already planning a cycle of environmental audits. Three firms in 1992 and 5 firms in 1993 had definitely decided to start on environmental auditing over the next five years whereas the number of firms considering this strategy as a possibility was 50 in 1992 and 51 in 1993. All other companies had expressed the view that they would definitely not begin such a strategy. This lack of activity once again reflects the low priority given to environmental management by a significant core of SMEs. However, when we consider the barriers to such a strategy in terms of time, expense and expertise required, the results should not be surprising. It was the view of many companies that they would start on an active environmental strategy if they could secure some funding to do so. This points to a possible strategy for local authorities which wish to promote environmental improvement in a particular area.

Such financial and other support might come about via industrial or regional grouping of firms interested in environmental strategies. At the time of the research there existed, in West Yorkshire, both the Bradford Business and Environmental Forum, and the Leeds Environment Forum, which encouraged the cooperation of businesses in discussing environmental issues and environmental strategies. In 1992, 5 firms belonged either to this sort of regional grouping or to some other industry-based grouping. In 1993 this had increased to 12 firms, demonstrating that such a strategy can, at least, get firms thinking about the environmental strategies which they might pursue. Moreover, a majority of firms did express a wish to be involved in some sort of regional or industrial grouping.

In line with beginning on a strategy based on environment reviews and environmental audits, there is a need to develop environmental management systems. This is an area which is clearly less well understood by businesses. The one company which had started environmental auditing had also begun looking seriously at its environmental management system. One other firm (in 1993) said that it would definitely begin defining its environmental management strategy over the next five years. Again, many firms thought that this was a possibility (50 and 52 in 1992 and 1993 respectively) but the same significant number of firms, amounting to 51 in 1992 and 49 in 1993, said they would not begin looking at such a strategy.

To try to identify some of the reasons for environmental action among these SMEs, and indeed, some of the impediments to action, it is interesting to analyse their views about the future direction of the markets in which they operate. The most important aspect here is the perceived behaviour of their customers in the future. When asked whether firms thought that environmental issues would become more important to their customers the following results emerged:

	1992	1993
Increasingly	25	40
To some extent	55	52
Not at all	22	10

Two aspects of these results are interesting. Firstly, the number of firms thinking their customers' demands would change increased substantially between 1992 and 1993. In many cases this actually reflected the experience of pressure from those customers, often in the form of requests for information about environmental strategies. Secondly, and very surprisingly, a very few firms thought that demand would not change at all. This seems to be in contradiction with the behaviour of many firms which had previously viewed environmental management as rather unimportant. For many firms this contradiction is very real, for others, it is less real and explained by the view that there was no environmental damage being done in the manufacturing process of their particular products.

Going on to the SMEs' experiences of specific environmental demands from customers, the results of the survey show a big change over the survey period. In 1992, 3 firms had experienced significant environmental requirements from customers and 7 had experienced some. By 1993 the numbers were 14 and 20 respectively. The SMEs most affected seemed to be those selling products to large retail chains. They had been required to complete questionnaires about their environmental activities. Environmental performance is often characterised as being pushed along the supply chain and a small number of firms surveyed had begun specifying some environmental requirements from their own suppliers (2 in 1992 and 8 in 1993).

It is often argued that to launch a new environmentally-friendly product will entail an increase in the price of that product. Whether this is true is open to some doubt, but nevertheless, the perceptions amongst firms about whether such a strategy would be achievable is worthy of consideration. When asked whether the firms would consider launching a new environmentally-friendly product into their profile, at the same price or at a higher price, the following views were expressed:

		1992	1993
At the same price			
	Yes	55	60
	No	47	42
At a higher price			
	Yes	3	6
	No	99	96

From this it is clear, therefore, that while an environmentally-friendly product might be launched at the same price, it could not be successful at a higher price. The perception seems to be that customers are price-sensitive and that, in general, they are not willing to pay more for a product with green credentials. Whether this view is true or not is less important than the fact that there is a perception that consumers are not willing to pay more for green products, since that is what firms will base their actions on. Indeed 82 firms in 1992 and 80 firms in 1993 stated that consumers would be less likely to buy green products if the price was higher.

Nevertheless, some firms surveyed had begun to introduce environmental strategies as a means of access to new markets. One firm in particular had been proactive, during the period of the survey, in promoting itself and its products as environmentally friendly (the same firm which had introduced environmental audits). Fourteen other firms in 1992 and 30 firms in 1993 had begun to use environmental attributes in their marketing as a means of access. This very large increase in such activity over the twelve-month period again highlights how quickly environmental issues have been moving up the business agenda.

That there are environmental pressures being exerted on industry is not disputable. Although firms may not take those pressures seriously, few would argue that they did not exist. Of interest, however, is where they see the main thrust of those pressures coming from. When asked about this issue the responses were as follows:

	1992	1993
Local government	30	28
National government	30	27
European Community	26	29
Customers	10	14
Pressure groups	3	2
Other	3	2

What is surprising here is that most of the pressure seems to be coming from the regulatory agencies rather than directly from customers. There is little to choose from between local government, national government, or the EC being the main source of environmental demands; but customers and pressure groups, while still perhaps important, are not seen as the major focus. Clearly, many firms are responding at a time when they have been faced with demands, as a result of the UK Environmental Protection Act (EPA) from both local authorities and Her Majesty's Inspectorate of Pollution (39 in 1992 and 42 in 1993 said that their operations were affected by the EPA), but the perception that the EC is also a major contributor to environmental pressures is interesting.

Part of the requirement of the Environmental Protection Act is to use Best Available Techniques Not Entailing Excessive Cost (BATNEEC) and for many firms this has been translated into a need to purchase clean technology when considering new investment decisions. This is reflected in the survey. In 1992, 30 firms had based their new investment decisions on the need to purchase clean technology over the past three years, and in 1993 this had increased to 39. On the other hand 20 firms in 1992 and 22 firms in 1993 had not considered the issue of clean technology. All other firms surveyed had not been involved in such a decision over the previous three years. Of the firms which had based a purchase of new capital equipment on the principle of clean technology, the overriding reason for so doing was the introduction of the Environmental Protection Act. A small minority of other firms had done so because of needs to meet customers' requirements.

One of the other major driving forces in the adoption of environmental management techniques is that of competitive advantage. Central here, therefore, is the perception amongst firms of what their competitors will be doing in the future. The same core of firms (52 in 1992 and 40 in 1993) who saw there being no reason to implement environmental strategies themselves were of the view that their competitors would share this approach. However, 25 firms in 1992 and 27 firms in 1993 thought that they would see a considerable change in their competitors' activities and 25 and 35 in 1992 and 1993 respectively expected to see some change. Clearly there is perceived to be at least some momentum building up across markets therefore.

The life-cycle assessment (LCA) approach to environmental management tells us that there is a need to consider the environmental performance of products from cradle to grave. In other words, there is a need not only to consider the environmental impact of manufacturing and processing, but also the impacts of procurement, use and disposal. Some firms surveyed had thought about the environmental attributes of their products during use, but rather fewer had considered the issues of disposal as the following table demonstrates:

		1992	1993
Have you considered changes to bring about environmental improvements in your product during:			
use?			
	Yes	31	38
	No	71	64
disposal?			
	Yes	1	3
	No	101	99

Central to the LCA approach is also the management of waste and strategies for the reduction of packaging which might be harmful to the environment. None of the firms surveyed were involved in the recycling of any of their waste, although 28 firms in 1992 and 31 firms in 1993, had introduced some form of waste minimisation strategy. Of these, 7 and 9 firms in 1992 and 1993 respectively had introduced treatment of waste on-site over the previous three years. Of the firms surveyed 2 had introduced considerable changes to their packaging. For one of them, this was as a result of the German Packaging Ordinance. If it had not done so it would no longer have been able to sell its products on the German market. Ten firms in 1992 and 14 in 1993 had introduced some changes to their packaging as a result of environmental pressures, but the majority of firms had not identified this as an area for action.

A key issue seems to revolve around the question of why SMEs are not doing more in identifying the impediments to environmental improvement. When asked to identify the key impediment to further environmental improvement the most important issues were as follows:

	1992	1993
Cost implications	10	22
Knowledge and skills	26	27
Not seen as important in the organisation	30	25
Other priorities more important	35	27
Others	1	1

It is not so much the lack of skills and costs which are seen as barriers herefore. There does seem to be a perception that there are other priorities before environmental considerations are dealt with. We must remember that this survey was undertaken at a time of recession and many of the companies were more concerned about cash flow and short-term survival. We should therefore see these responses as encouraging. Notwithstanding the fact that many firms did not see environmental issues important at all, one would surmise that, when other objectives have been met, there may well be a willingness to move on to addressing the environmental agenda.

The role of legislation in promoting environmental change is clearly important and we have seen a number of national and EC-wide initiatives aimed at promoting further environmental improvements. However, when asked whether firms saw this as of benefit, we found very different attitudes expressed about legislation when it is viewed from the perspective of the business, from society at large, and from individuals as the following results demonstrate.

		1992	1993
Do you consider future legislation on environmental protection to be good or bad for:			
(a) Your business?			
	Good	20	25
	No effect	22	25
	Bad	60	52
(b) Society as a whole?			
	Good	32	32
	No effect	45	46
	Bad	21	20
(c) You and your family?			
	Good	80	82
	No effect	20	20
	Bad	2	0

Once again this highlights a key contradiction between the wishes of individuals and the perceived benefits to society, and the views of individual SMEs. While environmental protection is viewed as being good for the planet on which we live, firms clearly perceive it to be an impediment to their normal operations which in many cases will have negative effects. It should be noted that it was the same managers who expressed these views. Clearly, on a personal level they are keen to see environmental improvement but they are less keen to see their businesses pay for this. This represents a fundamental contradiction between personal politics and corporate cultures therefore.

Much of the legislation in the EC is now turning away from command and control instruments towards the implementation of market-based strategies for environmental improvement. To this end the introduction of the EC eco-labelling scheme and the eco-management and auditing scheme are important initiatives. Linked to this approach the BSI's Environmental Management System Standard (BS7750) is based on the same voluntary approach aimed at certifying best practice in industry. When surveyed, the majority of firms had never heard about these standards. A very small number of firms had been thinking about them, but none had committed themselves to action by 1993. The fact that so few firms had even heard about the standards is an important reflection on the provision of information in this area.

SURVEY BIAS

To some extent we know that this survey is biased but we can correct for that. The survey questionnaire was sent to 200 firms in 1992 and there was a response from 103 of them. One firm went out of business in the period between the two surveys and has therefore been excluded. No reminder was sent to firms to complete the initial questionnaire but out of the 97 non-respondents, 10 firms were telephoned at random to find out why they had not responded. Nine out of the 10 firms were of the view that environmental matters were not important and had not managed to spare the time to complete the survey. The tenth thought that the issues were important but had still not completed the questionnaire. In effect therefore, we have to deflate all the positive responses to the questionnaire by up to 50 per cent, demonstrating significantly less action on environmental management than might be at first identified.

Nevertheless the survey should be seen as demonstrating that while the environmental issue is not of paramount importance in the SME sector yet, there have been significant changes over the twelve-month period between 1992 and 1993. Moreover, a small number of SMEs are engaged in positive environmental action and this looks likely to increase. This should be seen as extremely positive and further surveys will reveal whether this trend continues.

A BROAD CHARACTERISATION OF THE SME SECTOR

Although it is a minority of SMEs which are considering their responses to the new environmental challenges facing industry, it is nevertheless heartening to see that there are some who are responding in a proactive way. It is not surprising perhaps that this sector, particularly at times of recession, is lagging behind best proactive companies elsewhere, and we have identified that some non-active companies are not proceeding because they simply do not have the information, knowledge and skills so to do.

It is very difficult to draw strong conclusions or to make broad generalisation from a survey of this size, where responses have been very different among firms. However, in an attempt to characterise some of the developments in the SME sector and the behaviour of some of the firms therein, it is useful to think of a four-level characterisation of the SMEs surveyed.

- The largest group identified in the survey is the (around 40 firms) 'ostrich' group. They are characterised by burying their heads in the sand, not recognising the environmental challenge which faces industry. They assume that this is another passing phase, that their environmental performance has a negligible impact on the world and that the environmental issues are an unnecessary annoyance. Moreover, ostriches think that their competitors will also do nothing, and that even where consumers are demonstrating environmental awareness, they are unwilling to pay the perceived higher prices necessitated by environmentally-superior products.

- The second group of around 25 firms represent the 'laggards'. They recognise the environmental challenge but feel unable to do anything about it. There are other more pressing demands on them and their business strategy does not allow room for environmental considerations yet. They do not know how to proceed, they lack information; and, although they see the benefits of environmental improvement to society as a whole, they feel that they are powerless to react. These firms may change in future if they can see a dramatic change in the markets in which they operate, or in legislation.

- The third group of firms (around 25) are characterised as being the 'thinkers'. Not only do they recognise the environmental challenge, they know that in time they will have to do something about it. They still lack information, knowledge and expertise, but they are thinking about the sorts of actions they should undertake. The thinkers wait and see what others are doing because they are not yet willing to spend money in an uncertain area. Nevertheless, this is the group which is most likely to change from a reactive to a proactive stance over time and they will make sure that they are well prepared so to do.

- The fourth group of firms are by far the smallest, representing perhaps only 10 firms out of the survey. They are the 'doers'. They are beginning to put clear, proactive environmental strategies in place, they are planning ahead and see the need to change their products and processes in response to the increasing demands being put on them. Moreover, they are beginning to tell people what they are doing and beginning to include the environmental message in their corporate marketing strategies. Doers understand the links between the demands of society and the role which they need to play in becoming a successful company, widely defined.

Such a characterisation is clearly somewhat simplistic. It does nevertheless point out that it is a minority of firms who are being proactive, but that there are other firms preparing themselves, slowly, for change. Some firms need to be given a bit of a push, and the laggards still need to be convinced of the real benefits to undertaking environmental strategies. On the other hand, there is a large group of ostriches who are doing almost nothing and who still see the environmental challenge as an irrelevancy. These are the firms who will do nothing unless they are forced to do so. It will be a hard job convincing these firms that environmental issues are anything to do with them.

POLICY IMPLICATIONS

Policies with respect to SMEs need therefore to address the fact that very few firms are at all proactive in the area of environmental management. More than anything, those policies need to deal with what has been identified in this case study as the impediments to improvement. One clear starting point which would seem to receive support from many enterprises would be the development of regional or industrial groupings which could help firms deal with environmental issues. Such groupings, which are perceived as of benefit to many of the companies surveyed, would also have the benefits of stirring the laggards into action and providing help to the thinkers who need guidance in order to help them move on.

One key policy objective is associated with the need to help small- and medium-sized enterprises develop and become resource-efficient, competitive, technically advanced and environmentally friendly. We have already noted that it is very difficult for the small enterprise alone to achieve all these requirements. The sort of technical expertise which large firms will have in-house to help with their environmental management will probably be lacking, and few small businesses will have the money to buy in consultants to do these important tasks. A clear way forward for the SME sector therefore revolves around cooperation and networking. This entails creating links between small firms and between firms and institutions.

Small businesses themselves must begin to recognise the benefits which can be achieved from such a strategy. By networking and cooperating beyond even the boundaries of the firm, managers can learn from other people's experiences and errors. What small businesses therefore need is a framework within which to achieve such advantages. This can be created by the establishment of industry-specific or multi-sectoral forums or forums simply within localities, but the common element which will determine the success of any of these initiatives is cooperation.

Some business parks provide an excellent example of what might be achieved through cooperation and this might be extended into a concept of eco-parks. We have seen the establishment of many business parks (sometimes called science parks, or research parks reflecting their high-technology nature) and sometimes these are closely linked to one or more universities or other research institutions. Cooperation between those with expertise and knowledge in the university, and those with capital and experience of products and markets, feed into the system and can produce a powerful foundation on which to develop products in an environmentally-responsible way. The concept of an eco-park where like-minded firms are grouped together, share their experiences and expertise and produce products in an environmentally-sustainable manner is a natural extension of this.

There is also little doubt that the process of 'greening' requires innovation at the firm level if society is to reap the benefits of more environmentally-friendly products and processes. A great deal has been written about the innovativeness of SMEs in comparison with that of larger companies. On the one hand it has been argued that large scale and high levels of monopoly profits are required for research, development and innovation, while on the other hand it has been argued that small firms are more efficient at performing innovative activities and are the major sources of innovation. It is true, however, that very few SMEs engage in R and D expenditure. Nevertheless small firms and independent inventors have played a disproportionately large part in producing major twentieth-century inventions. However, at least half of these inventions owe their successful implementation to large companies. What seems to be stopping SMEs innovating in the field of green products is a lack of recognition of the importance of environmental issues, and a lack of skills and knowledge about the particular issues involved here. There is therefore a significant role to be played by communications and education, and this needs to be a major policy objective of local authorities and government.

The results of innovations aimed at environmental improvement will benefit the global environment only if they are shared. Such cooperation may at times conflict with competitive strategies, and there is therefore a need to provide incentives to small firms not only to innovate but also to share the benefits of such a strategy. There needs to be a framework whereby both technology transfer, and the transfer of information and knowledge, can be achieved if small businesses are to achieve the same levels of success as their large counterparts. To some extent there needs therefore to be a paradigm shift away from short-termism, which stresses financial controls and objectives, towards one which looks towards a more long-term sustainable future. Such a paradigm shift is difficult to achieve because it affects the very foundations of the economic system in which SMEs are forced to operate.

If there is a role for the Government and local government in helping small businesses become environmentally friendly, this has to be evaluated carefully. In the past some government measures to support small businesses have been ineffective. We must remember that small businesses are often run by entrepreneurs and that these people are more likely to be capable of gauging risk than public servants. Entrepreneurs also tend to be innovative, energetic and self-reliant and generally resent being coddled by so-called experts. On the other hand it is the case that the skills and aptitudes of most small proprietors of small firms are limited and, with this in mind, there is a clear role for the public sector to devise programmes to help small businesses introduce change aimed at environmental improvement.

The key strategy here has to be one of cooperation and not domination. We have seen how organisations such as the Groundwork Trust have succeeded in forging productive links between the private sector, voluntary initiatives and public agencies. We have also seen some links between the private sector and conservation groups. Urban regeneration, environmental education and community development have also brought with them benefits for the small business. But at the centre of all these successful strategies there has been an incentive for all involved to participate. Without proper incentives, which in most cases must go beyond mere altruism, we cannot expect small businesses to participate in environmental projects. On the other hand however, many small businesses have not recognised for themselves the benefits of cooperative ventures and have concentrated too much on narrow cost-minimisation strategies.

CONCLUSIONS

The environmental revolution, which began back in the 1960s and developed rapidly in the 1980s and into the 1990s, put much of the blame on large businesses and stressed the need for change in that sector. But increasingly it is to small enterprises to which attention is being turned, and for them, as well, environmental improvement will be an integral part of commercial normality in the future. Anyway, definitions of business success are likely to be wider in the future and every enterprise will have to demonstrate its contribution to the ultimate aim of zero negative impact on the environment. Even in the small business it will be increasingly the case that competitive advantage will be achieved not merely by keeping abreast of environmental developments, but also by initiating change within an organisation and responding with new environmentally-friendly products and production processes.

Even though governments are increasingly seeking to make all polluters pay, the success of environmental improvement will be determined largely by the responsiveness of business. There is evidence that larger businesses are, at last, responding to environmental pressures, but this survey indicates that smaller enterprises are, in the main, followers rather than leaders and are lagging behind.

The development of environmental networks amongst small businesses, voluntary organisations and the public sector, will enable controlled and sustainable growth to occur. Ultimately what we do with our environment affects us all and future generations. If the environment is important then we should recognise that the systems and processes used in businesses are also important. It has been suggested here that collaborative arrangements, multi-sector networking and cooperative strategies can help to meet the aims and objectives of a sustainable and developing economy to the extent that this provides us with a model for the promotion and development of sustainable industry. There is a need for small businesses to be given incentives to undertake environmental change. Some of these incentives are provided by the legislative framework and a need to survive in a more competitive and environmentally aware marketplace. In addition, larger firms will push environmental improvement along the supply chain. But there is still a need to convince small businesses that environmental improvements will reduce costs in the long run and this can only be achieved by demonstration of best practice. There is a clear role here for government and local authorities in supporting innovative developments and providing a forum where information can be exchanged.

Questions for discussion

1 What do you consider to be the main impediments to environmental improvement in the SME sector? To what extent do you think these also present problems to larger companies?

2 What do you think can be done to encourage the SMEs identified as 'ostriches' to improve their understanding of the importance of environmental management?

3 It has been suggested that there are benefits for SMEs working together in a cooperative way. How do you think this can be achieved in practice?

4 In what ways can notions of cooperation affect traditional ideas about competitive advantage? Which concept do you consider most important?

5 What strategies can larger firms play to encourage SMEs to be proactive in relation to environmental issues?

Note: For further information on the topics raised in this chapter, please refer to Chapter 9 of *Environmental Management and Business Strategy* by Richard Welford and Andrew Gouldson (Pitman Publishing, 1993).

CHAPTER 11

Environmental management at the regional level: the case of the Avoca-Avonmore Catchment Conversion Project and IDAS Trout Ltd[1]

Donal O'Laoire and Richard Welford

INTRODUCTION

The concepts of sustainable development, as introduced in the Brundtland Report (WCED, 1987), have become increasingly important. The linkages between environment and development are now well established, and have led to, amongst other initiatives, the United Nations Conference on Environment and Development in Rio de Janeiro, and the World Bank report on Development and the Environment (World Bank, 1992). The idea of sustainable development recognises that there is an interdependence between the economy and the environment, not only because the way we manage the economy has an impact on the environment, but also because environmental quality has an impact on the performance of the economy (Pearce and Turner, 1990). Much development in the past has left society with a degraded environment, often in areas characterised by economic decline, migration and community disintegration. The Fifth Environmental Action Programme of the European Community (1992) argues that in the past there has been a tendency to treat environment and development interests as being mutually hostile; today it is realised that they are mutually dependent. A soundly-based, comprehensive environmental policy can provide the preconditions for the optimisation of resource management, and the sustainability of almost all forms of economic and social development, and of the employment and welfare which they generate.

Throughout the Fifth Environmental Action Programme, it becomes clear

[1] This case was developed in association with Environmental Management and Auditing Services Ltd, based in Dublin, Ireland. Their developmental work in the Avoca-Avonmore Catchment Conversion Project has been funded by the European Community.

that the EC favours an integrated, comprehensive and cohesive approach in order to obtain 'sustainable development'. The basic strategy, therefore, is to achieve full integration of environmental and other relevant policies through the active participation of all the main actors in society (administration, enterprises, general public) through a broadening and deepening of the instruments for control and behavioural change including, in particular, greater use of market forces.

This case study outlines a potential new strategy for management at a regional level, which is based on company-level environmental management theory, and which attempts to integrate social, economic and environmental factors in a comprehensive manner. A market-led approach to regional development, using environmental management, is used to create area comparative advantage by differentiating area products and processes. The case examines the development of this strategy in a region of Ireland and examines the contributions made to, and the benefits derived from, the project by one particular company in that region.

BACKGROUND: THE IRISH EXPERIENCE

There is a long-standing association of green and greenness for which Ireland, the so-called 'Emerald Isle', pre-dates the more recent usage of 'green' as the general awareness of environmental issues. Indeed, the association of green and Ireland persists in the minds of consumers in many European Community countries. This fact is continuously borne out in successive market surveys conducted by various agencies, in particular, An Bord Bainne, the Irish Dairy Marketing Board. Throughout continental EC Member States and in the UK, images and themes of 'greenness', 'purity', 'cleanliness', 'close to nature', 'pre-industrial', 'natural beauty', 'clean air', and 'rugged Atlantic coast' are constantly echoed in market surveys.

By fact of history and geography, Ireland may have been spared the worst excesses of industrial development experienced in other parts of the EC and in the former Eastern Bloc. Ironically, its isolation and relative under-development may have provided a comparative advantage to Ireland as we enter the twenty-first century. This comparative advantage may be based on the abundance of environmental goods, such as clean air, clean water, open spaces and natural beauty, that are emerging as sought-after and scarce economic goods in Europe and other parts of the globe.

With a population of some 3.5m, the small open economy of Ireland must participate vigorously in the wider EC Single Market, if it is to prosper. This reality underpins much of Ireland's positive embracing of the European Community ideal. The scale of the general production base, compounded by its peripheral location, rules out market participation on the basis of scale, quantity, low cost and proximity to market – options that are becoming available to Ireland's emerging competitors in the market economies of Central and Eastern Europe.

Successive policy input reports for Irish industry have stressed that the only basis for participation in the Single Market, and in other Third Markets, can be quality and efficiency. The most recent report, which has been adopted by the Irish Government, the so-called Culliton Report (Benson and Associates, 1992), suggests that Irish industry and, in particular, the Irish food industry, can benefit from the favourable environmental perception. The report states that 'Ireland starts with the advantage of a favourable "green" image. Branded Irish products could benefit from the swing in consumer tastes provided this image is preserved and enhanced'. Recognising this opportunity, the Irish Industrial Development Authority (IDA) initiated a pilot project, involving a number of leading companies to examine the relevance and potential role of environmental management systems as a strategy for sustainable growth and competitive participation in the EC Single Market. This case summarises part of that project.

THE AVOCA-AVONMORE CATCHMENT CONVERSION PROJECT

The Culliton Report suggests that a product could gain currency in the market by virtue of its 'green' credentials. The Avoca-Avonmore Catchment Conversion Project set out to examine if a region could gain market currency by virtue of the high environmental quality of the area, its products and its production processes. The approach was proposed by Wicklow County Council through the Commission of the European Communities, who accepted and supported the project as a model to be emulated in other parts of the Community (the Avoca-Avonmore Catchment Conversion Project (EMA, 1992)).

The Avoca-Avonmore catchment drains an area of over 650 square km of County Wicklow on the east coast of Ireland, about 70 km south of Dublin. It can be defined broadly as the urban area of Arklow and its hinterland, extending into the upland valleys of the Avoca, Avonmore and Aughrim rivers. The river system comprises four main tributaries, fed by a number of secondary streams. The study area approximates to nine district electoral divisions, with a relatively stable number of inhabitants of about 15,500.

The area is well served by a network of national, primary and secondary roads, and has become more accessible for tourists and commuters due to recent roadworks. The river system forms an important connective thread throughout the catchment area. The quality of the Avonmore, Avonbeg, and Aughrim rivers is generally very high. However, as the rivers pass through the area, they become seriously polluted by leachate from abandoned copper mines, near Avoca village. For the last 9 km, the river system is biologically dead, forming an impenetrable barrier for migratory fish such as salmon. The pollution also damages the coastal waters and estuary where there was once a productive oyster fishery. Waste water from both industry and domestic premises receives little or no treatment prior to discharge, compounding the situation further. The future condition of the river could therefore be used as a measure of the success of environmental rehabilitation of the catchment.

The catchment has suffered in recent decades because the area has experienced a comparatively wide and rapid decline in traditional industry, leaving areas derelict, seriously polluted, and with severe social and economic problems. Unemployment is very high, almost 25 per cent, and development policies, which focus on attracting industries from abroad, have had limited success.

The Avoca-Avonmore catchment possesses a wealth of natural resources which are directly responsible for generating economic activity in the region. Land, soil, and water form the basis for the catchment's main economic activities. The river and seaport provide additional industrial and commercial benefits for the craft and chemical industries. All of these resources and their associated commercial activities are related to the present and future well-being of the economy and the people of the Avoca catchment. The future economic development of this catchment is about the management of these resources.

Within the European Community, the Avoca-Avonmore catchment is not unique. This makes the catchment an ideal location for research and innovation on economic and environmental conversion strategies that can be emulated in, and used as a model for, similar valleys and catchments throughout the European Community. One of the main tributaries in the catchment is the Aughrim River on which IDAS Trout Ltd is located.

THE CONVERSION FRAMEWORK

The underlying approach to developing a conversion plan for the catchment lies in the development of comparative advantage based on integrated environmental management, at both company and regional (catchment) level. The conversion plan proposes an integrated approach to dealing with economic, social and environmental issues. It necessitates a fundamental shift in culture towards the identification of the benefits which can accrue from the protection and management of the environment.

The concept, in principle, is that commercial and industrial viability in the 1990s and beyond is synonymous with quality at every level, including environmental quality. Rather than regarding new environmental control and legislation as a negative factor and a cost, the concept here is to turn apparent constraint into advantage. The conversion will take the shape of a regional or catchment management system which will provide a strategic link between environmental rehabilitation, development and the pressures and opportunities associated with environmental demands. The concept favours market driven, rather than legislation driven, development.

Recent EC environmental legislation has had a significant impact on the direction of national environmental policies, with many of the initiatives at national level concerning the implementation of measures adopted by the Community (Haigh, 1992). The Single European Act 1987 states that environmental protection requirements are to be a component of all other policies based on the indisputable fact that measures in the sphere of other policies may have a significant positive or negative impact on the environment (Kramer, 1990; Haigh, 1992). Legal changes are leading to a move away from dealing with environmental issues on an individual basis, i.e., air, water, noise, waste, etc., to the handling of issues on an integrated sectoral and regional basis, involving local communities and local and national governments. This approach fits with the regional conversion plan.

The critical differentiated added value for the study area is the emphasis placed on environmental and product quality at every stage of the production process, and every step in the production chain. The different production steps will increasingly take place within the same region including the disposal and treatment of waste. New opportunities may therefore arise in the catchment area. This may influence the necessity for development and implementation of environmental management systems at the company level. Increasing product quality, and achievement of environmental standards, will be ensured as a result. The regional conversion plan aims at focusing the marketing instruments not only on the company but also on the region in which the company is based.

It is recognised that the 'green image' of Ireland is underdeveloped in the European context and that there has been no positive effort to put structures into place to preserve, expand and exploit this image. In order to use the environmental 'green image' to penetrate the market and improve trade, it will be necessary to put structures into place that will improve the environmental credibility of companies (Roome, 1992). There is a growing recognition that the focus of 'green' marketing will switch from the product to the company level, or to the process behind the product (David, 1991; Charter, 1992). The adoption of environmental management systems (EMSs) within companies in the region will be actively promoted by the regional or catchment environmental management system.

From a regional perspective, concerns have arisen regarding the distribution of benefits which will stem from the Single European Market (SEM). The marketing weakness of indigenous Irish industry, coupled with the peripherality of Ireland relative to the main EC markets, contributes to the difficulties which Irish firms will face in attempting to exploit the opportunities presented by the SEM. As a result, an essential prerequisite to the development of successful domestic and export markets will be the establishment of a strong marketing focus and capability in Irish firms. The aim is that industry in the Avoca-Avonmore catchment will move to exploit the opportunities resulting from an increasing environmental consciousness by promoting the environmental integrity of Irish produced products and their environment.

In this respect, the concept which lies behind the Avoca-Avonmore project can only work within the context of European integration. Local markets alone will not provide a sufficient basis for a conversion plan. Inherent in the Avoca-Avonmore Conversion Plan is the development of a well-managed, environmentally conscious location where local organisational structures embrace a positive environmental philosophy.

COMPANY ENVIRONMENTAL MANAGEMENT

For many forward-looking companies, the new challenge of environmental responsibility has become an aspect of the search for total quality, and a clear link with Total Quality Management (TQM) has been made (Welford, 1992a). A close parallel may be drawn between TQM objectives and the concept of cradle-to-grave environmental analysis which involves a comprehensive evaluation of the environmental impact of a product throughout its life cycle.

Environmental management affects the whole business and requires a strategic response. Strategies based on the environment and 'compliance-plus' are consistent with current notions of quality management, but changes are required, even in those companies which follow a reactive strategy and operate to quality assurance standards. Compliance-plus companies take a proactive position on environmental management. A company adopting this approach seeks to integrate environmental management systems into the framework of its business strategy (Roome, 1992).

Industry clearly needs to adopt a more strategic view of environmental problems. It needs to move away from predominantly short-term solutions to problem solving, and towards the development of pre-emptive control strategies striking a balance between regulation and the need to turn those regulations into competitive advantage abroad (Winsemius and Guntram, 1992). Many companies now try to integrate environmental demands into their business objectives. Full integration can turn what has been a liability into an asset. Environmental management can be regarded as having a broad scope, incorporating not only environmental, but also social and economic factors. A properly designed and implemented environmental management system (EMS) can therefore form the link between strategic business objectives and environmental demands.

It is widely acknowledged that having an environmental management system is beneficial for virtually all companies (for an overview of the potential costs and benefits see Hutchinson (1991), ECOTEC (1992) and Welford (1992b)). Virtually all available evidence indicates beneficial effects on company balance sheets adopting environmentally sound practice (Chartered Institute of Management Consultants, 1990). Furthermore, it is clear that undesirable costs can result from not adopting such environmental practices.

However, the incentive to put an EMS into place, and the extent to which organisation changes have to be made, differ strongly between businesses. Two factors are of great importance (Roome, 1992; Welford and Prescott, 1992; Winsemius and Guntram, 1992). Firstly, the business sector in which the company operates, influences both the level of environmental risk to which the company is exposed, and the market opportunities for environmental protection. Secondly, the current operational system of the business: a business having established ISO 9000 or operating with a TQM system may find it easier to implement an EMS (Welford, 1992a).

The weight of opinion lies behind the need to adopt a new approach to environmental management. This ultimately involves internalising the costs of environmental protection (Pearce and Turner, 1990) and creating business initiatives and a comparative advantage from an increasing sense of corporate responsibility for the environment. This is the approach which is being followed in the implementation of the conversion plan for the Avoca Catchment. A high priority will be given to the environmental image of individual companies and the catchment as a whole, consistent with the establishment of a competitive advantage for products originating from the area.

THE CATCHMENT MANAGEMENT SYSTEM

There are inherent risks in treating economic forces and the environment as if they were separate and non-interacting elements. Economic policy which does not take into consideration environmental management, risks both environmental damage and economic instability.

There is a need to change from a piecemeal to a holistic approach and this is supported by the Fifth Environmental Action Programme of the European Community. The development of an economic conversion plan for the Avoca-Avonmore catchment is dependent on the mobilisation of indigenous regional and local resources facilitated through partnerships between individuals, institutions and agencies. In this context, it is important to facilitate developments in the business and wider community through education, training and the provision of support, advice, and capital for local initiatives. Any environmental management system starts with, and depends strongly upon, the development of understanding and commitment from all people involved. The catchment management system sees involvement from all parties operating and living in the catchment areas as one of the cornerstones of the whole concept.

The implementation of the catchment management system (CMS) should give the catchment a comparative edge, and lead to sustained economic growth and development. As a result of the implementation of the CMS, the area will be promoted as a 'green region'. A number of companies within the catchment may be able to take advantage of this 'environmental labelling' of the area. The message coming from the companies operating in the catchment must clearly communicate that the product comes from a region which is managed in an 'environmentally superior' way. Within the CMS, 'codes of conduct', minimum limits of environmental performance, are set, to which the companies within the region should perform. Companies complying with these set environmental standards are to be differentiated from companies that do not.

As a result of the CMS, the range of products which are produced in a way which is least harmful for the environment will be expanded. 'Green products' will not only be defined in terms of price and performance, but will convey real protection for the environment. In a market where consumers are increasingly willing to use their purchases as an environmental protection tool this can lead to a competitive advantage.

More of the synergistic effects of the CMS will only occur if all parties involved not only understand the conversion concept, but are also willing to cooperate and actively strive towards its success. Central guidance from the top downwards has to be given. However, the intrinsic benefits from environmental management at all levels will guarantee co-operation, once they become clear to all concerned. The main strength of the CMS lies in the integrative approach towards environmental, economic and social factors. The CMS will result in an ongoing cycle of improvement, with regular re-assessments taking place.

CONVERSION PLAN DEVELOPMENT AND IMPLEMENTATION STRATEGIES

The need for a conversion plan, its concepts, and its potential have been described above. During Phase I the catchment conversion concepts were developed based on a description of the catchment area and its industrial sectors, an assessment of its environmental status, and informative visits to companies and communities in the area. The conversion has to start with environmental rehabilitation, and the strategy focuses on the river and its quality. However, comparable strategies have to be developed for the land and landscape of the catchment area.

The CMS, as the main part of the conversion plan, will strengthen the existing County Development Plan (CDP) for the catchment area, and would be complementary to the operation of the plan in the rest of the country. During the development, or planning phase, representatives from the local authorities, communities and industry will develop a conversion plan. Close contact will be kept with industry and communities, to further identify opportunities and disseminate the conversion concepts.

The CMS can be regarded as a management tool, to be developed and used by the committee, and is aimed at facilitating implementation of the catchment conversion plan, and is comparable to the function of an environmental management system at the company level. The key characteristics of the CMS are:

- It is a management system for a specific region with well-defined natural boundaries.
- It facilitates environmental rehabilitation and protection.
- It offers a management framework for coordinated development, with a clear sense of purpose.
- It integrates environmental, economic and social factors.
- It emphasises the role of local industry and local community interest.

As a result of Phase I of the project, many people within the catchment are aware and supportive of the conversion plan. Their reactions to the plan are generally very favourable. Local industry is willing to cooperate and several companies have, in fact, started with the development and implementation of EMS. Clearly, the potential benefits of both environmental management systems at the enterprise level, and a catchment management system at the regional level are recognised.

The next stage is to develop a detailed conversion plan by a team which has members from the County Development Team, local communities, and local industry. Specific tasks for this team are:

- to further develop a catchment information system (CIS), including an environmental monitoring system;
- to conduct an extensive socio-economic study in the catchment area, with emphasis on topics such as migration patterns, effects of infrastructural developments, (un)employment, and the relative importance of the different economic sectors;
- to extend contacts and communication with local communities and industry, to develop internal strategies to promote information and education of all residents of the catchment area towards environmental protection and the benefits and implications of the CMS, and to stimulate community involvement and environmental awareness;
- to outline a draft catchment environmental policy, with specific standards and targets and to conduct a detailed environmental quality study, and to identify and prioritise areas for environmental rehabilitation;
- to stimulate and coordinate further development and implementation of company environmental management systems (EMS);
- to identify and prioritise areas for economic investment and growth, and to identify new economic opportunities, developing strategies to promote and market the catchment area externally.

Implementation of the conversion plan will be facilitated by the CMS. The steps involved in implementing such a system can be compared with the steps involved in developing and implementing a company EMS. Such an approach might be based on the BS7750 standard (BSI, 1992). After the development of commitment, an initial environmental review is performed (stage 1), and a catchment environmental policy is written (stage 2). Then the environmental, economic and social development committee and its support team start operating, and develop guidelines and regulations to achieve set objectives and targets, based on the policy. A management manual and operational control systems, based on the CMS, are developed (stages 2/3). Finally, the results of the conversion plan will be audited on a regular basis.

IDAS TROUT LTD

IDAS Trout Ltd is in the unique position of having a product that could potentially gain from the environmental management approach identified above and from being located in a region that was the subject of an experiment in regional branding, based on environmental performance of its products and processes.

This context, therefore, framed the approach to environmental management at IDAS Trout Ltd. The approach looked to environmental management as an opportunity and as a strategy for the future development of the company. The approach called for an interpretation of the environment in terms of (a) cost and production efficiencies, (b) market demand, and (c) legislative compliance in terms of laws and regulations in the market. In essence, it looked to environmental management as the catalyst to allow the company to grow in new markets in the EC on the basis of market-defined quality and production efficiencies.

In parallel with best management practice identified above, environmental management in the IDAS context was defined as total quality management (TQM) broken out under the elements of:

- Market-led demand in the target markets of Denmark, Belgium and Germany.
- Quality defined by these markets.
- Efficiency of production, in a sector of low margins, to allow the company to compete on price.
- Cultural change, conferring ownership of quality throughout the company.
- Improved communication within the company itself, with stakeholders and with its customers.
- Compliance with environmental laws set by EC, national and local authorities.
- Compliance with health, safety and hygiene regulations.
- Differentiation in the market based on environmental quality.

In essence, the approach set out to align the business objectives of the company with new environmental performance parameters.

The company was established in the 1950s along the banks of the Aughrim River, a tributary of the Avoca River, close to the village of Woodenbridge, some 12 kilometres east of the port town of Arklow on the east coast of Ireland. The company's primary resource is its clean and abundant water source which comes from the high mountain streams in the uplands of

Wicklow. The establishment of the IDAS Trout Ltd operation preceded the formal structuring of the aquaculture industry in Ireland by some twenty years. Its operation and its prosperity over the decades bear testimony to the common-sense and husbandry practices of successive managers and directors. The operation is now the largest producer of freshwater trout in Ireland.

Traditionally, the company has looked to the local markets where demand has been constant and steady over the years. Changes in Irish consumer patterns and the general growth of the aquaculture industry in Ireland has forced IDAS Trout Ltd to rethink its development strategy in the light of its strengths and weaknesses. The commitment from IDAS management to proceed with the implementation of an environmental management system was strong and unequivocal. Indeed, market research indicated that the demand for quality had gone beyond the product itself to the quality of the production system. It also indicated that consumers no longer took claims of environmental quality on face value but needed demonstrable proof of such claims.

An initial environmental review was undertaken over a three-month period and looked at all aspects of inputs, management, and outputs. The IDAS Trout Ltd operation had two distinct elements:

● Production units which produced smolts from eyed ova right through to market-ready fish.
● A smokehouse operation which smoked and packaged filleted trout.

The fish farm products therefore range from whole trout, filleted trout and a number of smoked products.

The initial environmental review identified the environmental issues in terms of inputs identified as water, livestock, chemicals, feed, energy, labour, and management systems. Outputs were identified in terms of product and waste stream, both from production and processing issues. All of these issues were analysed in terms of their potential contribution to resource efficiency and cost saving, market requirements and legal and licence compliance.

The issues encountered at IDAS Trout Ltd were typical of fish farming generally and these can be categorised as:

● Husbandry and management systems.
● Resource conflict issues.
● Waste management and disposal.
● Health, safety and hygiene.

The direct relationship between economic competitiveness and environment can be illustrated with reference to a number of these issues. One of the highest cost inputs into any fish farming operation is feed. The economic objective is to achieve the highest and fastest feed conversion rate so that good quality trout can be available on the market in the shortest possible time. The quality of the feed itself and the feeding husbandry practices have a direct relationship on this outcome.

The IDAS experience indicated a positive relationship between the relatively expensive, high-energy feeds and conversion rates. It was shown that it is a false economy to use lower energy-efficient feeds as these yield low conversion rates and higher levels of excrement and, therefore, pollution. The use of high-energy feeds, fed at times and in conditions when the fish are capable of absorbing all the feed, has the dual benefit of significantly increasing the conversion rate and reducing the excrement and pollution load to the water, making compliance with discharge licences an easier task. The link between quality and environmental issues is therefore clear in this respect.

During the course of development of the environmental management system, the local authority set up renewed licences from water abstraction to discharge parameters. The development of the EMS offered an opportunity and a forum in which to discuss the new management approach with the local authority. The result of this was a growing understanding by the local authority of the new emphasis of the four 'Rs' principles which were integral to the IDAS management system. The four 'Rs' were: resource reduction, resource re-use, resource recycling and resource reclamation. Instead of the traditional and more common conflict between local authority and industry, in this case both industry and local authority found themselves on the same side of the fence.

Predators are a constant menace to the fish farming industry. Traditionally, fish farmers treat them as a nuisance but may be reluctant to invest in relatively costly deterrents, such as fencing and nets. The IDAS review illustrated an economic dimension to the predator issue which is not generally recognised. While the heron or the cormorant may account for a relatively small number of fish kills, the stress caused to the rest of the stock during these attacks inhibits feeding and can contribute to disease. Protective investment in this light makes much more sense, and more emphasis was put on protecting the stock.

In addition, with a new concentration on the stock survivability rather than stocking rate, the traditional reliance on chemicals has been changed. The environmental management system brought out a new recognition that the over-use of chemicals and medicines reduces their impact, over time, on the diseases against which they are aimed in the first place. A reactive and limited chemical regime is now set in the context of other issues, such as close health monitoring, stocking density, water exchange, oxygenation and feeding and control of stress levels.

The Environmental Management System also led to a cultural change programme. This cultural change was aimed to confer ownership of quality right down to operative level and on the understanding that their job, their future, and their livelihood was dependent on their good and responsible environmental practices. In the case of IDAS Trout Ltd, a clear correlation between environment and development has been drawn and has led on to a new strategic development planning exercise which will involve the principles of applying added value to existing production to new product ranges and process development. This is leading to employment opportunities in the area and renewed acceptability of the industry as an important contributor to an integral part of the Avoca Valley economy.

The review set goals and targets for each of the issues identified and the environmental management implementation stage set out responsibilities and defined a management system to achieve those objectives. Even before the total system was implemented, IDAS Trout Ltd was able to make contact with a number of retailers in its target markets of Germany, Denmark and Belgium and invite them to examine the auditable and demonstrable environmental management right through the production chain. This has resulted in significant new orders in these markets – a fact which more than justifies their undertaking.

In addition, the work has presented a forum between IDAS Trout Ltd and the local authority to agree standards and set monitoring procedures for licence compliance. Most importantly, from IDAS Trout Ltd's point of view, the exercise has led to a separate strategic development plan for the company – a plan which will concentrate on defining and developing environmental quality at both production and processing levels to secure its niche in the target markets of the European Community.

This development plan will have the result of a significant increase in employment in the area and preserving the existing employment. The company's linkage into the regional branding project – the Avoca-Avonmore Catchment Conversion Project will, undoubtedly, benefit the marketing of quality trout products, and the high standards in IDAS Trout Ltd itself will, in turn, contribute to the overall achievement of the catchment collective goal of regional environmental quality reflected in future sustainable economic development.

CONCLUSIONS

In this case the concept of regional development through environmental management at a regional scale has been explored. The approach is supported by recent European policy, as presented in the Fifth Environmental Action Plan 'Towards Sustainability' (European Community, 1992). The approach can be characterised as both integrated and striving towards cohesion.

One prevailing view is that environmental management is synonymous with cost. The underlying premise in this case is to look to environmental management as a basis for competitive advantage, business development and profit generation. These principles are already being addressed in industry and international standards of environmental management are rapidly emerging.

In the context of the European Single Market, the peripheral regions of the Community have been spared the worst excesses of unsustainable development and may, in their relative under-development, have a comparative advantage over the core regions. Regional development planning in the Community has typically been blind to this comparative advantage and has emphasised the same approaches to development as practised in the core regions.

The principles of environmental management, which are emerging at industry level, have been generalised and explored as a strategy for regional development. In so doing, the concept differs from traditional approaches to development, which set the economy and the environment in opposing camps. It also reflects the new approach being applied by the Commission of the European Communities which consists of determining the balance between environment and development, rather than underlining the opposing aspects of these two policies. The experience of companies like IDAS Trout Ltd is that being more environmentally aware, and contributing to regional environmental management, has provided them with better management systems and operations and has also opened up new valuable markets.

The concept of environmental management at the regional level also moves the environmental debate beyond the legal domain of 'compliance', and sets it firmly in the market both as a motivator and a tool to pursue economic development. The framework is thus set for collaboration and complementarity between different industries whose common goals are now focused on spatial environmental management, specifically the Avoca-Avonmore catchment area. Collaboration, at this level, will undoubtedly open up other developmental opportunities as communication and understanding between these industries is raised. While this approach concentrates on the approach of environmental management for catchment development, the same principles are clearly applicable to urban and other settings.

Questions for discussion

1 This case study highlights the need to place environmental developments within the European framework for environmental action. Outline this framework and show how the plan complements it.

2 To what extent do you think the model outlined in this case is generic?

3 How can the integration of environmental concerns into a company's business objectives 'turn what has been a liability into an asset'?

4 Explain how the Avoca-Avonmore project will attempt to create a 'green region'. What are the advantages of such a strategy?

5 How can the Catchment Management System (CMS) be regarded as a management tool?

6 Explain the links between implementing a CMS and a company-based environmental management system.

7 What have been the advantages for IDAS Trout Ltd in being part of the conversion project and putting environmental management systems in place itself?

Note: For further information on the topics raised in this chapter, please refer to Chapter 10 of *Environmental Management and Business Strategy* by Richard Welford and Andrew Gouldson (Pitman Publishing, 1993).

References

Benson and Associates (1992) 'The Culliton Report', Dublin, Ireland.

British Standards Institution (1992) *BS7750: Specification for Environmental Management Systems*, BSI, London.

Charter, M. (1992) *Greener Marketing: a responsible approach to business*, Interleaf Productions, Sheffield.

Chartered Institute of Management Consultants (1990) *The Costs to Industry of Adopting Environmentally Friendly Practices*. CIMC, London.

David, R. A. (1991) *The Greening of Business*, Cambridge University Press, Cambridge.

ECOTEC (1992) *Industry and the Environment: the Implications of Environmental Pressures for Industry*. ECOTEC Research and Consulting, Birmingham.

EMA (1992) 'Avoca-Avonmore Catchment Conversion Project', Dublin, Ireland.

European Community (1992) *Towards sustainability*. A European Community programme of policy and action in relation to the environment and sustainable development. Fifth Environmental Action Plan EC, Brussels.

Haigh, N. (1992) *Manual of Environmental Policy: the EC and Britain*, Longman, Harlow.

Hutchinson, C. (1991) *Business and the Environmental Challenge: A Guide for Managers*, The Conservation Trust, Reading.

Kramer, L. (1990) *EEC Treaty and environmental protection*, Sweet and Maxwell, London.

NMP-PLUS (1991) *National Mileubeleidsplan voor Nederland*, SDU Stattsuitgeverij, Den Haag.

Pearce, D. W. and Turner, R. K. (1990) *Economics of natural resources and the environment*, Hemel Hempstead, Harvester Wheatsheaf.

Roome, N. (1992) 'Developing Environmental Management Systems', *Business Strategy and the Environment*, Vol. 1, No. 1, pp. 11–24.

WCED (1987) *Our Common Future*, Oxford University Press, Oxford.

Welford, R. (1992a) 'Linking Quality and the Environment: a Strategy for the Implementation of Environmental Management Systems', *Business Strategy and the Environment*, Vol. 1, No. 1, pp. 25–34.

Welford, R. (1992b) 'A Guide to Environmental Auditing', *European Environment*, special supplement, Autumn 1992.

Welford, R. and Prescott, K. (1992) 'Environmental Issues and Environmental Management', in *European Business, an Issue-Based Approach*, Pitman, London.

Winsemius, P. and Guntram, U. (1992) *Responding to the Environmental Challenge*. Business Horizons, Vol. 2, pp. 38–45.

World Bank (1992). *Development and the Environment: World Development Report 1992*, The World Bank, New York.

PART 4

Conclusions

CHAPTER 12

Which way forward?

Richard Welford

Environmental management based on principles of sustainable development challenges industry to take a more ethical and long-term view of their business activities. This requires industry to be more open, honest and credible than it has been in the past. We are rapidly developing a number of core techniques and concepts (environmental auditing, environmental management systems, life-cycle assessment, etc.) for managing change and environmental improvement and these need to be at the centre of any company's attempt to improve its environmental performance. Companies need to push along the learning curve, developing ever more effective strategies to protect the environment, also new measures of economic performance based on the central concept of sustainable development.

The case studies in this book have highlighted how environmental principles can be put into practice. We have seen that environmental demands are slightly different in every industry and that different firms have different ways of translating best environmental practice into strategies for change. Nevertheless we have seen that there is a core of basic principles which is being adopted in order to bring about environmental improvement.

At the individual company, industry and regional levels, we have seen that there are inherent risks in treating economic forces and the environment as if they were separate and non-interacting elements. Economic policy which neglects to take into consideration environmental risks and damage is not sustainable. We have seen in the area of transport policy that not enough is yet being done by government to encourage a more ethical response from industry and consumers, however there is still a role for action from the world's most important economic institutions.

Environmental strategy at the company level must be based on real commitment to environmental improvement. We saw that at the centre of BT's philosophy towards environmental improvement, there is great emphasis placed on the development of commitment across the organisation. Through its publications, management structure, and training and communications strategies it is trying to demonstrate that although BT is not a major polluter, it takes its responsibilities to the environment seriously.

In what has become an increasing trend in businesses, environmental management seeks to improve the environmental performance of companies in order that the planet on which we live remains habitable for future generations. Indeed environmental strategies have received increasing attention as the degradation of the planet has accelerated. At the core of this strategic approach has been the central role of environmental management systems where companies put into place systems and procedures which ensure that environmental performance is improved over time. Management systems aim to pull a potentially disparate system into an integrated and organised one. To that end, the system covers not only management's responsibilities but the responsibility and tasks of every individual in an organisation.

We have seen clear arguments in favour of a systems-based approach. An integrated system which covers the totality of operations helps management and workers clearly to see their place in the organisation and recognise the interdependence of all aspects of an organisation. Through establishing clear communications and reporting channels, it should pull a potentially tangled web of structures and tasks into a clearly defined matrix of relationships with clear horizontal and vertical links. This means that functions are less likely to be lost in a maze of mini-organisations, and that key aspects of an organisation's tasks are not forever lost in a black box labelled 'nobody's responsibility'. We have seen in the cases of the Bhopal and Alaskan disasters that a proper environmental management system accompanied by worst-case scenario planning is needed to avoid mistakes, accidents and such catastrophes.

An effective and all-embracing management system is therefore central to the avoidance of disasters, accidents and environmental degradation, in so much as it pulls together all the other tools and strategies for the avoidance of risks. Quite simply, a management system should be developed and implemented for the purpose of accomplishing the objectives set out in a company's or organisation's policies, and this must include the avoidance of environmental damages. Each element of the system will vary in importance from one type of activity to another, and from one product or service to another.

While accepting the need for management systems to control and monitor environmental performance, the case study on The Body Shop raises some wider issues, however. Indeed, it suggests that to concentrate on a systems approach alone may be suboptimal if our ultimate objective in society is to get businesses to behave sustainably.

Many of the firms discussed in this book have stressed what they see as natural linkages between quality management and the improvement of environmental performance. It is argued that this link exists through the need for environmental management systems and their associated auditing procedures, and that the general approach taken in philosophies such as total quality management mirror the desired approach for environmental improvement. The aim of both approaches is to achieve a continuous cycle of improvement achieved through the commitment of everybody involved in an organisation.

The theory behind a total quality management (TQM) system is that as

quality improves, costs actually fall through lower failure and a
and less waste. The concept that defects in the production proces
to remedy if a product has left the factory gates seems obvious, and
of generic approach integrating environmental issues, where pollutio
example, is viewed as a quality defect, has engendered a strong link betw
quality and the environment, and is increasingly becoming the dominant
ideology amongst industrialists.

This same link has led to the development of BS7750 and the EC eco-management and audit scheme. Such standards have been heralded as the major step forward which will provide incentives for businesses to improve their environmental performance. Fundamental to both schemes is a need to develop an environmental management system and to undertake periodic audits of undefined measures of environmental performance and the management system itself. Both standards specify environmental improvement as their aim rather than the achievement of a set threshold below which firms may not fall.

An alternative to stressing the quality approach which is based on management systems aimed at continuous improvement, might be to go back to the key concept of sustainable development and audit for sustainability. This approach, beginning to be practised at The Body Shop, is a holistic approach, and requires rather more fundamental change in business culture than we have seen to date. Organisations auditing for sustainability should be committed to integrating environmental performance to wider issues of global ecology, and make specific reference to the concepts associated with sustainable development.

Although we have seen the widespread use of the management systems approach, the key question relates to the extent to which environmental management systems can actually deliver sustainability. Where they are based on a continuous cycle of improvement, sustainability may take a very long time to achieve. Moreover, the auditing process encompassed in the quality-driven environmental management system, is dominated by the audit of the system, procedures, documents and management rather than environmental damage. Such an approach may take a business round in circle after circle of incremental improvement but, where the starting point for this environmental merry-go-round is fundamentally unsustainable, it is unlikely to result in the significant step-up in environmental performance which the world needs. The alternative approach is to undertake environmental audits based not on the principles of management systems but on the fundamental principle of sustainable development. That is not to suggest that management systems are not important, they are. But they should be seen as the vehicle which drives environmental improvement and not the measure of success themselves.

Auditing for sustainability requires firms to look at their overall impact on the environment, on equity and on futurity. It challenges firms to prioritise their actions in ecological terms rather than management systems terms. Moreover, it must be recognised that while bad systems may worsen

ppraisal costs
cost most
his sort
for
en

it is not the systems themselves which cause the
d services for which the system is designed. Rather
fore, we ought to place more emphasis on auditing
a central emphasis on the need for life-cycle assess-
it companies such as Volkswagen Audi are com-
vironmental performance of both their products
nufacture. The potential for the wider adoption of
it strategies is enhanced in many cases by the
nic self-interest of both the producer and consumer
erative that society has collectively placed on the
automotive industry to lead the way in developing sustainable modes of personal mobility. High standards of environmental performance within the automotive industry will therefore become an integral part of the industry's future
economic success. Through innovation at all stages in its product life cycle,
VW has emerged as a market leader in the field of environmental performance
in the automotive industry.

Life-cycle assessment brings with it a number of advantages often overlooked by traditional environmental auditing methodologies. The concentration on the product, rather than on the system, facilitates direct
measurement of environmental impact. Being directly linked to products also
means that environmental strategy can be linked into the marketing system,
therefore marketing and environmental strategy become intertwined. LCA
also widens the environmental analysis beyond management systems and site-
specific production attributes, which can so easily hide environmental damage
up or down the supply chain. The product-specific approach also aids environmental communication because of the clear link between LCA and
eco-labelling.

A concentration on products also allows us to track the inputs into the
production process; it allows us to track the sources of those inputs, and it
therefore allows us to say something about possible impacts on underdeveloped countries and the concepts of equity and futurity. Tracking the life
cycle of the product forward enables us to say much more about environmental damage than we can in a traditional assessment of processes. Again,
it fundamentally places the concept of futurity within our overall measurement
of performance.

Significant evidence exists that management trends which become popular
exert a strong influence on the ongoing techniques of corporate management.
New concepts which are successfully implemented in certain organisations
become accepted, become dominant and even when they are inappropriate
become the norm (Mintzberg, 1979). Three explanations for this phenomenon
are offered by DiMaggio and Powell (1983). Firstly, organisations will submit
to both formal and informal pressures from other organisations upon which
they depend. Secondly, when faced with uncertainty, organisations may model
themselves on organisations that have seemed to be successful and adopt the
sorts of techniques which they see being introduced. Thirdly, normative

pressures which stem from a degree of professionalism amongst management can cause the adoption of 'fashionable' management techniques. Universities, training institutions, standard-setters, professional associations, and books like this one, are all vehicles for the development of these normative rules.

These are precisely the trends which we are seeing in the adoption of the quality-driven approaches to environmental management. This approach may not be entirely appropriate to the concept of sustainable development in that it does not go far enough. But this approach is becoming the accepted ideology because it is being adopted by leading firms, espoused by academics and legitimised through standard-setters such as the BSI and the EC.

A change in ideology is, of course, difficult to achieve because environmental management standards have been set by industry itself. To date, they have been designed to be voluntary and designed so as not to conflict with the ideology associated with profit maximisation in the short to medium term. Arguments such as the ones outlined above, suggesting that industry has not gone far enough, might therefore be treated with derision by industry and side-lined. The power which industry has in the current economic system could be a barrier to further development of the concepts of sustainable development.

It may well be that there is a need for tougher legislation which would include requirements on businesses to measure their environmental impacts widely defined. Moreover there is a need for national legislation which not only protects domestic economies but also those of developing countries. Such an approach represents a radical shift in the foundations of industrial policy and firms will, of course, complain that the real requirements for sustainable development will impose severe costs and competitive disadvantage on them. They will not, however, disagree on the need to create the ubiquitous 'level playing field' and the clear implication of this is that industry itself should have a vested interest and should be campaigning for a tougher legislative stance on the part of governments across the whole world.

Increased legislation is, however, unlikely in the present political and economic climate. Nevertheless we must recognise that environmental management is not a 'pipe-dream', it is not an added extra, it is not a luxury, it is fundamental to the future of our planet. We must therefore look towards best practice in industry as a model for future development. The Body Shop has proved that we can reshape the way in which we do business and that we do not have to continue to degrade the planet, be cruel to animals and exploit indigenous populations. The Body Shop provides us with a path along which we should expect other businesses to tread.

The development of environmental networks amongst businesses, voluntary organisations and the public sector is fundamentally needed. It will enable controlled and sustainable growth to occur. It has been suggested, in our discussion about small- and medium-sized enterprises, that collaborative arrangements, multi-sector networking and cooperative strategies can help to meet the aims and objectives of a sustainable and developing economy. This concept should apply across the global economy with a stress on the concepts of equity and development in the Third World. There is a clear role here for governments and local authorities to support innovative developments and provide a forum where information about best practice can be exchanged. Moreover, it has been suggested that the principles of environmental management, which are emerging at industry level, can be generalised and explored as a strategy for regional economic development. This reflects the new approach being applied by the Commission of the European Communities, which consists of determining the balance between environment and development rather than underlining the opposing aspects of these two policies.

The concept of environmental management at industry and regional levels moves the environmental debate beyond the legal domain of 'compliance'. There is a need to balance traditional economic forces and short-term demands with an approach based on the concepts of partnership, collaboration and complementarity between different industries whose common goals can be focused on spatial environmental management.

What we have identified in this book is best practice in environmental management as it currently stands. There is clearly a lot more to do. We have pointed towards some impediments to improvement and have tracked one possible way forward through discussion of environmental strategies at The Body Shop. Current best environmental management practice is good, and innovations, such as the EC eco-management and auditing scheme and BS7750, provide principles which all firms should work towards. The issue is whether we have yet gone far enough. The answer to that has to be no. A responsible and proactive approach to the environment may require additional, more radical approaches to doing business.

The challenge for the leaders in the field of environmental management, identified in this book, is to go still further. Rethinking business strategy along the lines of sustainable development is the only way forward, and that will require a change in corporate cultures. That, in turn, opens up new opportunities to reassess other aspects of business. Issues that need also to be addressed in line with environmental demands include worker participation, democracy in the workplace, the fair treatment of women and minority groups, animal testing, public accountability, and the impact on the Third World and indigenous populations. Indeed, these issues should not be seen as separate entities but as part of a new overall strategy to doing business ethically and holistically. Many of these issues will necessarily challenge the very foundations of the system which we too often see as immovable and will therefore be opposed by vested interests. Nevertheless, such ideas are achievable and indeed fundamental to the very existence of the planet on which we live.

Note: For further information on the topics raised in this chapter, please refer to Chapters 5, 9 and 10 of *Environmental Management and Business Strategy* by Richard Welford and Andrew Gouldson (Pitman Publishing, 1993).

References

DiMaggio, P. J. and Powell, W. (1983) 'The Iron Cage Revisited: Institutional Isomorphism and Collective Rationale in Organisational Fields', *American Sociological Review*, Vol. 48, pp. 147–160.

Mintzberg, H. (1979) *The Structuring of Organisations*, Prentice Hall: New York.

PART 5

Exercises

Nigel Roome and Richard Welford

A. DUKE PLC AND THE GREAT CRESTED NEWTS

The Conservation of Wild Creatures and Wild Plants Act 1975 establishes a schedule of endangered plants and animals in England and Wales. It is illegal to move, disturb, take or destroy any of the plants and animals on the list without the consent of the Government's conservation advisers – English Nature (in England). The Great Crested Newt is a rare British amphibian and is on the scheduled list.

You are the Chief Executive of a major British construction company, Duke Plc. Your company is involved in property development as well as construction. It has become heavily involved in the development of industrial estates as a vertically integrated business – buying, developing and leasing sites. However, the main culture of the organisation is rooted in civil engineering. The company operates a short-term, financially driven strategy based on decentralised business units each with financial targets negotiated annually.

In the early 1980s Duke Plc acquired a 80-hectare site to develop an industrial park. The site is located in an attractive wooded setting in a metropolitan borough. The advantage of the site is that it is only 400 metres from a major motorway. The development costs are low because it is a large site on a good green-field location. The local authority has just established a Development and Enterprise Unit which is keen to see economic developments of this kind diversifying the area's employment base.

In 1986 the company applied for planning consent to develop the site. The local authority planning department considered the proposal against a backdrop of some local opposition. The main arguments against the site were that it was in attractive, open countryside and had some merit as a habitat for wildlife. On balance the needs of industry were seen as paramount and consent to develop the site was granted.

The recent planning history of the site is complex. Outline planning consent was initially granted for the whole site, then detailed planning consent was sought and given for half the site, which will be called site A. The balance of outline and detailed planning consents fitted with Duke's intention to undertake a phased development of the site.

The whole estate is therefore divided into two roughly equal parts: site A with detailed planning consent and site B which currently has outline consent. Access to the estate is by an access road on site A which now supports a number of factories and offices. Site B will be developed at a later state as and when the market demands.

Site A has been developed and plots have been let to a number of locally important companies. In addition, Duke Plc has succeeded in letting a number of plots to blue-chip companies. One of these is in the banking sector. The other is the main UK depot for a German truck manufacturer.

Duke Plc has worked closely with the Development and Enterprise Unit of the local authority. The depressed image of the area has been seen as unattractive to most companies wishing to relocate. This is despite the quality of the transport network, the competitiveness of the rents and the extremely attractive countryside. In contrast to the prevailing image of the area, it has recently scored very high on a national survey of quality of life.

Unfortunately the quality of the new landscaping on the estate has not been very good. As part of the development the natural vegetation of site A has been cleared and facilities laid. A green landscaping scheme was undertaken by a contract landscape architect who introduced the type of industrial estate vegetation you might find in any new industrial area in inner city Britain. It has shown little respect for the traditional landscape of the area.

In 1988, the parish councils in the area around Duke's Industrial Estate became part of a national scheme in local community environmental action. The local parish councils, together with the local authority and the Countryside Commission, initiated a project to explore the potential for environmental action to protect the countryside through local action.

By 1990 the project was highly active. A number of events had been held which gripped the attention of the local community. Environmental action was the issue of the day and the close-knit community was enthusiastic to follow the cause, both by undertaking projects and by asking for their voice to be heard over matters affecting the future development of the area.

More locally, Duke's Estate became one of a number of focal points for attention. Members of the community wanted to see a higher quality of site landscaping, with greater respect for the earlier vegetation and landscape. There was a feeling that the site was still 'green' but had become sterile. It was viewed more like an urban park than a bit of green-belt countryside yet, unlike a park, it was no longer accessible to the community, despite the complex set of rights of way across the site.

Representatives of the community together with the parish council argued that a more naturalistic landscape regime for the Estate would lower maintenance costs, improve the wildlife, enhance the value of the site and the reputation of the companies, including Duke Plc. The local community representatives were well received by the prestige German company, who agreed to host a seminar for other site owners, and the site manager from Duke Plc. The aim was to establish a local liaison group between community and the owners of sites on the estate.

At this time Duke's applied for detailed planning consent for site B. The local activists examined the application and surveyed the area. It was realised that there was an interesting raised pond on the line of a proposed road linking sites A and B. The pond was regarded as important to local people as a wildlife and leisure area. Additionally it was hydrologically rather unique, being raised above the surrounding area. The sides of the pond were naturally embanked and the pond appeared to be fed by a spring which was linked to a natural supply on higher ground. The result was that the water level in the pond was 3 metres above the surrounding land.

Protecting the pond would require either the diversion of the road, or the construction of a concrete embankment. Retaining the pond would also take out about 5 hectares of land from site B. The local planning authority had not recognised the value of the pond when the original outline consent was granted. The recent plans for detailed consent were then drawn up to the specification of the original outline plan. Modifying the road would require site B to be redesigned and then resubmission of these plans for planning approval.

The site manager now faces a potential delay of at least six months; the possible need to draw up new plans; additional costs and the loss of immediate land value. The site manager is concerned about meeting his yearly financial targets and is becoming irritated by the local activities. He wants to get on with the plans as agreed. There is support for this from the local authority where officers are embarrassed about their earlier recommendation to grant outline consent.

The events on the site have not been a direct concern to the Chairman's Office. Reports of local planning difficulties and some delays have filtered through but you, as Chief Executive, understand that everything is on target and the site manager has events under control.

You are feeling rather pleased. Business is good, profits have been healthy and these will be reported at the forthcoming AGM. Last week you agreed to sponsor a Youth Environmental Award as part of a sponsorship scheme with a major environmental group. The Community Affairs Department had argued that an environment-related company, such as Duke's, should assume a higher profile on environmental issues.

But this is not the only event raising Duke's environmental image. Today you read in your copy of your newspaper under the headline 'Company in Battle over Endangered Newts' a piece about the site owned, and in the process of being developed, by Duke Plc. It is the centre of a local controversy. Local residents concerned about the loss of a local landmark have been advised by a team of ecology experts that the pond they are seeking to protect from development is the home of a large community of Great Crested Newts.

Questions

1 What is your assessment of the issues faced by Duke Plc at its site?

2 What further information do you require before you take action?

3 What action do you plan to take?

4 What opportunities do you see for your company to gain from these events and how do you propose to realise them?

B. STAKEHOLDER ANALYSIS:
THE CASE OF ORGANO-PRODUCTS PLC

Organo-Products Plc is an organic chemical manufacturer, founded by an enterprising chemist in the 1960s. The company was acquired by a multinational American-based specialist chemicals manufacturing group four years ago. Organo-Products has a plant in South Africa and a plant in the north of England. In the early 1990s Organo-Products is seeking to expand through the acquisition of a company in Northern Europe. This is being steered by a new managing director supported by a recently appointed technical director. They aim to reshape Organo-Products' structure, systems and values.

The headquarters of Organo-Products Plc are based at the north of England site. The UK headquarters of the parent company are centred on plant in another northern town. The parent company operates Organo-Products Plc as a decentralised business unit. The parent has recently reorganised its divisions to create groupings of business units which are more heavily focused on markets. This replaces the technology-based organisational structure of the past ten years.

In addition to the new market focus there is increasing awareness, throughout the parent company and its groups, of the need to achieve high levels of environmental performance. The product lines for the whole group include organic chemicals, solvents and pesticides. These products and their allied processes place the group in the front line of popular concern about the environment. They also make the group a subject of increasingly stringent European and domestic environmental legislation. The group is part of the Chemical Industry Association's Responsible Care Programme and there is concern to ensure that all divisions and business units operate above a set of minimum acceptable standards.

The parent company takes a long-term view of its business. Major capital expenditure programmes are normally subject to central agreement. Targets for profit on turnover and return on fixed assets are part of an annual planning programme between Organo-Products and the parent company. The parent company normally accepts Organo-Products' plans without intervention.

Organo-Products is performing well in the recession of the 1990s. It has more than 10 per cent profit on a turnover of £30m and its return on fixed assets is over 40 per cent per year. The company is restructuring its management to ensure that it has the market focus to maintain growth in the 1990s. The company's core technology is the production of very specialised organic chemicals. The company has developed a technical edge through specialisation in this field. It has developed its own process technology and is used by some of its customers as a route to new product development.

The company's products are used in diversified markets. These range from industrial catalysts, industrial and domestic cleaning products, and personal care products. It has some highly specialised and profitable industrial product lines. It has also gained preferred supplier status with major customers. Some of these have a regular annual supplier audit of the company and appear to use the supplier audit of Organo-Products as training material for new managers. However, the company itself does not have its own environmental audit programme.

Some of Organo-Products' competitors have recently received considerable publicity because of their involvement in the production and manufacture of phosphates, and because of infringements of their consents to discharge waste through pipelines. This has attracted adverse publicity from environmental groups. There are currently important questions being asked about the production and use of phosphates and this has received close scrutiny from the European Community.

Organo-Products has managed to achieve a significant share in its markets through its flexibility of production with short, specialist production runs and customer-led product development. The company is also seeking to meet the quality assurance standards needed for major suppliers in the personal products market. The difficulties here are that their chemical plant does not easily meet the biological assurance standards which are increasingly expected in this market. The company has an active investment programme to achieve the required standards demanded in this part of its market. In addition it is about one year away from applying for the quality assurance standard BS5750.

The Organo-Products plant is located on a 2.5 hectare site 600 metres from the centre of a satellite town of a major northern conurbation. There is a long history of chemicals manufacture at the site and in the adjacent area. Previous uses of the Organo-Products site include a cloth manufacturer, a dye works, and now the current use. The site is adjacent to another chemical company, which is part of a French multinational group. Other close neighbours include a municipal waste transfer station and a metal products manufacturer. The town itself is set around a central core of shopping and service facilities. The centre of the town is in a valley bottom. The residential area of the town comes close to the company's site and the whole of the Organo-Products' complex is clearly visible from most other parts of the town.

The main local river runs to the rear of the site. In the past, spillage of detergents (accidental and intentional) from the site has caused persistent foaming in the river at a weir 700 metres downstream. This is now controlled to the satisfaction of the National Rivers Authority but there is still a local concern about releases from the site; in the main these occur after heavy rain because of surface soil contamination. To the front of the site is open ground where a long-disused canal and canal basin are located.

The local authority has ideas to reopen the canal basin and develop it as a leisure and recreation area. This plan is conditional on European Community Regional Aid funds. Other local authorities in the north have been successful in attracting multi-million pound grants for similar projects.

The Organo-Products site is scheduled under the Environmental Protection Act 1990 and is regulated by Her Majesty's Inspector of Pollution. It has a consent licence to operate under the EPA with a discharge limit of 5 kg of sulphur dioxide per hour. The site is also registered as a hazardous site, controlled by the Health and Safety Executive. Registration as a hazard site means that the company must assess the risks of accidental releases of chemicals and prepare an emergency contingency plan. This plan involves the emergency services, also the local community, who might be affected by any release. The company is in the process of phasing out the use of trioxide on the site and developing its own sulphur-burning-based technology in response to the hazard issue.

In the short term the planned extension of a local primary school and the expansion proposals of a local service sector business are being delayed because they are zoned as too close to the hazardous site. The canal basin is also within the hazard zone. Overall, the hazard zone includes more than 300 existing houses, other companies and the local school.

One outcome of the establishment of the hazard zone contingency plan has been the formation of a local company/community liaison group. This group has met once and was characterised by fairly vitriolic comment about the past performance of the company. There is a significant air of mistrust.

Questions

1 Who are the stakeholders in Organo-Products' operations?

2 What do you see as the interests of these various stakeholders in Organo-Products' developing position and strategy?

3 What do you assess as the most important interests that Organo-Products' senior management need to take into account, and how might they do that?

4 What sort of strategies would you suggest the company adopts to improve its relationship with its stakeholders?

5 What strategies would you suggest should be adopted to improve the company's environmental performance?

C. RESPONDING TO ENVIRONMENTAL PUSH: THE CASE OF ARTCO TEXTILES

Artco Textiles is a small firm producing high-quality textiles for the European market. As a small company it has never thought about the environmental impact of what it is doing although it is commonly considered that textile production does have harmful effects on the environment, especially in dying processes. Artco has existed for five years and employs twenty people. It takes raw materials, mainly high-quality wool from local producers and manufactures a limited range of products. One reason for its limited range is that its business is concentrated in supplying just three main retail outlets: in Germany, Holland and the UK.

Recently Artco received a letter from one of its large customers informing Artco that the company was putting in place a complete environmental management system which included specifying new environmental demands from its suppliers. As part of the letter the Environment Charter of the retailing company was expressed as:

> This company shall in future seek to purchase goods from manufacturers who themselves can provide evidence of internal strategies for environmental improvement. It will seek to purchase products which have not depleted the stock of non-renewable raw materials and will favour products produced from recycled materials. In the longer term we aim to cease buying products which are identified as having an excessive negative impact on the environment whether this shall be through the manufacture, distribution, use or disposal of the product in question.

Artco has been asked to respond to this letter, informing the purchaser of its strategy for environmental improvement over the next ten years. At a board meeting of Artco it was decided to be honest with the customer in stating that to date the company did not have an environmental strategy, but to map out a plan of action in response to this demand for environmental improvement. The board identified a number of concerns:

1. Its products were sold as being high-quality products (indeed the company had recently gained accreditation through BS5750), and as such it was worried about changing its source of high-quality virgin wool.
2. As a small company there was a question over the extent to which it could afford to employ consultants to analyse its problems, and how they would fund the new environmental strategy.
3. There was a general lack of knowledge relating to how to proceed with a programme of environmental improvement.

It was decided to ask the Quality Manager to produce an outline strategy laying out the actions which were considered to be possible and desirable in the short term (up to one year) and in the long term (up to five years). After two weeks the Quality Manager came up with the following ten-point plan:

Short term:

1. Artco should switch to using recycled paper in its offices.
2. Artco should introduce energy-saving light bulbs and begin a campaign to turn off lights after use.
3. Artco should state its commitment to environmental improvement in its mission statement.
4. Artco should ask its own suppliers what they are doing to improve environmental quality.
5. Artco should begin looking for new customers in case this particular customer terminates their contract.

Longer term:

6. Artco should measure and assess the environmental impact of its products and improve their environmental performance where necessary.
7. Artco should purchase materials from firms who can also demonstrate environmental improvement strategies.
8. Artco will introduce a marketing campaign telling its customers and potential customers about its positive environmental performance.
9. When new investment becomes necessary Artco will try to invest in cleaner technology if it can afford so to do.
10. Reduce the annual dividend to shareholders to pay for the ongoing costs of environmental improvement.

The board thought that many of the recommendations were good but that their customers might not think they were doing enough. The Technical Director was therefore given the task of improving the strategy.

Tasks

You are the Technical Director and you are asked to consider the following:

1 Comment on the appropriateness and effectiveness of the Quality Manager's strategy.

2 Outline your own plan for the short-term and longer-term strategies which you think will be important.

3 Discuss how you will be able clearly to demonstrate to your customer that you are genuinely aiming for environmental improvement.

4 How do you consider Artco should respond directly to the supplier's Environmental Charter?

D. PLANNING A STRATEGY:
THE CASE OF ENGELS AND COMPANY

Engels and Company (E&C) are manufacturers of fine organic compounds. They operate a single plant on the south side of a conurbation. Major products produced at the plant are speciality compounds used as ingredients in pesticides. It buys its feedstocks from major chemical manufacturers and sells a large proportion of its production to the North American market. Its customers include many multinational corporations. The company is therefore extremely sensitive to fluctuations in foreign exchange ratios. As a small operator it is also squeezed between multinationals. In practice the company operates at the pleasure of its multinational suppliers and customers. It can do so because the company has established markets in line with its core technology in the processing of pesticides. Turnover is around £25 m but returns on turnover are highly variable with exchange rates. There is no borrowing, but there is also little capital available for investment. The company has been prevented from developing new markets in fine organics by the lack of capital for investment in product development.

The plant is located on a 26-acre site. It is about 2 kilometres away from the site of another chemicals manufacturer, which is separately owned. Both plants manufacture chemicals which have a distinctive odour. One characteristic of these chemicals is that they can be detected by the human nose at extremely low levels of concentration. Indeed, outside the laboratory, humans are able to detect these compounds at concentrations which are lower than those which can be detected by most monitoring equipment.

The plant itself was built on the site of earlier chemicals works. Its origins can be traced back to a picric acid plant which supported the munitions industry in the First World War. There is therefore a degree of long-standing site contamination by chemicals due to the site's earlier use.

In addition to the odour problem and the site contamination, the production of herbicides within the company's range of products has influenced the vegetation around the site. There is significant and obvious stunting of trees and shrubs, and poor herb growth down-wind of the plant. Some of this damage is caused by the dispersal of emissions through the plant's chimney stacks. The plant is itself being progressively modernised but has the appearance of a large-scale chemicals works – pipe-work, stacks, fixed storage tanks, a large drum storage area and low-rise, flat-roofed office buildings. Products are transported from the site exclusively by tanker. Tankers normally travel on local roads for 1 kilometre, through a suburb of the local city, and then by B road to the nearest motorway connection.

Waste products have tended to accumulate over time and there is a large number of old and rusted 55-gallon metal drums of waste products which are poorly labelled. Many of these go back over ten years and the site on which they are stored is not properly bounded. They are recognised by management as a hazard and they are being analysed and repackaged in new drums, for disposal by a reputable waste disposal contractor. Most of the analysis and repackaging is being done by employees of the company.

The company employs a Health and Safety Officer who has been with the company for twenty years, working up from a job as laboratory technician. E&C has recently appointed a Technical Director with overall responsibility for Environmental Protection and Health and Safety. The postholder recognises the need for action on the safe disposal of the accumulated toxic waste.

The nature of the products used and manufactured at the plant makes it the subject of regular inspections by the Health and Safety Executive (H&SE), who are the professional staff of the Health and Safety Commission. A particular concern to the H&SE is the control and regulation of chlorine stored at the site, under the Control of Industrial Major Hazard Regulations 1984. However, products are manufactured using 'Scheduled Processes' and a number of product lines are classified as Scheduled (or red list) substances. These processes and substances are regarded as particularly hazardous because of their toxicity or persistence. They are regulated by Her Majesty's Inspectorate of Pollution.

The discharge of pollutants to the water course is currently controlled by the National Rivers Authority and the Water Company Plc. The Water Company calculates the permitted level of discharge to the water course, sets a consent level and monitors performance against this standard. E&C pays a discharge fee to the Water Company and it is liable to prosecution if it exceeds the consent level.

The company employs 120 people. It is a family-owned business but with an increasing awareness that the high level of technical and managerial skills required by the business will involve the appointment of new senior management at board room level. Hence the appointment of the Technical Director. Most of the manual staff are recruited from the local area which has a distinct sense of its own village identity, despite being part of a larger city.

There has been a history of local opposition to the plant and its operation from a small, but increasingly vocal, local group. Other members of the community, who are bound to the company through employment, are ambivalent to the problems of smell and the visual impact of the site. The majority in the tightly-knit community have come to accept the plant and tolerate its presence.

The particular events which precipitated this case are linked to a planning application by a local developer for a housing estate 750 metres at its closest point from the plant. An application for planning consent was submitted to the local planning authority in late 1985. It is the legal duty of the authority to consult with a range of statutory bodies when planning applications are made. At the time, it was necessary for the authority to seek advice from the Health and Safety Executive because the application was for residential development within a 1.5 km zone of a hazardous site – hazardous because chlorine is stored on the site.

In prevailing H&SE advice, this zone is regarded as the normal exclusion zone for housing development, given the possible problems associated with the accidental release of stored chlorine. However, there is uncertainty about the power of the Health and Safety Commission (HSC) to enforce any recommendation it might make to prohibit new housing. General legal opinion is that the local planning authority would have to consider this advice together with other planning issues. The HSC advice is therefore not seen as binding on the local planning authority, rather it is seen as advisory.

The local authority decided to refuse consent for the planning application on the grounds that the site was inappropriate for housing development; this was partly because it was in the green belt and partly because it posed a risk to safety should there be an accident involving the chlorine storage tank. The developer decided to appeal against the refused planning application. Given the technical nature of the issues involved, the Inspector appointed by the Secretary of State for the Environment to consider the appeal, opted to hold it as an Inquiry in Public. The Inquiry was held in the hall of the local Town Council.

At the Inquiry expert witnesses were called from, among others, the local planning authority, officers of the Health and Safety Executive, the Factories Inspectorate, the Company, and local residents opposed to the new building. The planning and risk issues were rehearsed in public and the Inspector's report agreed with the local planning authority that the site was inappropriate for residential development, although the grounds were taken as, first and foremost, the question of risk and, then, the loss of land from the green belt. The Inspector's decision to refuse the planning application was made some eighteen months ago. However it effects are still felt within the company and the community.

The Inquiry received local and national publicity because of the uncertain relationship between the role of advice from the Health and Safety Commission and the position of the local planning authority.

The application also received much local interest for three reasons. First, it provided a platform for those opposed to the plant to voice their objections to the continued operation of the plant to the media circus that attended the Inquiry. Second, there was already a number of established housing estates within the 1.5 km advisory zone around the site and its chlorine storage tank. Third, the local village primary school was within 450 metres of the chlorine storage tank.

The education committee of the local authority was reluctant to accept the need to relocate the school, while the planning authority was unable to accept the proposed new housing development on grounds of risk to the new inhabitants.

These events gave fresh emphasis to the nature of the site, its products and the processes carried out there.

Tasks

1 Assume you are the Technical Director. Outline your assessment of the company's position in the form of a brief environmental review. You should consider products, processes and the management of the site in relation to the company's stakeholders.

2 Set out a strategy for responding to that position.

3 Set out what you consider to be the major costs and benefits associated with your chosen strategy.

E. MARKETING GREEN PRODUCTS: THE CASE OF LUMBERING LTD

Lumbering Ltd is the British subsidiary of an American-based multinational. It has an annual turnover of about £300m from three main areas of business – chemicals, the wholesale distribution of building materials for use in the interior design of commercial buildings, and timber treatment. These areas contribute 42 per cent, 35 per cent and 23 per cent respectively to business turnover. 70 per cent of Lumbering's business is based in the UK.

The Timber Treatment side of the business has recently been reorganised under a European Business Unit in anticipation of the opening-up of European trade. The emphasis within this reorganisation has been to develop a keener market focus. The sales team is based in the north of England at the company's Head Office. It deals principally with a franchised dealer network.

The company has chosen to develop its business with a particularly visible ethical stance. It has divested its South African holdings. It is active within the local communities within which it operates, undertaking projects involving local health care and environmental initiatives.

It has recently sought and gained BS5750 for its management systems. The company has a similar concern for quality in product performance. The timber treatment side of the business has a core business based on timber preservation and wood finishes. Chemically treated timber carries a 'lifetime' guarantee which has helped to establish the company in the marketplace.

Company organisation for timber treatment

The Company has a centralised chemical production processing operation for its timber treatment. This plant is located on the same site as the Head Office of the Timber Treatment part of the business. All timber treatment services are run from this site. The company is operating in a highly visible end of the chemical business. Its activities have to be regulated by Her Majesty's Inspectorate of Pollution and it produces products and uses processes scheduled under the Environmental Protection Act. The nature of the business is to manufacture and use products toxic to flora and fauna. The plant which produces chemicals for timber treatment is also a CIMAH site, controlled under the Control of Industrial Major Accident Hazard Regulations 1984. These require an assessment of the hazards on the site, the preparation of contingency plans in the case of an accident, and the dissemination of the plan within the company, the hazard services (fire, police, etc.) and the local community.

The timber treatment products from this plant are placed in the market through a network of franchised dealers. These timber merchants treat timber using chemicals and pressure impregnation equipment, provided as part of the franchise. They operate to standards specified by the franchise contract. The dealer network is also responsible for presenting and promoting the product to the market, using material prepared by Lumbering's sales team.

Market position

The company is sensitive to its environmental position and its record on treated timber. There are a number of points here. The pressure treatment of timber enables soft wood to have an extended life in use. It is then used to replace more traditional timber products, especially oak, cedar and mahogany. However, the chemicals used are toxic. This has generated some consumer resistance in areas where the products are used in sensitive environments. The highly localised contamination around treated fence posts has led to an advisory ban on their use in fencing around Sites of Special Scientific Interest to wildlife, Nature Reserves and National Parks.

Moreover, Lumbering Ltd are increasingly having to deal with requests for information from companies they supply about the environmental performance of their products. While Lumbering Ltd believes its products have a distinctive market edge, and that the advisory ban can be disputed, it is concerned about the more general need to establish a better information base about the environmental impact of its products.

The company has recently promoted a young member of its staff, with an environmental background, to a senior management post responsible for Environmental Management. He reports directly to the Technical Director responsible for the timber treatment side of the business. The Environmental Manager wishes to respond to what he sees as an increasing 'green' edge in the commercial and domestic market for timber products. He is keen to use this to promote a more wide ranging environmental stance within the company. The Technical Director has asked him to prepare a report for the main Board to consider the greening of the business, starting with timber treatment.

Questions

1 What are the issues the company faces in developing and promoting a greener image for its products and for the company?

2 How would you market the environmental image of the company and its products, and what forms of structural and organisational change would you contemplate as part of this initiative?

3 Are there any key initiatives which you think the company should be involved in?

F. GROPING IN THE DARK:
THE CASE OF BRADMOPP

Bradmopp is a medium-sized company, employing 300 people on a single site, and selling a range of cleaning products and cleaning equipment (including mops, sponges, cleaning cloths, etc.). It is aware that many of its cleaning products contain substances which might be considered harmful to the environment. It has phased out CFCs as an aerosol propellant but still buys and uses a number of chemicals, which in large quantities at concentrated levels, do pose health, safety and environmental hazards. The manufacture and assembly of equipment are considered less harmful to the environment, although a significant range of its products are sold as disposable, designed to be used then thrown away.

Bradmopp has recently been asked to supply information about its environmental performance by a number of its customers. It had never before even considered its environmental impact, except for having to go through an exercise for registration under the Environmental Protection Act because of some of the hazardous chemicals it was using. The company is situated on the outskirts of a large city on an industrial park. Bordering the park is a large suburban estate. On one side of the factory is a tile manufacturer and on the other is a large plant which makes light bulbs.

Worried by requests for information by the company's customers, the recently appointed Chief Executive of Bradmopp employed a consultant to provide an overview of the environmental impacts of the operations on the site. The consultant came up with a whole list of areas where she thought there was need for further investigation. Some of these are as follows:

1. There is significant wastewater from the plant which goes directly into the sewer. Although this may not be illegal, given the generous consents which have been allowed, a number of diluted chemicals and dyes are being washed away.
2. Chemicals are stored outside in a locked paddock but the gate to this area is often left open and unattended, and locks on the top of safe drums are often left open.
3. All products are packed in polythene, further packed into batches of twelve and then put into cartons. As a minimum, therefore, there are three layers of packaging for transportation.
4. The very fact that many products (especially dishcloths) are produced to be disposable is of concern.
5. All solid waste from the plant is put into skips and taken to landfill.
6. Although there is a clear management system in place, managers appear to

pay little attention to environmental issues and seem unaware of the increasing importance of environmental management.

7. There is no environmental policy statement and the company is providing only partial, and at some times inaccurate, information in response to requests for details about its environmental management strategies.

8. The company seems to be driven by short-term profit motivation and there is very little evidence of any overall long-term strategic planning.

When the Chief Executive received the report, he was shocked to find it showed so little environmental awareness and was even more dismayed when the consultant told him, in private, that there were some areas of the company's activities which were probably illegal, and where it might be deemed that managers and directors were acting negligently. She reminded him that if a major accident occurred and it was shown that directors had been negligent, then prison sentences were possible.

Tasks

Imagine you are the Chief Executive:

1 What is your first action on talking to the consultant?

2 Make a list (in order of priority) of the actions which you are going to take as a response to the consultant's report.

3 Outline a longer-term strategy which will both ensure that this situation does not occur again, and which will provide you with reliable information to give your customers.

G. FORMULATING AND IMPLEMENTING ENVIRONMENTAL POLICY: THE CASE OF METALLIC PLC

Metallic Plc operates two lines of business. The first involves the recovery of precious metals, gold, platinum, and silver coatings from base metals. This business is done on a contract basis, where the owners of scrap metal with a high precious-metal content negotiate a value of recoverable precious metal and pay a contract fee for the recovery process. This business requires smelting and chemical extraction, enabling the purification of metals.

The other side of the business involves the development of metallic coatings. The most familiar of these are gold and chromium plating. Metallic Plc produce the chemicals which other plating companies then use for plating work. Metallic Plc are involved in R&D to support new product development in electro-chemical plating.

The company operates from one highly secure site. This is the base for the chemicals side of the business as well as the headquarters of the operation. The workforce of around 60 comprises scientists and technicians involved in Research and Development, operators highly skilled in metal smelting and recovery, a general factory workforce, clerical support and a young and innovative integrated management team. The workforce is recruited locally, except for senior management posts. The company has a reasonable profile in the local community but has taken no special initiatives in community affairs.

The site is on a modern industrial estate on the outskirts of a rural market town. The town is close to a National Park and internationally famous for its spa waters. The spa arises because the town is sited on porous limestone bedrock. The industrial estate is adjacent to open countryside. The site itself is highly secure and includes an office block, laboratory and small-scale chemicals-treatment and production laboratory, as well as a metal-smelting and recovery plant. The site is larger than Metallic's current needs, and is partially landscaped with trees and shrubs.

The site includes a purpose-built enclosed chemicals store, where highly corrosive concentrated acids and highly toxic chromium compounds are kept. The recovery process for metals means that considerable quantities of metal scrap are also stored on the site. The smelting process can involve the release to atmosphere of metal impurities: these include heavy metals such as cadmium, zinc and lead. The recovery process also produces liquid chemical waste which is disposed of, after treatment, through the sewer system according to a consent licence granted by the Water Authority Plc. The site has its own closed storm drain system to collect accidental spillages. All chemical storage areas are bounded so that accidental spillages are contained.

The company turnover is about £50m per year and it is regarded as within the top three companies in that business. The business has a quality image because of the association with precious metals and purity, quality products, quality finishes, quality service and craftsmanship. For this reason the company has begun to progress the idea of Total Quality Management.

As part of the TQM exercise, Metallic's Board members have become sensitive to contradictions in the company's image. The idea of purity and quality of the precious metals is in contrast to that of chemical processing and potential environmental pollution. There are also contradictions between the threat of environmental pollution and the historic image of the town – based on pure spa water. The company is committed to the development of a comprehensive environmental policy.

Questions

1 Identify the main stakeholders involved in this case.

2 What do you consider need to be the key features of the company's environmental policy?

3 What other strategies do you think would be worth exploring in this case?

INDEX